Product of a Postcode

A True Life Story to be Shared

CW00550642

Written by Gary Hutton & Zoe O'Leary

Dedicated to Kim Hutton

Table of Contents

CHAPTER 1

A Boy - A Product of my Environment and Circumstance

It was 13 May 1993 and I was on my way to Wood Green Crown Court in North London. I was only 24 years of age and been told to look forward to a long stretch at her majesty's pleasure. I had already spent three months on remand at Pentonville prison the year before being granted bail, after being nicked by the South East Regional Crime Squad based at Scotland Yard. I arrived at the court early, clean shaven, smartly dressed with a tidily trimmed barnet, I looked the respectable part. I felt relaxed and was having a cuppa and a chat with my brief when I heard my name called to the dock.

I had been pre-warned that the judge was a nightmare, but I'd already figured this out for myself at the pre-trial. The pre-trial had been to find out what the prosecution had against me and my co-defendant. It transpired they had a fucking shitload, so I was pleading guilty. The jury had been sworn in for a long trial a month beforehand, so were probably chuffed when I pleaded guilty. I was told I would be returning in a month for sentencing after reports had been completed. My reckoning was that if I had a trial I would get a 10 to 12 year stretch, so I thought fuck that and went for a guilty plea.

Judge Jarlath Finney entered the court and everyone stood to attention, but I was already on my feet looking at the judge, thinking has this cunt got the hump, did his wife fuck him off this morning and put him in a bad mood? He sat there looking stern and superior wearing all the gear that a top judge wears including wig. He was an old man in comparison to me, with a very pointed face, grey hair, sideburns a farmer would be proud of and had a very regal look. He then turned to me and said 'Gary Hutton how do you plead on count one?' to which I replied 'guilty'. I was asked the same question three times and each time I repeated 'guilty'. At that point I felt my hearing cut out, I couldn't hear a fucking thing apart from a ringing noise in my ears. I was looking at the judge, his mouth was moving, but I couldn't hear what was coming out and it felt like whatever he was saying was happening to someone else and I was hovering above everyone. I think I had gone into some kind of shock because it felt like I was having some sort of out of body experience. I was looking around thinking what the fuck is going on, then all of a sudden, the noise in my ears returned and I heard those dreaded words 'take him down'. I then felt a tap on my shoulder and as I turned a screw said 'follow me son'.

I was then taken to a holding room and the screw who had escorted me from the court told me I was extremely lucky and I'd had a result. A result would have been not having to go to court that day and instead be sitting in the sun somewhere because it was a lovely day outside. It was at that point I thought 'how the fuck have I ended up here?' I'll fucking tell you how and I'll tell you in my words, in my way and I won't be holding back. I may not be able to mention some names and places but read the story of my life and you'll see exactly how the fuck I ended up here, and I'll let you be the judge of whether I'm a product of a post-code.

My mum and dad (I hate calling him that so from here on in he will be referred to as Bin Laden or Bin for short - I hate the cunt and for many good reasons of which we will come to) were both from Ireland. My mum was from the south of the country; Cork and Bin Laden from the north; Derry. Both were Roman Catholics. Mum came to live in Brick Lane in the East End of London with her mum, three sisters and two brothers in the 50s. To this day I'm not sure why they moved to England.

My parents met in Brick Lane in the mid to late 50s after Bin finished his national service in the army. My mum was a wonderful, beautiful, warm woman and a very strong lady who protected her children with a passion. She sadly died at the young age of 41 to leukemia. During the time she was married until the day she took her last breath, she had 11 children; eight boys and three girls. In the area we lived our family wasn't that different to others, it was unusual to not come from a big family and strange if you were an only child. Our mum doted on us and really took care of us, we were always clean and smartly dressed. Mum would always dress us the same to our nearest same-sex sibling in age, we were all so alike we'd look like twins when dressed the same. All throughout growing up as a kid, everywhere I went, people would say 'god you're a Hutton' and I was always mistaken for one of my brothers.

Bin Laden, on the other hand, was no father, he was a selfish, drunken, manipulative, drunken cunt and knowing what I know now, I wouldn't piss on him if he was on fire. I would actually carry on walking if he was dying on the floor in front of me which I did later on in life. At one stage he'd had a heart attack and I didn't bat an eyelid and five minutes later someone told me an ambulance had arrived and he was on his way to the hospital. My response was 'tell someone who gives a fuck'. I will come back to what a vile creature he was a little later.

CHAPTER 2

Home – The East End and Hutton Clan

I was born into the world on Tuesday 4th June 1968 at London Hospital, Whitechapel, and given the names Gary Vincent Hutton. Most of my brothers and sisters were born at the same hospital, Jimmy being the biggest baby at well over 12lbs. My mum delivered me into the world at a healthy 8lbs and took me home to No. 1 Spelman House, Spelman Street, London, E1. This is where my life began with love and happiness. I still live in the Brick Lane area to this day and am proud of my roots. The East End has a lot of history, most of it great and some of it not so great.

Brick Lane for centuries has become home to many immigrants. In the 17th century, the French Huguenots moved into the area and developed the clothing industry and in the 19th century came the Irish and Jewish. The Jews continued to arrive through to the 20th century having fled their homelands from the Nazi persecution and settled as a prominent group in the area.

They dominated the East End with their trades and professions and had their own Synagogue, which in 1976 was converted into the Brick Lane Mosque. Prior to their purpose built Synagogue, they would pray in non-recognisable buildings, so not to be noticed during the war. I have very fond memories of the famous Beigel Shop on Brick Lane because my mate's mum worked there and used to give me doughnuts.

I wasn't always so good to the Jews nor the Bengalis who moved in the area in the latter part of the 20th century, not in a nasty way, but I will come on to that later. It wasn't a race thing, the

Jews were rich in the area and easy pickings for a few quid. Brick Lane is and always has been a melting pot where people see people not race. As cockney as I am I would always be called the Irish boy when growing up. Most of the Jewish community earned their money and moved out to the leafy suburbs and any remaining in the area integrated with the rest of the Brick Lane community so much so, I'm not sure if any of my friends were Jewish or not. Brick Lane is still owned by the Jews who now rent it out to the Bangladeshis.

A famous firm for many years in the East End was Truman's Brewery, where Bin worked for a number of years. It is still famous around the East End today. It was founded as early as 1666 when Brick Lane was just a track flanked by fields. The brewery grew as the East End grew and then beyond into what is now East London. There is a difference between the East End and East London - E1, E2, E3 and E14 are the East End and the remaining is East London. Truman's remained independent until succumbing to the merger craze of the 80s. In 1989, the brewery and pubs were sold and Truman's was closed, but the area is still a busy spot for all sorts of businesses such as arts, fashion and bars. The Lane has a new buzzy life and feel.

Brick Lane's name suffered during Jack the Ripper's reign of terror. A series of prostitutes were brutally murdered and mutilated by some sick bastard. To this day it is still unconfirmed how many victims there were and the psycho was never caught. You can spot many tour guides day and night around the East End streets showing tourists where victims were found. Personally, I can think of better touristy things to do when on holiday. I still refer to the Lane as the ghetto because brasses still work the streets and there are dealers selling their shit openly all around. I feel sorry for the women selling themselves to survive. Even though it was a century ago that the Ripper struck, there are still plenty of nutters out there and these women put themselves at risk either to feed their kids or to get their next poisonous fix. The Lane was and still is a hot spot for crime and resident villains. The most famous criminal outfit in the area where I grew up were the Krays who ran London's Underworld in the 60s a few streets from where I lived.

In 1917, London's postcodes were redefined into sub-districts. This happened when unfortunately World War One began. The local postmen at the time were conscripted and division into sub-districts became a necessity to make it easier for the women of war who had taken over the sorting and delivery and didn't have the local knowledge that their fathers, husbands and brothers had. Nowadays you can tap a postcode into a sat-nav and it will tell you where you can take a piss – I bet our war veteran heroes are proud they fought for such a privilege!

Brick Lane today has two sides, there is the northern end which has its private clubs and spas and is frequented by the rich and famous and then the southern end to the extreme poverty of the renamed Banglatown with council estates across Tower Hamlets homing some 70,000 Bangladeshis.

Brick Lane is probably today most famous for its Indian restaurants where you will find 'pullers' outside selling their food as the best and at the cheapest possible deal. If you have never visited trust me they all say the same thing, but it hasn't got the famous title of curry capital of the UK for nothing. The 'pullers' sell it that well you think they are going to pay you for eating their food!

Brick Lane is more than curry restaurants when on a Sunday morning it becomes a street market selling almost anything including counterfeit DVDs and cigarettes! It's comical to listen to the market traders' gift of the gab, selling their random items which they will swear blind you won't find cheaper in the country. The reason behind Sunday markets in the area is because of the Sabbath where Jews do not work on a Saturday for religious beliefs. Another similar local Sunday market is Petticoat Lane, which isn't its official name. In 1830, Petticoat Lane was renamed Middlesex Street but still today it is known by the old name. Similarly to Brick Lane it has bustling crowds and many market stalls selling various items. By the mid-Victorian period the Lane was not only the place to buy new and used clothes, it was a place to buy all sorts of second-hand goods and the nearby Brick Lane and Club Row markets made Spitalfields the market of London.

We were a large East End family and very well known. There wasn't much of an age gap between us siblings, less than a year in fact. What with mum and Bin Laden being Roman Catholics, contraception was a no-no. As I've said there were 11 of us and in order we were Georgie (who died as a child), Jimmy, Michael, Paul, Terry, Tracey, Kim, Rodney, me, Darren and Jackie. I would always look out for my younger brother and sister similarly as my older siblings would look out for me. In the early years, we were a close-knit brood who stood together when we were not fighting each other. We had an unwritten rule that we were allowed to knock seven bells of shit out of each other, but no-one outside of our family could lay a finger on any of us without consequence.

Jimmy was a quiet kid but like us all had a short fuse and a bad temper and could really have a fight and hold his own. He was given a lot of respect in our area when we were growing up which was given because he would always be bashing some kid, but he adored and loved our mum and was as soft as shit around her. He was almost 16 when she lost her own personal fight. He was always bunking off school and I don't think he really knew what school was about. As he was much older than me I only got to know him later in life. I remember as a kid I'd watch him in awe play football, he was seriously gifted. Jimmy's talents were fighting and football.

Michael was also very quiet as a kid, but again was always out fighting and living in Jimmy's shadow. Those two would stand strong and toe to toe with anyone who got in their way. Michael was very similar to Jimmy as in he never went to school and if he did it would be for a row. I think we all inherited this fighting spirit from our mum. It wasn't that we were looking for trouble, we just didn't take any shit or back down from something that stood in our way. Michael left home shortly after mum died and moved in with a family not far away, so I didn't know him too well as a young kid, but later in life we became very close for a time.

Now with Paul, I don't know where to start. Paul was a mummy's boy and was permanently at her heels. Where mum was, Paul was within a few feet. Paul went on to live a very sad life on the streets. He was an angry child after mum passed away and would beat anyone up including girls, he didn't care who he hurt. He was and still is really messed up.

Terry was a shy laid back boy and again a very good footballer. If he had to have a row he would, but preferred not to. Terry loved the girls and they loved him in return. I was close with Terry and he would look out for me as my big brother.

Tracey I felt a bit sorry for but didn't understand at the time because I was too young. Tracey inherited the role of becoming mum which stole a chunk of her childhood. It's very sad when I look back because she was a very quiet girl who hardly ever left the house to play with friends. Tracey went to school every day, studied and did very well for herself.

What can I say about Kim apart from wow, what a girl. She was truly different. As a young girl, she was a tomboy and the best footballer I'd ever come across. We would play in the same team and she was better than boys from miles around. Still to this day my mate says that she was the best footballer when we were kids and I reiterated this at her funeral. I will explain her passing later. She was a stunning girl but my god could she have a row. She would fight boys with no fear whatsoever. It was probably second nature to her what with having eight brothers to contend with on a daily basis. This must have been tough on her, especially losing mum so early.

Rodney was the closest brother to me in age, so we were dressed the same but we were complete opposites in personality. Rodney would always want to do girly things so never wanted to play football. Mischief was Rodney's game of choice and he was always game for a laugh. Later in life he came out as gay and went on to own his own hairdressers in Stepney Green.

I'm next in line as the seventh son and ninth child. What can I say about myself? I'd say I was a likeable, loveable street urchin! I was a talented footballer like my siblings, with a passion for life. I always have and always will stand by and help anyone and trust me I've stood by some low-lives which you will read about later.

Darren was a lovely young boy who sadly never knew mum and grew up to be angry for it. He loved boxing and still boxes to this day. I looked after Darren and would have to go out and fight his corner for him and got nicked for it once. Darren had got into some trouble with three blokes and I had to wade in. One of the fellas I picked up and put in a barrel of water and the other two I knocked out - no-one had a go at my little brother without any come back. Luckily, I wasn't charged because they wouldn't press charges against me. Darren was a good child and very quiet. I used to play pranks on him and he could tell you some stories of what I did to him.

Last but not least is Jackie who is the baby of the family and was spoilt as fuck! I'd spoil her rotten as we all did trying to make up for her not having a mum like her friends had. I used to give her £30 a pop for ironing one of my shirts. The cheeky cow grew to milk it and would ask to iron my trousers as well for a score. She could do no wrong in my eyes when we were younger. For a long time, she was the apple of my eye.

CHAPTER 3

Early Memories of my Protective Mum

Mum did everything for us kids as Bin Laden was either at work or drunk as a skunk in a pub somewhere. He worked at Truman Brewery in Brick Lane, which was not a good place for a piss-head to work. While we were living at 19 Spring Walk as well as bathing and dressing 10 children, cleaning the house, cooking meals and running a tight ship, my mum had an evening cleaning job working at some offices in Commercial Street. When I think back, I have no idea how she managed all this in a day. Where she got the energy from and how she carried on going, I will never know. She never had a minute to herself. Mum used to take me and Rodney to work with her and we would help her out by emptying little bins while she would be running around cleaning. One day Rodney and I were helping mum out and we heard this high pitched scream. When we turned round mum was running around like a mad woman waving her arms in the air. We had no idea what was going on and after mum calmed down, she told us that a mouse had run across her foot. We left that place quick sharp and I don't think she ever went back. I laughed afterwards with Rodney, but mummy didn't find it funny at all.

At that point living in Spring Walk, we were very happy and well fed even if a little overweight, but I have real fond memories of Spelman House, we had a lot of joy there. I remember an old lady, Mrs. Cole, who lived next door who always gave me chocolate biscuits. I used to knock at her door all the time because I was a greedy little git. Opposite our home was a chicken factory which was a slaughterhouse. I used to stand and watch all the goings on over there and remember the noises as the men would go about their jobs. During their lunch hour, they would be eating their sandwiches and chopping off chickens' heads at the same time. The noise was atrocious and not really for a kid's ears, and the smell was disgusting. At this point, I was still too young for school so I used to sit and people watch, which is still my favourite pastime today.

Mum was an extremely fiery woman which is where I think me, my brothers and sisters inherited it from. Mum had a crazy temper, she would do her nut if anyone spoke to us kids rudely or treated us with disrespect, but would also scold us if we treated anyone with a lack of regard. Mum was very much a 'treat people as you would wish to be treated' person.

I recall a very well respected shop owner, an old Jewish man called Mr. Gollops who ran a shop selling sweets and newspapers with his wife on the corners of Spelman Street and Chicksand Street. He would be there every morning and as people passed by they would say 'good morning Mr. Gollops' in their fine cockney tones. I used to sit on a step and watch him wish everyone good morning in return. One morning I decided I would have a go, I saw him on the opposite side of the street walking along and innocently shouted 'morning Mr. Bollocks'. The next thing I knew I was being dragged backwards by my shirt collar through the door and my mum was shouting at me. I remember being so confused as to why mum was raising her voice. She asked me why I shouted that word across the street, so I told her I was just repeating what others had said to the old Jewish shopkeeper. Mum then went on to tell me that Gollops is not the same as bollocks! Mum was mad that I had picked this word up and blamed my older brothers and she also threatened to take me to see a priest to ask forgiveness. I really thought that was his name and that's what I'd heard people call him every morning. I grew to understand cockney tones a lot better from then on. I was only used to hearing my mum talk and she spoke with a strong Cork accent.

I remember another time when me and mum were out shopping down Whitechapel Road where there are market stalls and shops still to this day. I was following mum through the bustle of people while she was shopping and occasionally stopping to talk to people she knew. We then went into a butcher for some meat. Back then butchers would have sawdust on the floor and this was a large butcher so there was plenty of it. While mum was queuing I was having fun gathering all the sawdust up with my feet, pushing it into a big pile and then taking a running kick like I was taking a penalty. The butcher who was young and only in his 20s shouted at me 'oi, you little shit cunt stop fucking doing that'. I froze scared to the spot. My mum calmly took my hand, walked me to the front of the queue and said to the butcher 'this is my son and you will not talk to him or any of my children like that'. My mum looked down at me and said 'tell the man he can't talk to you like that, go on'. She was egging me on to tell the butcher. I remember being scared that mum would tell me off if I did and told her that, so she promised me she wouldn't be mad. It was at that point I found my voice and bottle and I let him have it. I called this bloke all the cunts, wankers and tossers under the sun. He was completely dumbfounded. Having older brothers came in handy that day because this is the language I had picked up from them. After my outburst, my mum went on to tell the butcher that if he ever spoke to me or any of her children like that again she would drag him by his hair out onto the street and knock seven bells of shit out of him and trust me my mum could have done that easily. The butcher's face was priceless. After telling the butcher his possible fortune, mum took my hand and said come on son and we left.

We were walking along the street and I was feeling full of myself thinking I certainly told that bloke. As we got around the corner, my mum spun me round and started going off her head asking where I'd learnt such language, telling me I needed to go to church, asking what the lord Jesus would make of my foul mouth and telling me that my brothers were going to get a serious hiding.

My mum would lose the plot if someone upset her kids. I saw her beat men and women up for it. She had no fear, just pure love and passion for her children and their happiness.

One day my oldest brother, Jimmy, was at secondary school and was talking at the back of the class as a lesson was about to begin. The woman teacher, Mrs. Bentley, did no more and got a bunch of keys and threw them directly at my brother's face, which marked him underneath his eye. He got up, walked out of the classroom and went straight home to mum who, of course, went mental. We didn't live too far from the school; St Bernard's RC just off of Bethnal Green Road. It was quite funny when I went to prison as I found a lot of the inmates came from that school. Mum marched up to the school with Jimmy in tow and straight into the class where the lesson was taking place. She faced Mrs. Bentley, grabbed her hair as all the boys in the class looked on in shock, pulled out a black Kat like air gun and placed it to Mrs. Bentley's temple and threatened to kill her. As you can imagine, Mrs. Bentley was crying and screaming in fear and rightly so. After mum said what she had to say, she left and returned home and carried on what she was originally doing.

Of course, later that day the police came to our house and searched for the gun. Mum was a smart cookie and earlier had taken the gun out the back and dropped it in a pot of paint and resealed the lid so they never found it. That gun was forevermore blue. They couldn't charge my mum as she had denied there was any gun, so the police left it as the teacher's word against my mums. It's a shame the system doesn't work like that now, you couldn't deny a fart with the poxy CCTV in every street nook and cranny these days.

There is nothing like a mother's love.

CHAPTER 4

A Life Changed Forever

In 1971, we moved a short distance from Spelman House to 19 Spring Walk. We moved from a flat to a four bedroom maisonette with a garden. It felt huge. I was three years' old and my mum was pregnant with my little brother Darren. We didn't have a removal van or removal men to help. We moved by piling everything up on to a market barrow; the old ones made of wood with the big red wheels and green frame. The barrow belonged to an Irish bloke by the name of Sailor and he helped us move. Outside the front of the house was a big grass area where all the kids on the estate would play. I absolutely loved it there and to this day I still think about some magical times spent playing on that green. All the kids were in the same boat, we didn't have a pot to piss in but we all made do, got on with it and were happy with the cards we had been dealt – we didn't know any different.

We had great big windows in our kitchen and mum would watch, through the windows, us kids playing together and larking about. All the kids loved my mum as she would be in the kitchen cooking all the time. She would cut up a sack of spuds, make chips and wrap them up in newspaper like a proper chip shop and call us over one by one and pass them through the window. She didn't do this just for me, my brothers and sisters, but for all the kids who were playing on the green. It was only recently that an old friend in his 50s said to me he still remembered my mum's chips. Mum never thought about herself, only others, which was a quality that made everyone love her. She had all these kids and for a while she took on other kids she knew needed help; one such person was my cousin Johnny, my mums brother's son, who was on the run from Borstal prison at the time and who came to live with us and became like a big brother to me. Even now, people I see out and about still talk about her memory.

Our house as you can imagine was packed and cramped, but it was fun and we never complained. We had two in a bed, top and tailing and we loved it, it kept us warm in the winter. The house had a flat roof so when it rained heavily, water would sit on the roof and over a period of time would leak into our bedrooms, so we had to move our beds around and place a bucket on the floor to catch the drips. Mum always kept a tidy home and was forever washing clothes, cooking and cleaning. She would bathe us one after the other in the same bathwater to save hot water and I can still remember how she would rub soap into the flannel and scrub my body from head to toe.

My first born brother, Georgie, sadly died at the age of four, so I never knew him. I recently placed a three foot angel at the head of his grave as it has always just been a piece of grass amongst lots of other unfortunate children and baby graves. I did this for my mum more than anything because at the time he passed away we were poor and could not afford a headstone. Saying that though that fat cunt Bin Laden was getting drunk every night. My mum was broken by the death of Georgie and Bin did nothing to help or try and soothe her pain.

There were a couple of times that mum nearly lost me also. Rodney woke me up one night from a deep sleep and told me to follow him. He told me he knew where there were lots of sweets for us to eat. We both crept downstairs very slowly so we didn't wake anyone. I was thinking fuck it if there are sweets about; I'm in. We got to the kitchen and it was pitch black so we quietly switched the light on. I asked Rodney where the sweets were and he pointed to a locked cupboard which was high up and out of our reach. Rodney then told me he knew where the key for the lock was and got it. Saying no more, I got a chair and climbed up, Rodney passed me the key and I unlocked the cupboard. Touch!

Inside were lots of sweets in little jars in all different colours; red ones, blue ones, yellow ones, pink ones, you name it they were there. We laid them all out on the table and shared them between ourselves by saying 'one for you, one for me' until we both had the same amount. Even at six years' old I was a fair little boy. We started eating them sweet after sweet and were laughing and started to make a lot of noise and we got louder and louder and woke the whole house up. As we heard footsteps coming our way, I remember thinking we are in big trouble and we were!

We were taken on a trip to London Hospital to have our stomachs pumped as we had been stuffing our faces with tablets. We were both buzzing out of our nuts telling our mum we were good boys because we had shared them into equal portions at which point she screamed in despair. Silly bollocks Rodney and his fucking sweets.

As kids, we all used to play pranks on each other and I used to play some funny pranks on my younger brother Darren but some of them were not so funny. I remember I thought it would be funny to put a solid dumbbell on top of the bedroom door which was slightly ajar. I called my little brother upstairs and as he pushed the door open, the bell dropped straight through the wooden floor. If it would have hit him, he wouldn't be here today. It hit the floor with such force, the house shook and all I could do was laugh. I got a good beating from Bin for that.

When I was five years' old during the summer months my brothers Jimmy and Michael decided to play a prank on me. Sharon, our neighbour, who was a little older than Jimmy and Michael asked my mum if she could take me to the launderette on Whitechapel Road. Mum agreed and off we set. Jimmy and Michael were around the corner and started to show off in front of Sharon. They took my top off and put it on our dog Patch, so I was topless. The dog started to run around so I was running around after him and my brothers were killing themselves laughing at this. Patch decided to run off and was heading toward Valence Road which was a busy road. Patch ran across the road with me in tow, I didn't look and was hit by a car and thrown in the air. I landed on the back of the car and bounced onto the floor. I remember laying still, not moving. I was a tiny little boy back then. My brothers were told to fetch my mum while I was taken to London Hospital. I was kept in the hospital with two broken legs (one bone had pierced through my skin) and two broken arms. After I was settled, mum asked me what had happened, so I told her. At that point, she started to go mad and I couldn't work out why. Jimmy and Michael hadn't told her what they had done and had said that I had just ran out into the road for no reason. They got a good hiding for that and to this day poor Sharon still feels guilty.

Shortly after that accident, mum became pregnant with my little sister, Jackie, and 18 months later mum would leave us and our lives would change forever.

Anyone seeing their mum sick in hospital finds it devastating, but for a seven year old boy it is also very confusing especially when not being told why your mum is in hospital or that she is even sick. I was not being told anything about what was really going on and had no fucking idea what was happening. We would all be issued a hospital white mask, green gown and hat to stand by my mum's bedside. I can still see myself standing there, completely lost in the scene, watching my older brothers and sisters talking to my mum in her hospital bed. Back then I don't think hospitals really knew if you could catch or pass on my mum's illness hence the hospital clothing.

Mum had so many visitors which showed how much love people felt for her. School teachers would say in school that they had been to see her and priests and nuns would come to our house and pray with us, I didn't know why at the time. The day we were told mum had gone to live in heaven will stay with me forever, it was 30 December 1975. I still hate New Years to this day.

I remember being called to the kitchen and sitting around the table with my brothers and sisters. An Irish woman who lived around the corner had just returned from visiting mum at the hospital. Bin Laden spoke and told us that mummy had gone to live in heaven. There was no emotion, no cuddles of comfort and no words of reassurance that we would be OK. Someone spoke, I think it was me and asked 'are we not going to see her again?' we were told no.

We all left the table sobbing and ran upstairs. I remember asking my sister Tracey what was happening. I couldn't get my head around what I was being told. We all cried and cried and tried our best to comfort each other the best we could. For a very long time afterwards if one of us cried we all followed suit and burst into tears.

One day you're hanging on to your mum's apron strings feeling so much love and then you're told she has gone to live in heaven and you will never see her again. You cry and cry and cry, but no tears will bring her back. You promise you will never be naughty again, but nothing you say or do will grant you your

26

one wish, a wish I still have nearly 40 years later. Today I find myself thinking how nice it would be to sit with my mum and have a cuppa and a natter. Everyone in life has that one person they need at various times to confide in. Sometimes we lose that person so we lose our confidante. There has been times when I've needed to speak with my one person, in my case my mum, who I trusted 100%. Just occasionally I needed her unconditional love, warmth and understanding as it always made me feel better as a boy. As young as I was when she left, I still feel that strong bond and have never found anything in comparison since.

I cried a river every single day for a very long time which was extended by what followed my devastating loss. I will go further into what happened following my mum's passing in the next chapter. For a while, I didn't even have my brothers and sisters to cuddle or feel their love, warmth and comfort. My life felt like that for such a long time and all days seemed to roll into one. We were sent to school as normal wearing our uniforms of grey socks, grey shorts, light blue shirt and the school blue jumper.

One particular day shortly after mum died, I set off for school and it was a normal day or so I thought. I was seven and a small child in so much emotional pain. This is a pain that has stayed with me my whole life and I know will never go away. I arrived at school and nothing appeared any different so as usual I sat down in my classroom with the other kids. The next thing I knew Sister Joan, the head of school, popped her head in the door and told my teacher she was taking me out of class. I had no idea what was going on.

I arrived at Sister Joan's office and Rodney was already there so we looked at each other and immediately wondered what we had done wrong. All of a sudden Kim appeared and Sister Joan told us we were going to pray and started the prayer, so we joined in. We prayed a lot in school and used to go to church all of the time because the church was only 10 yards from the school gates. We also used to go to church with mum a lot too. We prayed for roughly 10 minutes and then Sister Joan told us that today we were going to church so we walked with her.

As we were walking I noticed lots of black cars lined up outside the church. As we entered the church doors, the whole school was there, sitting quietly and sullen and then I noticed my whole entire family at the front. It was a huge church and it was packed to the rafters with faces I recognised all throughout my young life; aunts, uncles, cousins, etc. I then saw my mum's coffin placed in the centre, directly in front of the altar. It was at that point I dropped to my knees as it hit me what was happening. Nobody had told me what I was walking into. I was on my knees, a seven year old boy, crying and bawling my eyes out uncontrollably. Sister Joan picked me up off the floor and we sat together. My mind was racing, why did no-one tell me what was going to happen today? Why the fuck would they surprise this on me?

Mass was said and it seemed like it was over quickly, it was all a blur and I sobbed all throughout the service. I was standing with Sister Joan and the coffin was placed in the hearse. My aunts and mum's friends came over and kissed me, Rodney and Kim to comfort us as we stood outside the school gate with Sister Joan. I felt completely numb.

We were then taken back to Sister Joan's office for more prayers. Sister Joan called us over to the window and what I saw is still imprinted in my mind. Underwood Road is a long road that leads on to Valence Road and as we stood there, we watched the cars drive away with our beloved mum. That was our farewell to our mum and the last time we would feel her presence amongst us.

Up until my early teenage years I would open doors thinking she would be on the other side and also walk around corners expecting to see her smiling face. I would do this daily, walking the streets, looking for her face in the crowds. I just wanted to see her face but, of course, never found her.

It wasn't until I was 14, seven years later, that I would visit my mum's grave. Michael took us younger ones and on the way there some young blokes wanted to start trouble. Michael stood firm as we all did. We never came to any harm that time and arrived at mum's grave safely but were shocked at what we found. There was no remembrance to say she was there; no words, no pictures, no nothing. When we asked Bin when we got home why this was, he told us it was because our uncle owned the plot and would not allow it. That was bullshit. It wasn't until I was in my 20s that me, my brothers and sisters clubbed together and put that right with permission from our uncle who was absolutely fine with it.

I later found out from my uncle Jimmy, my mum's brother that Bin had stolen the deeds to one of the houses my Nan had owned and when my Nan had died Bin had sold it. There were never any pictures of our mum in our house while we were growing up. We were never allowed to talk about her openly and grieve, she was gone and that was that. All through the years I've kept and cherished her memory fresh in my mind, my mum, my rock. Later on, Tracey divided any photos we had but only gave me photos of myself. I'm gutted that to this day I still have no photo of my mummy.

That was the point my life changed forever. It was a massive turning point. From then on my life would turn to shit and shit would be all I knew. It was like this, you're living in a bubble and the bubble becomes the norm. I wouldn't get my life back on track for years and years to come.

-

CHAPTER 5

Holiday Home

Just after mum died, me, Paul, Terry, Kim and Rodney were put into care and sent to separate children's homes. Paul and Terry were sent to a home called Dave Adams House and me, Kim and Rodney were sent to another called Windermere House. Now this was fucking hard as a kid. I genuinely don't know what is worse being a bit older and understanding that you're not wanted, or being the young age I was and having my whole world torn apart by being separated from what was love and family in my life and all I knew. We read and watch films about kids who have been in care and go off the rails and trust me I fucking get how they feel and how it happens. No kid asks to be born but to be given life and not be wanted destroys your heart and self-worth. It's true what they say, you have to love yourself before you can love others.

Is all I could think about was a few weeks previous we were sitting in our kitchen with our mum and she was telling us all about Ireland and teaching me and Rodney Irish rebel songs, which I still remember. It must have been the worst feeling in the world for mum to know she had no choice on her life outcome, that she would one day soon be leaving us and not be around. I can only imagine that that is what a true broken heart feels like. It shows her strength of character because not once do I remember her ever crying or breaking down. She must have taken some comfort in thinking that Bin Laden would take care of us and raise us correctly; I don't think she had a clue who this man was. I'm not knocking my mum or accusing her of being a foolish woman because she certainly wasn't, I just think her life's attention was spent on us kids and she didn't see the real him. This

31

man was pure evil and I would go on to find out just how evil he really was. Have you ever seen the film 'Who Will Love My Children?' If you haven't, it is about a mother of 10 children who becomes terminally ill. She makes the agonising decision to find homes for her children before she dies. I look back and wish my mum had done that for us.

I recall sitting in the front room at the age of seven and me, Paul, Terry, Kim and Rodney were told by a woman we had never met in our lives that we were going to a children's home. She told us to pack some clothes as we were leaving straight away. My thoughts were 'who the fuck is she' and 'what the fuck's a children's home'? I was confused and started to cry. I felt lost as to what was going on, my life had drastically changed yet again in a split second. I wasn't the loved little boy I once was blanketed by my mum. I was entering into a new life, one of survival that I would live for the rest of my childhood.

I never asked at the time as my mind was racing, but I was trying to think about what we had done wrong. We hadn't been naughty or been disobedient at school. We were all petrified and had no clue whether we would ever see each other again. This felt so wrong, but I had no fucking choice, or so I thought at that particular point. Myself, Kim and Rodney packed some clothes and were told if we forgot anything it would follow. We were taken by car to Windermere House, I was scared during the ride as I had no idea where I was, what county I was in, or even what planet I was on. Windermere was a strange building, it was two flats knocked into one. It was run by an older lady who scared the shit out of me at first.

We were standing in the hallway and it didn't smell very clean at all. There were kids running about and initially it didn't appear too bad. Bin Laden was there, he put our bags down and was talking to the old lady in charge. It was time for him to leave after all of five minutes. Kim started to cry uncontrollably and scream at the top of her lungs shouting 'no, no I'm not staying here, please take me home'. Me and Rodney were crying because she was hysterical. I was thinking 'oh fuck this place must be hell if Kim doesn't want to stay here', so I also thought I didn't want to stay there. Bin looked at Kim and she begged him not to leave her behind. Well, I couldn't fucking believe it, he said OK he would take her home, to our family home, and off they went and left me and Rodney behind. If I had known that all you had to do was ask to be taken home, I would have asked the same question but it was too late. Looking back my sisters were always treated differently but especially Kim.

Me and Rodney were shown to a room and were told what time we would be eating, what time we would be going to bed and were also warned we were not allowed outside of the home. It was a rundown of rules that were all bollocks to me. We set our bags down and were told that dinner would be ready in half an hour. The old lady then left the room and left me and Rodney standing there completely dumbfounded. This must have happened on a Saturday because we didn't have school the following day. I told Rodney I would not be staying there and he just looked at me and asked why Kim had been allowed to go home? I was as confused as he was and I remember thinking we're obviously not as loved as she is. It was a reminder that I would never hear those four special words again; I love you son.

The home had two sets of stairs one being called 'apples' and the other set 'pears'. One was for going up to your room and the other for coming downstairs. Me being me would run and down both sets of stairs while Rodney would do as he was told and use the appropriate stairs that were ruled out to us. I didn't give a fuck and used whatever tickled my fancy at the time. When we were called we went downstairs for some food and it was the first time we met the other kids living there. They looked normal, but I didn't know what to expect. I was scared, confused, feeling unloved and completely in the dark of knowing how long we were going to be there for. We settled in after having something to eat and slept until the next morning.

On the Sunday morning, the frightening old lady took us to church because we are catholic and she had been informed that we attended church all the time. The church was full of 'born again' type people and I thought everyone was nuts because they were singing, dancing and waving their arms in the air. I wasn't used to this shit and we had certainly never done this at any mass I had attended. I wasn't sure if I was alive or in a bad dream, but it was real and happening. Me and Rodney were not happy or impressed. After a while, we were thankful to be leaving the happy clappy church and thinking and hoping we would never see those people again. I worked out the old lady didn't have a clue what a Roman Catholic was, a church was a church to her.

When we got back to the home, there was a young lady cooking and the food smelt really nice, it was a roast dinner. The young lady cook came over to talk to us and seemed a nice person. Rodney was chatting to her and they were getting on and she was saying that the home was a nice place and they did lots of activities there. Rodney built up a friendship with this girl during the time we were there. I just sat there listening not saying a word, thinking I didn't give a fuck and didn't care how nice she wanted to be to us, it was not somewhere I wanted to be.

Later that day, we got our stuff ready for school for the following day and went to bed early. I cried myself to sleep every night, an uncontainable amount of tears I would shed every single night missing my brothers and sisters. All I wanted was to be with them and see that they were alright as I didn't know where anyone else was apart from Paul, Terry and Kim. I felt as though my heart and world were broken.

The following morning we were taken to school by the home's own minibus which dropped the other kids in turn at their schools. I wasn't engaging with the other kids, I was staring out of the window not knowing where I was and not recognising any of the streets. Is all I knew was it wasn't the Brick Lane area, my home.

When we arrived at school, all the kids were staring at me, their mums were looking at me with pity. It was obvious they knew what had happened. I still felt numb and missed my brothers and sisters desperately. I was still crying myself to sleep every night and most of all I missed the warmness of my mum and would cry at the drop of a hat thinking of her. While at school, I couldn't concentrate. Nothing there seemed to have any meaning or matter anymore. The dinner ladies could see I wasn't right and would give me extra food to try and comfort me in their own way. One dinner lady would bring me in a bag of sweets every day and give them to me at playtime. Two mums at the school – Rita Quinn and Eileen Peel – who knew my mum well, would also give me sweets when picking up their kids who were in my class. They would sit on the steps of the church and call me over as I walked out of the school gates. I was grateful for their kindness.

After a week or so of being at the care home, I knew I had to get home because I knew my family, including Bin, must be missing me as much as I was missing them. I thought to myself I'm off at the first chance I get, and that chance came. I ran out of the home and pelted it as fast as I could through the streets. I had no idea

35

where I was going but was following the minibus route it took to school every morning. I knew once I got to my school I could find my way home from there as I'd walked that route with my mum many, many times. As I was running through the roads, I felt so happy and elated thinking I'm going to see the people I love and who love me. I was jumping on and off the curb in the road feeling so free with the sun shining down on me. I had never been out on the street by myself before so this was an adventure. Looking back it was only about a mile from my family home, but at the time for a small boy it felt like 100 miles.

I eventually arrived home and was so excited when I burst through the front door. I shouted at the top of my lungs 'I'm back' and cuddled my little brother and sister, Darren and Jackie, and told them how much I'd missed them and that I would not be going back to the children's home or leaving them again. My triumphant joy did not last long as Bin was fuming and scolded me. He took me straight back to the home in a black cab. I couldn't believe that following my brave adventure to get home that he was taking me back to where I had escaped from. Unbeknownst to me, in time we would all be back together but only once Bin had been on his holidays to Derry to visit his family. What a cunt.

When I eventually was returned home, we could never be sure if we would eat after school. Pretty much every night Bin would be in the pub which was 300 yards from our house. The pub was called the Queen's Head, it was a little pub full of hardened drinkers and Bin was one of those pissheads. It was our first port of call if we got home from school and no-one was in. I'd sit outside the pub on many a cold evening and watch all the goings on of men singing and fights breaking out. Someone would always usually buy me a bag of crisps and a coke. When I used to get home from school, I'd be so hungry; sometimes I didn't care, but other times my stomach would be screaming at me. There was fuck all in the house to eat and I mean fuck all. If I went to a mate's house, their mum would offer me something to eat, but I'd never accept it because we didn't want other people knowing our secret. I remember me, my brothers and sisters telling each other what we had been offered at our friends' houses and talking about how nice it looked and smelt. We all wish we had accepted the kind offers, but we all felt the need to protect Bin.

Bin used to tell us all the time that everyone outside the house was no good and we were to keep quiet unless we wanted to end up in a children's home for good and never see each other again. He even turned us against our mum's brothers and sisters. He twisted all of us kids into thinking they were horrible people and it was us against the world. There was only one person that would come to our house and that was my mum's brother, John (John uncle to us kids). He would pop round most mornings. He was a lovely man who was quiet, but a man who had a temper and could have a row and would fight the best of them. I now know Bin was scared of him. John uncle would check that us kids were OK and I know that put the fear of god into Bin in case one of us piped up.

We used to sometimes sit there in the dark with no money for electricity while Bin would be getting pissed in the warm, lit pub. We soon learnt how to stop the wheel from turning by fiddling it with a match so the electric would stay on. We used to be able to hear him staggering his way home singing some shit song at the top of his voice about his beloved Irish homeland. It would take him 30 to 40 minutes to make a 300 yard journey at silly o'clock in the morning. He was an embarrassment. I know what people thought around our area, they thought aaaah he should enjoy himself getting drunk as he has lost his wife and has all those kids to bring up on his own. The cunt played on that and milked it for everything he could.

We would take it in turns to wait up for him so we could take him upstairs, undress him and put him to bed. We would walk behind him up the stairs because he was in no fit state. We were terrified that he would fall and hurt himself so thought if he did fall by one of us being behind him we'd break that fall.

I used to pinch the change out of his pockets and he wouldn't have a clue the next morning because of the alcoholic block. I used this change to win more money playing 'money up the wall' with my mates. He always had a hangover the next day and we'd wait on him hand and foot making him cups of tea and running to the shops for bottles of lemonade. Hindsight is a great word. When I look back, we were completely brainwashed by the prick and the outside were not allowed in. Tracey and Kim were like his wives. Tracey would cook dinner and if he didn't like it, he would throw it up against the wall. On nights he was drunk, Tracey and Kim would hide and lock themselves away in their room when he called out for them.

CHAPTER 6

Primary School Menace

I absolutely hated school with a passion especially when it was around Mother's Day. All the kids would be making cards for their mums and it would kill me to be around that, so being angry I would play up. The teachers didn't think about how I was feeling and just thought I was an out of control little boy with the temper to match. By this time, I had become a little tramp. I was unwashed, head running alive with lice and wearing dirty clothes full of holes. At home, there was piles of unwashed clothes everywhere and no-one was taking on the responsibility. We were too young to look after ourselves and too tired through being hungry.

I remember one particular day I had a PE lesson, but I had no sports kit, so the teacher told me I'd have to do the lesson in my pants and bare feet. I was horrified because I knew once I took my shoes off, everyone would be shocked at the sight of my feet. One thing that Bin did teach us was that the outside world was not allowed to know anything about us and I was to keep it that way. At the time, I was keeping my trainers together with tape and had cardboard from a cornflakes box cut out and inserted because of the holes in the sole. I felt like a rabbit caught in the headlights when the teacher told me what I must do. I made an excuse that I needed to go to the toilet, so once I got to the boys' toilets I walked into a cubical, shut the door behind me and took my shoes off. Imagine a homeless person's feet, well that was how my feet looked, filthy dirty. I put my feet in the toilet bowl and pulled the chain and scrubbed my feet because they were black and I mean black as black. I repeated this until my feet were as clean as they could be. At home, I was never told to

39

wash or have a bath because when mum was alive she had done this for me. As we all know young boys don't wash until you force them. I went back to the lesson feeling humiliated that day.

I was angry at school and would snap at anything especially if someone said something about my mum which is what kids do. I would go off my head and beat the shit out of whoever it was. Really I was just misunderstood and lashing out in the only way I knew how. I didn't give a fuck, I'd send kids home with black eyes, bruises, scratches, ripped clothes, you name it I done it. As you can imagine, a lot of parents didn't like me.

One particular day I was playing football in the playground. I used to go to school early just to play football for an hour before lessons would start. There was a Church of England school across the road and the kids from that school would walk by the fence of my Roman Catholic primary school. Some of my mates from the estate used to go to the other school. One particular day this boy was walking towards the other school and I kicked the ball which hit the fence, he jumped out of his skin and more or less shit himself. He then started swearing at me and called my mum a whore and all sorts of names. I saw red mist and went nuts. I ran towards the fence and told him I was going to kill him and I was deadly fucking serious. The wanker just carried on walking.

I was so livid, I went and found a knife in the school kitchen and marched right up to his school. I stuck out like a sore thumb because in my school we wore a uniform, but in his school they wore their own clothes. I was walking through classrooms looking for this kid and finally found him at the back of a class in the third room I walked into. I started to jump over desks to get at this little prick who had insulted my mum, but before I could get to him, the teacher managed to catch me and get the knife out of my grip. All the while I was screaming 'I will get you' to the kid.

I was taken back to my school and delivered straight to the head, Ms. Monday, a large stern looking lady with bobbed mousy dark blonde hair, very butch looking and wobbled when she walked. Did I give a shit? Did I fuck. The head was going mad at me shouting with spit coming out of her mouth. She was new to the school as Sister Joan had left to go on a mercy mission in Peru. Ms. Monday told me I was the naughtiest boy she had ever come across blah, blah, blah in one ear and out the other. She called every classroom in the school to the main hall where she went on to tell every kid present how bad I was and how she would not accept such behaviour in her school. Then out it came, the cane. I thought to myself give it your best shot, or dozen. She caned me four times across my hands and I didn't flinch or make a noise. I could see a lot of the kids putting their hands over their eyes not wanting to see what I was feeling inside. I could tell the stupid bitch was pissed off that I didn't cry. I looked up at her with a face that said 'are you finished yet'. She then angrily told me to go and sit down.

In my last year of primary school, Ms. Monday was taking my year on a week's trip to the Isle of Wight. I wasn't going because you had to pay for it and if we couldn't afford a tin of beans we certainly couldn't afford an all expenses trip to the Isle of Wight. Ms. Monday surprised me by telling me I could go and that the school was paying for me – touch! The only condition was that I had to behave. She told me she was taking a chance on me and that she knew I was a good boy deep down. She felt sorry for me because she had been told of my history and she wanted to do something nice for the underfed skinny, dirty little kid. At that specific point, I remember thinking 'I must be good for Ms. Monday and I'll have a great time with my school mates'.

We arrived at the Isle of Wight and it was a really nice place. We were having days out and being fed really well. I was thinking what a life, this is great and a much better living than on the estate I lived on in the East End. Unfortunately for Ms. Monday, me being me, saw that there was money to be earned. One particular day we were taken on a trip, there were lots of families on holiday, plus other schools, so there were people everywhere. I was sitting on a bench people watching and overlooking a busy looking square. It was a lovely sunny day and people were smiling, chatting, laughing and enjoying the weather. There was a steady stream of people wandering through the square I was watching and I noticed most of them were stopping and throwing money into a pond. I was hooked by the sun hitting the coins and thinking to myself that this was a goldmine.

I was walking towards this pond with another kid and we were on it. I was thinking on my feet and working out how to stop the flow of people, so I got my mate to stand at the edge of the square and told him to only let some people through in groups. At this point I started to put on a show in front of the pond, giving it my best street patter of a fly pitcher and my audience started to throw even more money in. I was telling them all to make a wish and promising that their wishes would come true. I was on a roll and I'm sure they were all thinking I was part of the holiday entertainment.

I then told my mate to stop letting people through which he did, I took my trainers off, rolled up my trousers and was in the pond cleaning out the silver coins quick sharp leaving behind the coppers. We kept this up for a little while, letting people through, stopping the flow, taking the coins and starting again. It was perfect. I now had spending money like the rest of the kids, or so I thought. I then found out that someone else liked people watching, Ms. Monday.

As she marched and stomped towards me, I thought 'oh fuck'. She had been watching us for 15 minutes and thought I'd put on quite a show. This woman was livid, I swear her head had swollen in rage, she was beetroot red and not happy at all. She went on to tell me I was being sent home. She grabbed me by the scruff of my neck and was going nuts. We got back to the place where we were staying and she was screaming at me that she had never been so embarrassed in her life. She was telling all the other teachers of my little money making scheme and they were looking at me horrified.

What I didn't know and soon found out was that the wishing well was for a cancer charity. I felt like the biggest cunt when she dropped that bombshell. The bitch made me put all the money back in the pond. I was gutted at the time, not because of being in trouble but because I'd worked damned hard to get people to throw their money in and that money was rightfully mine, but once I was told it was for a cancer charity I felt like shit and didn't want it.

She stood me in front of all the kids and teachers on the trip and they all looked at me like I'd just killed their mums. Again, she told me I was one of the naughtiest kids she'd ever come across and blah, blah fucking blah. Instead of being sent home, she decided to cane me in front of everyone and again, I thought give it your best shot. She gave me five of her best on each hand and again I didn't flinch or make a sound. I was feeling a little bit gutted to be honest and was feeling inner pain rather than what she could do to me. Cancer had taken my mum.

School to me was like an extension of a youth club with the added twist of food, so somewhere for me to eat and if I wasn't at the youth club after school I was sitting outside the Queen's Head. No-one told me at the time just how important school would be for later on in life. Education opens doors for people to a better life. Today it upsets me when I see inner-city kids go on to a path leading to incarceration or other such sad existence. I must say I came across Ms. Monday a lot later on in life and I greeted her with a smile and a very big warm cuddle which she returned to me; a very nice lady.

In a way we were quite happy that Bin spent most of the time in the pub because we could do as we pleased and have fun and mess about with each other without him stopping our fun. Sometimes it did go too far and we would end up fighting which could get really out of hand. Thinking about it, it would be a naughty affair because we all had terrible tempers.

One night me and Kim had a falling out while Bin was at the pub getting pissed. Kim seriously lost the plot, got a kitchen knife and stabbed me in my upper left arm. As soon as she done it she was screaming and calling for our older sister. Tracey took me into the bathroom where she looked at the wound and all the while Kim was screaming 'he's not going to die is he'. Tracey was very cool and calmly patched me up and told us that we were never to tell anyone what had happened because we would end up in a children's home.

This was Bin speaking through Tracey, not that she realised. This would be what he would threaten and use against us and we never wanted to be apart so did what he said. We would never tell the outside world anything and this would all work in his favour. That day I should have been taken to the hospital for stitches, but, of course, if that had happened the outside world would have asked questions and found out. I still have a scar on my arm from that day which remained a well-kept secret.

CHAPTER 7

Mixed Emotions

From the age of eight up until I was 11 I was taken away for holidays on farms during the six weeks' school holidays. This was organised for underprivileged children by a charity and every year it was the best two weeks of my life. When I think about it now, it was obvious Bin wanted me out of the way so he could do what he liked which suited me down to the ground. A week before the underprivileged kids were packed off on their farm holidays we were all given a medical by a doctor at Toynbee Hall where the charity was based. The doctor would give you the once over and send you on your way with flea shampoo and whatever else you may need. This wasn't for our own personal care, but for the families we would be staying with.

It was petrifying the first time I was sent away because I never knew where I was going. We'd be told what mainline station to go to and be put on the train with our bag and a cardboard nameplate pinned to your jacket. The train would be packed full of other kids in the same boat. The noise on the train would be deafening because we were all so excited to be going on holiday. There would be no warning, we'd arrive at a station in the middle of some sleepy little village full of green trees, fields you could run for miles in and it would smell so clean and fresh and someone would call your name out. You would then get off the train and there would be a husband and wife full of the joys of life waiting for you and telling you that you'd be staying with them for a couple of weeks and off you'd go. As scary as it was initially, they were the best times of my life.

Rodney and I were sent away together two years on the trot and on the third year me and Darren were together and for those three years we stayed with a really nice husband and wife; Dee and Alastair, who had two children younger than me. To us, they lived in the middle of nowhere. We were used to city streets and this was another world where there was space everywhere. My eyes had never seen so far and the views just went on and on with not a block of flats in sight. Dee asked me back every summer for three consecutive years. No-one could replace our mum, but Dee did her damned hardest to be second best during those summer holidays. This lady could cook and she would tell us what she was going to cook and tell us how step by step. She would laugh at me because some of the food I'd never heard of before, let alone seen or eaten. Alastair was a British Airways pilot on a Boeing 747 and took us flying on his private jet. One day he let silly bollocks Rodney take the controls. Rodney was always full of mischief and would do funny things to get a laugh out of people. This particular day when he had the controls in his mischievous hands, he pulled on them so we were flying upwards and then he pushed back so we then shot downwards. I was in the back of this little plane shitting myself and screaming at Rodney that I'm going to kill him. The bastard was laughing his head off asking how to do a loop the loop. I was willing to show him a loop the loop with my fucking boot. It was the worst fucking rollercoaster ride I have ever been on in my life. Dee's dad owned a pig farm so we would go and watch the pigs being born and as kids this was amazing. They really were special times.

Me and Rodney also stayed on a dairy farm which was really exciting for two young boys. The first time I saw a cow being born was out of this world. The farmer put a cow which was about to give birth into a barn. Me and Rodney watched this in amazement at how the baby calf came to life, watching it drink its mother's milk and finding its legs and trying to walk. The dairy farmer was a nice bloke and his wife was lovely and treated us well, but they had a son who was a few years older than us and he would get very upset that we were getting special treatment. He got very jealous and would be fucking horrible to me and Rodney, so me being me had enough and told Rodney this. There was a big barn full of bales of straw from floor to the roof of the barn, so we climbed to the top and started to move the bales around to create a hole ten foot deep. We called the boy into the barn and told him to climb up. When he got to us, I hit him with my best punch right in the face and he was in such shock he cried like a big poof. He had been bullying us for a whole week. I ran into him at the same time as my brother, he didn't know he was right over the hole we had made and he dropped right into it, so me and Rodney got the bales we had moved and covered him up. Me and Rodney were killing ourselves laughing as we climbed down. We could hear him crying and calling for his mum. He did get out eventually and grassed us up to his mum and dad who didn't believe him.

We were living a different life by being fed and washed every day. Dee would also buy us clothes because we would turn up with holes in what we owned. Up until I was released from prison I kept in contact with Dee, she was a really special part of my life. She gave me some hope even though it was short lived.

After mum died, my two older brothers who were 15 and 16 would go out to work and were never at home. They would collect their wages and give it to Bin who would, of course, squander it down the pub as they also did. As they were older and earning money they never felt the shame of having clothes full of holes. They now say they do not remember that bullshit, but in my opinion they choose not to remember those times. I can see why as they are painful memories.

Rodney found fun in everything he did and everywhere he went. Once we were in our back garden and the neighbours had left their backdoor open. Rodney told me that Alice our neighbour had gone shopping and told me to follow him. We climbed over the fence and went into her house. Rodney came up with the idea of changing the house around, so off we went and started moving stuff around. We started with moving the TV to the opposite side of the room, then went on to move chairs out of place, swapped pictures around, etc. We were pleased with our handy work because it looked really good. We left Alice's newly laid out home and sat outside the front of our house and waited. It wasn't long before we saw Alice coming back with bags of shopping, so we ran out to the garden and hid. The next thing we heard was Alice screaming out 'what's happened' and crying out for her husband, Stan, who wasn't home. Me and Rodney were hiding and crying with laughter on the floor. Rodney was nuts with ideas like that. To this day I think the show '60 Minute Make Over' got their idea from Rodney! 30 years later, I told Alice what we had done that day and she laughed just as me and Rodney had done all those years before.

I was struggling at school, I couldn't concentrate and my head was all over the place. I was missing my mum so much and that was all I could focus on. I was not allowed to grieve by talking openly so it was all trapped inside me. Bin was unwilling to acknowledge and help my pain. He made it feel like she never existed and any time she was spoken about, he would shoot whoever it was down. I would go through photo albums all the time just to look at her and keep her fresh in my mind. These albums were hidden and there were no photos on the side or on walls. In my opinion, there should have been photos displayed all over the house but there were none.

This played on my mind so much, so when I was in school, I was unable to take in English, maths or any other lesson. All I wanted to do was get up and scream at the top of my lungs and the last thing I wanted to do was as I was told. Me being naughty was my way of telling the world to fuck right off. If I was sitting in a Religious Education lesson, I would be thinking 'if there was a god, why would he take away a mum from her 10 kids when they needed her so much'. I actually thought God was a tosser. I felt like school was just somewhere I was told I had to go and if I didn't go, I would be sent back to the care home. My love for my brothers and sisters was too strong to bear the thought of being separated from them again. I worried too much about Darren picking on the wrong bigger boys and who was going to look out for him. School for me was about eating as much food as they would give me and surviving.

Another special person in my life was West Ham Joe who showed me the love and kindness I lacked at home and in my life in general. It was a cold night in 1978, and I was sitting with my football outside the Queen's pub hoping to get a bag of crisps. Joe came out of the pub and asked me what football team I supported. At the time, I supported Manchester United, so that's what I told him. Joe wasn't impressed and went on to tell me that I could not support a northern team seeing as I was born and bred in the East End. Joe was Irish but was nuts about West Ham hence the nickname West Ham Joe. Out of the blue Joe told me to meet him at 12:00 that Saturday and that he was going to take me to watch West Ham. Joe said he knew my dad and that he would ask his permission first. Bin didn't give a shit what I got up to so it was a done deal.

We met that Saturday morning and made our way to Upton Park, home to West Ham FC. We jumped on the No. 15 bus on Commercial Road and that took us right to the ground. On the way there, Joe told me the history of the club and lots of football stories which I loved because I was passionate about the game. When we got off the bus, the atmosphere was buzzing. There were supporters everywhere wearing West Ham tops, scarves and hats. I fell in love straight away. Joe filled me in on all the goings on and told me about the famous 'I'm forever blowing bubbles' anthem, which he said I must learn so I could join in with all the supporters.

We went for breakfast in a café on Green Street next door to the ground and Joe said I could have whatever I wanted, which was music to my ears and a love song to my belly. After we finished breakfast, we made our way to the ground and Joe bought us both programmes. He had paid for us to get in at the turnstile. Once we were in the ground, we made our way to a great view where we could see the whole pitch. More and more supporters were arriving, singing songs at the tops of their voices and it was deafening, but I was now hooked. There were 30,000 people singing one song; 'I'm forever blowing bubbles' and the atmosphere was out of this world. The game then started and I was glued to the pitch while Joe gave me a running commentary on what the players should be doing and he knew what he was talking about. Half time came and Joe got me a cup of hot Bovril to warm me up because it was a freezing day. That day was one of the best days of my life and I fell in love with West Ham and also with Joe. After that, we would meet up for every home game for two and a half years. It was our ritual and I still go over to West Ham and do the same things that we used to do.

Joe became someone I really loved, he showed me such kindness and wanted nothing in return. He really opened my eyes and I wanted to have his outlook on life. Eventually, I grew out of Joe taking me to West Ham but I did carry on going. I would always see him out and about around the East End with his West Ham hat on. In my 20s and 30s if I bumped into Joe I always gave him money to go and have a drink. There was no price on what Joe had done for me as a kid, but I just wanted to try and pay him back a little bit to say thanks for the memories. Joe was a big drinker but not once did he drink in front of me when I was a kid.

I'd always look out for Joe and so did my pals if they saw him around. Joe would always tell me that he'd seen one of my mates when he was out, but he never got their name. There was a time when I hadn't seen him around for a few weeks so I asked about and no-one had seen him. I eventually found out he was in the London Hospital so went over there. I found him in a hospital bed not looking good at all and he'd lost weight and looked frail. He was really pleased to see me and we had a chat and he then told me he was suffering from TB, but was on the mend.

I asked Joe if there was anything he needed and anything he wanted I would bring for him. The only thing I could think of on my own was a West Ham top. Joe was a very private man and never told me anything about his life. He asked if he could use my phone because he wanted to call his sister in Ireland. I knew he had family over as he would say from time to time he had just been to visit her. We both spoke to his sister and she had no idea who I was. I explained to her the story of how we met and how Joe had introduced me to West Ham and she was a little taken aback. The next day I turned up at the hospital and there was a bloke I didn't know sitting next to Joe's bed and talking to him. When I walked in Joe's face lit up like it always had done and he told me the bloke was Andy, his grandson. The three of us started to talk about West Ham and anything we asked Joe he would know the answer. I would google things on my phone to try and catch him out at times, but this man knew more than google. I'd

51

seen this man win money because he knew about all football not just West Ham.

Me and Andy left the room for a little while to have a chat and I asked him what was wrong with Joe and my god he fucked me with what he told me. Joe was dying and was riddled with cancer and only had a few weeks to live. Andy told me that his family in Ireland told him about me and the whole family were shocked and wanted to know who I was as I was caring for Joe. I told Andy that his family did not have to worry while Joe was in hospital as I would take care of him. Andy and his mum lived in Halifax and the family wanted Joe to move to Halifax so they could take care of him, but they also didn't want to take him away from his beloved East End, the people he knew and now that I had showed up, it made the decision even more difficult for them. I told Andy that the family had to do what was best for them and I would visit Joe no matter where he was. Andy said that his mum would feel much better now that he had spoken to me. I knew Joe had a daughter, but that was all I knew.

Over the next week, I pumped Joe for information about his life and my god did he surprise me. Joe was now 89 years' old and told me that he had been at Normandy on the beaches in World War II just two days after the main landings. I was gobsmacked by all the stories he told me and saw Joe in a completely different light. He told me that he didn't want to go to Halifax and that he would be fine in a couple of weeks; he didn't know that I knew just how ill he was and I didn't let on. He knew how ill he was but kept it from me.

One day Joe asked me to go to a lady's house as she was holding some money for him and because he was going to a care home in Halifax, he couldn't 'land there with no money' – those were the words he used. I met this lovely woman and I'd spend time with her taking her to visit Joe in Halifax. This particular day I went to Joyce's house and she told me she was in contact with Joe's family and they were questioning her about me, so I told her our story. On our trips, to see Joe we had good chats and I found her to be a lovely old cockney lady with a heart of gold. Joe had told her he was terminally ill, but had told her not to tell me. I also met Joe's daughter, Margaret, and found out that she had been separated from Joe from a very young age and was brought up by Joe's sister in Ireland. We came to the conclusion that Joe had done for me what he couldn't have done for Margaret. In my eyes that makes me and Margaret brother and sister. Joe was more of a dad to me than Bin ever was. He told me that when he first saw me, he saw a skinny little street urchin with hardly any clothes on for that time of year and he told me that he wanted to help me.

The last visit I made to Halifax to see Joe alive, I stood at the end of his bed and I knew I was never going to see him alive again, so holding back tears, I sung the one song I know he loved at the top of my voice; I'm Forever Blowing Bubbles. He sat up, told me to shut up because I'd get him fucked out of the care home and we both laughed.

> **For West Ham Joe:** I can honestly say you helped me at a time in my life when I desperately needed to be helped and I am forever grateful. I will go through life with all the lessons I picked up from you and I know I'll be a better person for it. Thank you Joe. West Ham Joe.

I met Joe in 1978 and 35 years later in 2013, I spoke at his funeral in Halifax, West Yorkshire and I was humbled to do so.

CHAPTER 8

Cheeky Urchin in a Turbulent Environment (CUTE)

Me and my mates on the estate were little rogues and tearaways! We'd get up to all sorts and I mean all sorts at a young age. We loved to play football and were from families all in the same boat. There weren't many families on our estate that had just the one kid. My pal Ronnie, who I'm still friends with today, had more brothers and sisters than I did and that's saying something! Our passion was football and we were very good players. Wherever we were a football was close by – it may not have been our ball, but a ball was close all the same.

We used to go to the Valence Youth Club along with all the other naughtiest of naughty kids on the Chicksand Estate. What a place it was, I have many fond memories of it. We would play football matches against the other clubs in the East End. At the time, we were eight years' old and would watch the older boys play. It always ended up in a fight. I'm not talking just a slap, it would be a full on street fight. Where I come from there were some game young blokes including my older brothers; Paul was stabbed in the arm during one fight. The clubs were a breeding ground for no good, not for all, but for most and mainly people ended up on the wrong side of the law. A lot of clubs didn't like coming to play football at Valence Youth Club on Chicksand because of the trouble.

As me and my pals got older we followed suit to what we'd witnessed as eight year olds. We played a team called New Cambridge from Shoreditch once and us boys tried to turn their minibus over. Violence was all around that particular day and we'd gone nuts.

Growing up on Chicksand could be quite intense sometimes. There were some very hard young men who wouldn't even think about taking a backward step if in the face of confrontation. The pain of running away felt much worse than the pain of a good hiding and in the early 80s Chicksand proved that they ran from no-one. There was an invisible boundary around Chicksand and you only came on to the estate if you were welcome. There is lots of written bollocks in the media now about gang cultures around the country and it's written in the papers like it's a new thing. There have always been gangs in London.

Outside of the Chicksand boundary was a much bigger area; Bethnal Green. One night a few boys from Chicksand went to a party and got into a fight over a girl. A fight kicked off and one the Chicksand boys beat the shit out of someone from Bethnal Green. This wasn't taken well at all and over the next few weeks a major street war started to brew. It was coming up to bonfire night and the older boys on Chicksand were on high alert as they'd been told that Bethnal Green were coming to Chicksand for revenge. The older boys were tooled up and waited every night for a week, but Bethnal Green never showed. They'd had scouts out who'd found out about this and they also found out that Bethnal Green would not come on to Chicksand on their own and had been asking other gangs from all over the East to help them. In total, there were 15 older boys in their late teens from Chicksand and they were all game for what was coming their way. During that week of waiting they'd set a bin alight in Hanbury Street and stood around it to keep warm while waiting for something to happen.

Bonfire night came and word went around that Bethnal Green were on their way, so the older Chicksand boys were ready and waiting. One of the older boys took me and a few of us younger ones to the top floor of Kingward House on Hanbury Street and gave us two milk crates full of petrol bombs. Our job was to throw the petrol bombs as soon as Bethnal Green got within 40 feet of us which was where the older boys were standing around the warm bin.

What I saw next shook me and I thought our older boys were going to be killed. Deal Street is a road off of Hanbury Street that runs up to St Anne's School and from where I was standing on the top floor of Kingward House all I could see was a sea of heads bobbing up and down, heading our way and they kept on coming. I could no longer see the road and as they got closer, the noise they were making was unreal. There must have been a good 400 of them and they were all tooled up and feeling brave. I don't think one of us thought they would turn up so mob handed.

The older Chicksand boys were waiting for them to get nearer so us younger ones could throw the petrol bombs and then they could take care of the rest. Me and Ronnie were a part of the group of younger kids and were ready and waiting. There were gangs from all over the East End coming towards us and what happened next meant that no matter where you went in the East End, if you were known to be from Chicksand you were also looked upon as someone not to be messed with. As they got closer the 15 older Chicksand boys ran at the sea of tooled up gangs screaming like madmen and like they were on a death wish. I remember being at the top of the block of flats, looking down on the madness and thinking they're going to die. I couldn't bear to look because my older brothers were amongst those boys. It turned out I had nothing to fear because every single one of Bethnal Green and their associates turned around and ran and kept on running. A few of them got caught and got a good hiding, but not once did they come back or seek revenge. Over the years, I've spoken to many men that were in that 400 strong group and they've all said that for 15 young men to be running at 400 they knew that they didn't fancy getting caught by one of those 15 boys. This was like nothing I've ever seen or likely to ever see again and for an 11 year old it was a massive lesson learnt.

Me and Ronnie were proper little street urchins, if something was movable we'd have it. When we were younger there was a dustmen strike in 1979 which meant bins were not emptied for a long time. There were piles of rubbish building up everywhere you looked. At that time, there came about the marvellous invention of black bags and they were hard to get hold of. Me and Ronnie at the age of 11 found out where Tower Hamlets were stashing their stock and we soon became a godsend to every local business. We would rob boxes and boxes of black bags and sell them on. We were savvy not to pinch the lot and would take just enough so they would refill the stock. We'd then return the next day and take another 20 to 30 boxes. One day we hit jackpot because when we went back for more black bags there were boxes of electric fires. That day we only took one box of electric fires and our usual take of black bags. We took our loot to our buyer and showed him our new line of goods and he said he would have as many as we could get. Me, Ronnie and Mark were doing really well out of this and kept our little earner to ourselves. If we were out with our other mates, we would just slip off and do what we had to do.

Another good earner for me, Ronnie and Mark was bonfire night. The weeks leading up to it, kids all over the place were making their 'penny for the guy' dummy and working out where they were going to plot up. All the kids were sussing out the best places to sit which would be outside corner shops and tube stations. Kids all over London were at it. Me, Ronnie and Mark, on the other hand, took it to another level. The best plot which was our plot was on Whitechapel High Street next to Aldgate East tube. We were right outside the biggest Jewish restaurant Blooms which proclaimed itself as "the most famous kosher restaurant in Great Britain". Jewish people would come from all over London to eat there and you had to have a few quid to do so and Jews would be pulling up in Rolls Royce's. We would work that pavement like three well-tuned street urchins, grafting and squeezing top bob out of every person that passed us. If you got out of a car to eat in Blooms, you got special treatment. We would open the door for the lady, help her out of the car and walk her to the restaurant door where we would open the door for her. She would smile and say 'oh what lovely boys' and at that point we'd turn to the bloke and say 'penny for the guy please sir?' Bang, she would then say 'aaaaah look after them sweet boys'. We had it made. Sometimes the bloke would empty his pockets of all his change, or give us a crispy pound note which happened a lot. The head waiter would come outside on his fag break and watch us work the pavement. He'd be laughing and tell us how smart we were. Our penny for the guy was the nuts, it was a traffic cone with one of our jackets thrown around it, with three bits of plasticine for the eyes, nose and mouth. We didn't have time to make a proper guy like all the other kids, so we improvised and if someone asked where our guy was we would point at the traffic cone and they would laugh and give us more money.

Us three had money lining our pockets and would go over to West Ham to watch the game. We loved to buy a red bus rover ticket. We would go over to Aldgate bus garage and buy our tickets early on a Saturday morning and jump on and off of buses all over London. We had no fear, could hold our own, didn't give a shit and had the best time.

One evening, we got the last bus back to Aldgate. We wanted to get a little nearer to where we lived, but it was only a five minute walk along Whitechapel High Street. When we got back to Aldgate, it was pitch black and quiet in that part of town because it was the weekend and the square mile was a ghost town at weekends. We noticed three blokes standing around the open boot of a car and Ronnie said he didn't think they looked right and Mark agreed. They started to cross the street, but me being a cocky little fucker said 'bollocks they don't scare me' and I started to walk towards them. I was getting closer to these blokes and I noticed they had their hands by their sides. I looked over at Ronnie and Mark and they were giving me the eye to cross the road towards them, but me being me ignored them. As I got to where these blokes were one pulled at me and then, they were all pulling at me. I managed to grab a lamppost and lock my arms around it and held on for dear life. One of the blokes then started to hit me with a rolled up newspaper so the others joined in and one was shouting 'get him in the boot'. They were pulling at my legs and trying to unlock my arms from the lamppost, but I was locked on and not letting go. I could see Ronnie and Mark looking on at me while it was all going on and they were shouting for the old bill or anyone who may have been around. As quick as it all happened, it was over and they jumped in their car and sped off. I picked myself up, ran over to Ronnie and Mark and we walked home. I remember Ronnie turning to me and saying 'I told you they weren't right flash bollocks'. We laughed all the way home and still laugh about it to this day.

Just after that incident a young boy named Jason Swift was kidnapped, sexually abused and murdered by a paedophile gang from Hackney. I still believe, to this day, that it was the same men who had grabbed me that took Jason's life. Even after what happened to that poor boy I still never had any fear, I just didn't care about myself.

Having no fear was a good quality when taking part in crime and at that point I was involved in petty crime at the young age of nine. That was the age I was first nicked, but I wasn't nicked for my first crime! Me, Ronnie and Mark would roam the streets of E1 looking for opportunities. There was money to be taken everywhere. Where we grew up there were world famous street markets such as Petticoat Lane and Brick Lane. People would come far and wide to buy what these places had to offer. Sunday was the most popular market day because the Jewish community did not work on a Saturday because of the Sabbath. Shoppers would buy bags and bags of stuff and a lot of the time could not carry it all so would return to their cars, offload and return for more stuff. We would follow them and take what they had left in their car. It was easy pickings when they were parked in the backstreets because it was quiet with no-one about.

One sunny day just behind Whitechapel Tube Station, we found a loaded car so one of us popped the window. As we were emptying the car, two plain-clothed old bill jumped out, nicked us and took us to Bethnal Green Police Station. All I could think at the time was shit, I've been arrested for the first time, and Bin is going to kill me. I was crying thinking of the beating coming my way. He was a sadistic bastard and would come at you with belts, shoes, bamboo sticks, mops, anything he could get his hands on. When he arrived at the police station, he was happy to see me, which unnerved me. He asked me if I liked the cells which confused the hell out of me. I then realised the cunt was drunk. The old bill was in shock that he had turned up in such a state, little did they know it was his usual state. They gave us a police caution as we were too young to be charged. The top copper sat us down and gave us a bollocking one by one while our parent was with us.

That was the first time I found out Bin had been to prison. Because he was drunk they ran a check on him and had a go at him as well. He had previously been sentenced for smashing a paving slab over a copper's head after beating him up. The old bill were not best pleased with him.

Did my first arrest change me or teach me a lesson? Did it fuck. That day Bin saw something in me that would help feed us all and keep him afloat of beer tokens. After that, I was told to go out thieving and bring money home. From that day until the age of 24 that's what I did to feed my siblings and Bin's greed for drink.

CHAPTER 9

Misguided Survivor – A Way of Life Becomes My Norm

We had no food in the house, this was pretty much how most of my childhood went if I didn't do what I had to. I was one of 10 children and it was my role in my family to do my best to feed by brothers and sisters in any way I could. When you have no money because your old man is a fucking drunk and spends what little you have on alcohol, of course robbing is the only solution and the norm. One week I took my usual Thursday trip to Tesco's on Bethnal Green Road, I hated doing it but in a way was forced to and it was either that or starve. Off I set at the age of 12 with my older sister Tracey. I was given a shopping list on which Bin had written down the basic food items and said that after collecting them, it was my choice what to nick – what a nice bloke he was! I was also given the usual shopping bag and a black four-wheeled shopping trolley with red wheels like the old dears use for shopping. I had now been doing this for a couple of years and knew what had to be done. What annoyed me was that it always had to be in the evening when I wanted to play football with my mates.

Me and Tracey entered the supermarket with everything we needed apart from the money to pay and starting from the top of the list started to load our old dears trolley. After a while, I noticed two old battle axes were following us around the store. I told Tracey what I'd noticed, but she told me to shut up, stop being silly and finish what we'd came to do so we could leave. We had loaded up and were walking towards the exit, just like I did every Thursday, and I noticed one of the women standing by the sliding doors. I can still see her now, a big fat woman with black greying hair. I carried on walking not a care in the world of what I had just done and was carrying. In a way I knew it was wrong, but my worst fear was having no food in the house and in my eyes not eating was more so unfair. As we were about to leave, the two battle axes and other staff stopped us and asked us to come to the back room. Oh fuck here we go, I remember thinking.

We were in the back room and Tracey was crying, so I whispered to her 'just tell them it was all me and you won't get into trouble'. That was our plan. Two young kids who had been caught stealing to feed their family. They told us that they had been watching me putting food into the trolley and the bag. The bag we had was huge and I'd have to put it on top of the trolley to fill it up because it became too heavy to carry. They then started to empty our bag and trolley onto a long table and I remember thinking 'oh fuck' as there was piles and piles of food. All this food in front of my eyes was for my brothers and sisters to eat and survive on. To be honest there may have been piles of it, but the food didn't last long because as I've said there were 10 hungry children. The shopping totalled over £150 which was a lot of money back then. If you spend that now you still get a shitload but back then, it was a fucking ton of food.

The store detectives, well I think that's what the two battle axes were, were in complete shock at the amount we had tucked away. I think they took pity on us, but still off to Bethnal Green nick we went. I told them that Tracey had no idea what I was doing. She was still crying, but slagging me off at the same time for good measure. In the end, they let her go. At the station, I was told I would be released in a little while and would be taken to a juvenile court where eventually I was given a one year conditional discharge. I was also banned from Tesco, big fucking deal, hello Sainsbury's! All I could think about was how we were going to eat for the next week. I did this every week for roughly two fucking years and even though I was caught and got in trouble, I wasn't told to stop once by Bin. Once I was caught in one store, I'd just move on to another. For me this was the norm just as it's the norm for you to go and fill your trolley and go to the checkout to pay for it. It was my way of life to fill the trolley and bag and leave the store.

I spent a lot of my childhood being embarrassed of how poor we were, but it was my life. My mate's mum Stella, who worked in the beigel shop on Brick Lane and gave me doughnuts was a lovely woman and took pity on me and my family as a lot of people did where I grew up. Bin would send me to the beigel shop every Sunday morning. I would walk up Brick Lane, through the market and the hustle and bustle where street traders were selling their goods. The noise was unbelievable with people shouting at the tops of their voices. There was a big fruit stall on the corner of Cheshire Street where my mate Mark, who lived next door to me, had a Sunday job. I'd always nick a bit of fruit as I was passing on route to pick up our beigels. I remember it would be packed full of people – I don't know if you have ever been to the beigel shop on Brick Lane, but on a Sunday as a kid the queue waiting to be served would be half way up the Lane. Little me would jump the queue, walk to the front and catch Stella's eye as she would be rushed off her feet serving customers. Once I caught her eye, she would give me a warm smile, call me over and give me a sack full of beigels, loafs of bread and bread rolls and send me home after insisting on giving me a kiss. Off I'd trot home and nick a different bit of fruit from my mate's stall. Stella sadly passed away a few years back and I'll never forget her kindness and generosity; a real lovely special lady.

As kids we would go swimming in Goulston Street Baths, we'd slip in one by one until we were all in. After swimming we would be hungry, so we'd go to Tubby Isaac's fish stall and ask

Tubby for something to eat. He would give us stale bread which we would saturate in salt and vinegar and happily wolf it down. We would then walk along Whitechapel High Street to Blooms, walk around the back and knock on the kitchen door. The chef would give us hot latkes which we loved. This was something that was passed down from generation to generation that kids from Chicksand did the same thing for many years, it was a way of life.

In our house there were lots of clothes laying about because nothing was ever thrown away. Another way to earn a few bob would be Bin ordering me to bag some of the clothes up and take it to the ragman on Cheshire Street. I hated doing this, it was a fair old walk and the bags were heavy, but it had to be done for food for the table. There was an old bloke behind the counter, as cockney as you like, who would weigh our tattered clothes and tell me how much he was going to give me. Me being a brash boy would always try and get a bit more out of him and sometimes he would have it and other times he'd tell me to jog on. I'd return home and give the money to Bin, he'd count it and then send me to the shop to buy him fags.

I used to always get up early for school and do my best at getting myself dressed and ready. I'd hear the milkman outside doing his rounds and once he disappeared into the other blocks of flats to make his deliveries, I'd slip out round the corner and find milk and bread on doorsteps and help myself. I recall one such freezing morning, I popped out and pinched some milk and bread and when I got home, I made my little brother and sister sit in front of our three barred electric fire and hold the bread in front of it to make toast before setting off for school. The toast was dry as we had no butter, but at least they had something in their bellies.

Looking back, this was the norm and nothing out of the ordinary. I remember when I was 10 years' old we were going on holiday. We were staying in Ronnie's parents' chalet in Leysdown on the Isle of Sheppey. We were so excited and happy that we were going on holiday together as a family. We arrived in Leysdown and were buzzing by the lights of the arcades and the sticks of rock on display. Little did we know, Bin didn't have a fucking bean in his pocket or enough food for us to eat. We made do though, we picked apples and berries off the trees and made pies. There was a shop on the caravan park we were staying on called Happy Days or Happy Valley – how fucking ironic is that. I spent our time on holiday stealing food out of the shop so we didn't starve. Bin didn't give a shit about us kids having a good time, but we got on with it and had a great time on the beach messing about with each other as kids do.

As well as being poor as a kid, I was always getting into fights, it was just part of my make-up and following in my brothers' footsteps. It wasn't too hard for me to get into a row because I had short fuse. One day when I was about 12, a particularly strange fight happened. I knew a family that had moved from Brick Lane to Bow and they asked me if I would fight with another boy who lived in Bow and of course I said yes. I was told that this boy loved to have a fight, was always in a scrap and he'd heard that I would be a good fight.

As we were making our way to Bow, I remember thinking that I didn't even know the boy, he didn't know me and he hadn't upset me so how was I supposed to fight him. I'd only ever fought someone who had upset me which led to me losing my temper. We got to the boy's house, my mates knocked at the door and a tall skinny kid opened the door. My mates told him that they'd brought me to fight him. He told us to wait a minute because he had to get the keys to his dad's car, which I thought was fucking strange. He walked over to a car, opened the boot, pulled out a pair of steel toe capped boots and put them on. I'd never seen anything like that just before a fight.

We were both looking at each other, sussing each other out and he said to me 'come on, I'm sure you haven't come all this way to look at me'. He was a little bit older than me, but not by much. I walked towards him and we started to fight. It was a good fair fight, we broke a couple of times and then went back at it. After a little while we were broken up because it was felt that we would have kept on fighting all day because no-one was winning or losing. It was weird for me because it was the only time in my life that I've fought and not lost my temper. Over the years that boy turned out to be a much feared man and still is but we still have respect for each other.

CHAPTER 10

Bin Laden the Dictator

I have touched on Bin a little bit so far, but I want to open your eyes fully to what an evil slag he really was. The man, which he has no right to be called, was one sick and wicked bastard. As a kid, I would feel sorry for him. I would think to myself that if he was feeling just a little bit of what me, my brothers and sisters were feeling he must be in pain. I would think he must be hurting because he has lost his wife. I really would put this man on a pedestal like Jesus Christ. Many people in our area thought he was a good and great man. He was all we had as kids and we worshipped him and could see no wrong in him. What I did find strange growing up was not once did he ever visit my mum's grave, I could never understand that along with no photos of her in our house.

I would do my best to be a good boy and do everything he asked, like make him tea every five fucking minutes when he was in the house, go to the shop and basically follow any order he barked. He'd had my mum run around after him all their married life and now he had an army of slaves answering his beck and call 24/7. If we didn't do as we were told and defied him, he would hit us and I'm not talking a pat on the bum. If it wasn't a beating, it was some form of mental torture.

As I was growing up from a kid towards teenage years, I was becoming a boy full of fun and occasionally got up to mischief. The cunt would try and beat the fun and personality out of me with mops, sticks, belts, shoes and anything he could lay his hands on at the time. He once made me sleep in the bath with nothing but my own skin to keep me warm. Before he had sent me to the bathroom and shut me in, he had given me a good hiding and all because I had been messing about at bedtime with my little brother. We had been doing what usual boisterous boys do, running along the bed and fly kicking each other. Unfortunately, when I kicked my brother he slipped and smashed his head on the wall. It was an accident, we had just been playing kung fu.

At one time it felt like we had two families as Jimmy was never home, Michael had moved in with another family to a block of flats opposite our home, Terry floated in and out and Paul was in a world of his own talking to himself with full on mental problems. That left me, Tracey, Kim, Rodney, Darren and Jackie and we really felt the brunt of Bin's punishments. One night we were larking about jumping from bed to bed, chasing each other play fighting and having fun. Bin walked into the bedroom and beat me with a thick bamboo stick. He beat me so hard, my body from head to toe was covered in lumps and welts. I was in so much pain but he didn't stop there, he wasn't satisfied enough. He then grabbed me by my hair still beating me with his other hand and dragged me down the stairs. He threw me in the garden where our pet dog would sleep in all weathers. This particular night was fucking freezing and all I was wearing was my pants and a t-shirt. I did think about fucking off, but reality set in and I realised I had nowhere to go. I paced around the garden trying to warm up and thinking to myself that I could not sleep out there. I could not warm up and my arms, legs and body were hurting from the beating I had just taken. I then walked over to my dog and sat with him, I cuddled up to him feeling his warmth and held him close. He seemed happy to see me as he pretty much spent every day and night on his own in the garden. We both soon drifted off. Our dog was later taken by the RSPCA for being underfed and neglected. It's a pity they didn't take kids for the same reason.

I took many beatings like that over the years and so did Darren. We were very much the same as boys and had energy and personality. Bin didn't like it and would use any excuse to beat the life out of us. He once beat Darren so much he broke his nose. Even after all that endurance we still worshipped the ground he walked on. We were completely brainwashed into Bin's way of thinking. Deep down we knew it was wrong, but couldn't do anything about it because it was the only growing up experience we'd had.

We had a coal cupboard right next to the front door, which was handy as we got older because we would store weapons in it in case they were needed. The cupboard was a fair size but there was no light and it was pitch black so you couldn't see your hand in front of your face. Bin would use this cupboard to lock us in and wedge the door shut with a stick. He would leave us there for as long as he saw fit. He didn't just leave you sitting there in the cold though, he would encourage your siblings to tease you while you were in there. Another one of his favourite places for locking us up was in the garden shed full of spiders and mice and again you would stay there until the fat cunt was ready to let you out. He also liked to ground me for weeks on end. I wasn't allowed to watch my brothers and sisters outside playing and if I got caught looking out of the window, I'd get a good beating.

He was that twisted he'd play us off against each other. He would tell my brothers and sisters to not take any notice of me, or trust me and say that whatever I said was a lie. He didn't just tell them this, he drummed it into them. I'm the most trustworthy out of all of them and him saying that at the time killed me. That would come back to bite the evil vile bastard later in life.

Bin was a professional in his field of being a cunt. Not only was he a manipulative, abusive, sick, pisshead, arsehole, he was also a conman. He would con money out of anyone he could. S.A.F.A. was a charity for ex-service men and women who had fallen on hard times and genuinely needed a helping hand. The proceeds of buying a poppy went to help these poor men and women who genuinely it, but Bin didn't give a shit. This charity had offices in Old Ford Road, next to York Hall the famous East End boxing venue. Bin would march us there and play the victim and fucking hell did he lay it on thick. They would look at us kids and the state we were in. You could see in their faces what they were thinking – oh my god, what little tramps. We were unwashed, had rags hanging off of us, shoes that had seen better days and were underfed and skinny. We were allowed to stay off school on these particular days because it helped him out. He would ask them for money for washing machines, cookers, carpets, clothes for his children, anything at all that would get him money. They would then post him a cheque and he would go to the pub and drink the lot. He would do this scam at various places and the DSS was a favourite of his.

I remember going to East Ham with him and he would get money from a little old man called Freddie who was the brother of his sister-in-law. One day he walked Freddie to a TSB and Freddie withdrew £500 and gave it to him. This wasn't done just the once either I was taken to Freddie on many occasion.

This following story even I find hard to believe and I lived it. It's so fucked up. We all remember playing out with our mates as kids and being called in by your parents at dinner time, but not wanting to go in because you're having too much fun, but your mates have been called in too. Well, Bin took sick to a whole new level. Us Huttons would be called in and told dinner was ready and to sit at the table. Bin would be busying himself around the

71

kitchen in front of the kitchen window by the sink and cooker, but be busy doing fuck all. We would all be sitting there for a time and after a little while he would say to one of us 'OK you have now finished now go to the front room'. Another two or three minutes would pass and then Bin would turn to someone else and they would be told the same thing about being finished and going to the front room. This would go on until no-one was left at the table. We were told to sit in the front room and let our food go down and digest before we were allowed back out to play. Now this is the sick bit, THERE WAS NO DINNER, we hadn't been given anything to eat. It would be a fucking Monday, Tuesday or Wednesday and there would be no food left from the previous Thursday's shoplifting spree. The shoplifted food didn't take long to disappear. After we had not eaten and waited for the imaginary food to go down, to pass the time we would run around the house touching every wall until he told us we could go back outside to play. Still to this day I can't get my head around that one – it's just pure evil.

If I eat in company now people say to me 'for fuck sake Gal you eat too fast, you couldn't have enjoyed that plate you just polished off'. If I'm with a pal and we're in the pie 'n' mash shop, I finish a double pie and double mash before my pal has finished one pie. The reason I eat so quick is because when I was a kid sitting around the table and we did have food, if you ate slowly everyone else would snatch food from your plate, so I learnt to eat fast – doesn't mean I'm not enjoying it, I'm just enjoying it quickly!

Growing up mentally abused, starved, beaten and manipulated I didn't really stand a chance. They say smile and the world smiles with you. I'd do this in the outside world, but the world was never allowed to know what went on inside. Please bear this in mind, you can live next door to someone and not know what sort of life they are living, what's happening or what they are doing. None of us know what goes on behind closed doors.

CHAPTER 11

Secondary School Menace

I didn't really have a good start at secondary school. I went to St Bernard's RC for boys. The school was made up of two buildings. One housed the 1st, 2nd and 3rd years on the old Bethnal Green Road and the other the 4th and 5th year boys on Cheshire Street, just off of Brick Lane. I followed in the footsteps of my older brothers going to St Bernard's, so before I'd even started I had the Hutton reputation. To be honest I didn't help myself because I was caned on my first day for fighting – give them what they expect eh! As well as my older brothers going to St Bernard's a lot of kids from my primary school St Anne's, also went there so I wasn't on my own. As I was a ringer for my older brothers everyone knew who I was.

It was my first morning in big school and we were being sent from class to class up until lunchtime which was our first break as there had been no morning break because they were rabbiting on about rules and class timetables. We were finally allowed to go to lunch which was a godsend because I was starving and could smell the food being prepared. I lined up in the queue and was given a ticket for my free lunch I was about to receive. I was told I must pick up a ticket every day otherwise I wouldn't be allowed a school dinner. I remember thinking yeah right like that is going to happen, try and stop me. I noticed there was a game of football going on outside and thought I'll have some that and it would be my chance to show off my skills. I wanted to play for the school team, so finished my lunch in record time and went out to the playground.

I joined in the game and it was a free for all, the ball was all over the place, no-one was passing the ball and no-one had a fucking clue whose side they were on. I managed to get the ball and then some black kid kicked me right in the shin. Well, I wasn't fucking happy and told this kid exactly what I thought of him and then whacked him to show him what I meant. There I was on my first day in secondary school, fighting in the playground and giving some kid a good hiding. To be fair, he was trying to have a go. We were pulled apart and broken up by three teachers, so I just stood there but this cunt was still trying to have a go even though I'd just beaten the shit out of him. I was standing there taking the telling off from the teacher who was shouting at me and all of a sudden the black kid appeared out of nowhere and kicked me straight in the bollocks. Now I wanted to kill this kid.

We were separated and taken to the head of the lower school's office, Mr Fleming, a skinny nerdy looking bloke with square silver framed glasses. He wasn't happy and berated me for starting school on the wrong foot, which was probably the same foot I wanted to plant on the other kid's chin. Mr Fleming then told me my arse was going to get caned and that he was sure he would be seeing a lot of me in his office in the coming years. He then told me to bend over and well this cunt hit me three times across the arse cheeks and fuck me it stung at first. I didn't give a fuck though because after five minutes it was fine and I'd grown up with Bin doing the same but much harder. I did think to myself that if the first day was going to be like that then I wouldn't be there long but not because they'll throw me out. I think if you wanted to be thrown out of that school you would have had to burn the place down.

After the first day, I settled in to school and attended every day. I was enjoying it because it was a laugh and there was food on offer. I used to walk to school with Rodney and a few kids from the other flats around the estate. After school we would get up to mischief and go to shops and pop in to shoplift sweets as it was something to do. I found nicking the odd Mars bar easy as I was used to stealing for a family of 11 from Tesco's on a weekly basis.

I got through the first year trying hard with school work, but I was playing catch up because in junior school my head was all over the place. I still missed my mum and thought about her every day, but I was getting on with life. Being a thief, looking out to earn a few bob and having clashes with other kids had now become the norm.

My next door neighbour Mark moved to my school and into my class as he didn't like Stepney Green school. Mark moved next door when he was five years' old with his mum Alice, his sister Sharon who wanted to take me to the launderette when I got run over and his other brothers and sisters, there being six of them in total. When Mark moved to my school, we became the best of friends and stuck together. We had such a laugh at school and where one of us was, the other wasn't far away. We spent most of our time in the headmaster's office and if we were not in there, we were in the same class which was the most misbehaved class you could ever imagine. Is all we wanted to do, along with every other boy in our class, was play up and make it fun. Rodney was in the year above me and one day a couple of his mates stood outside of our classroom and couldn't believe what they were seeing.

We had an Asian maths teacher, Mr Khan, who was feared by kids in the school as he would lose his temper and either hit you or literally throw you out of his class. One day I decided to let him meet his match, so I told everyone in my class that I'd had enough of this prick and today was the day we were not taking any of his bollocks. The lesson began and we all started talking so Mr Khan started to go off on one and was shouting trying to get order in the room, he had no chance of that. I jumped up on a table and everyone else followed suit and we all started running and jumping from table to table making so much noise. Mr Khan was going nuts and grabbed one boy and threw him out of the class telling him to go to the headmaster's office. We all carried on running and jumping on desks, so he grabbed another boy and told him to do the same. He could not get control of the class so grabbed another boy and dragged him to the headmaster's office shouting to the rest of us that he would be back with the head.

When he returned with the headmaster, Mr Hawkridge's face was a picture as we were all standing up against a wall being cool and not saying a word. The head was open mouthed, completely confused and eyeballing us all. He then singled me out because in his mind it would have been me who was behind it and to be fair he wasn't wrong. He said in a stern voice 'Hutton where are all the tables and chairs'? I called him over to where the window was and said 'there they are sir'. When Mr Khan had left the classroom I had decided to open a window and chuck a chair out of it and everyone else followed with other furniture. As we were throwing the tables out we were laughing and shouting out pleased at the possibility of being sent home because of our actions.

Mr Hawkridge turned to me and said 'right Hutton this is what is going to happen. You and the rest of the class are going to pick up all the furniture and put everything back where you found it, by that time your lesson will be over and you are going to come to my office, not all of you, just you Hutton'. Off we all went to pick up the tables and chairs and also stopped to have a sly fag. I arrived at his office and he invited me in and told me to sit down. This was a first as he would normally have me and Mark stand in front of his desk and he would go into a long speech about how he has taught all of my brothers and how Bin was such a good man and I'm the naughtiest young man he's ever come across blah dee bloody blah. He would never actually tell me off directly for what I had been sent to him for. This particular day I sat down and he was talking to me, going on and on about god knows what. I wasn't taking a blind bit of notice, but nodding and saying 'yes' and 'no' when I thought the time was right.

After that incident, he called me into his office every single day between 11:00 am and 11:30 am and would give me money and send me to Pellicci a café on Bethnal Green Road frequented by TV and film personalities. Besides all the trouble I'd caused, for some reason Mr Hawkridge liked me. He was an alright bloke really and used to send me to Pellicci to fetch him a sandwich and cup of tea for lunch. I would order his sandwich and tell Neville the old cockney Italian waiter my order for myself and I'd sit and eat. Neville would then give me Mr Hawkridge's sandwich and I'd walk back to school just in time for school dinner. Me and Mr Hawkridge had an unwritten agreement that I would keep his change. I think it was an unwritten agreement i.e. he never asked for his change and I certainly didn't offer it! I never did thank him for paying for my breakfast every morning. I would take Mark along sometimes and he couldn't believe my luck. I'd return to the school and deliver Mr Hawkridge his sandwich, he'd thank me and I'd leave his office. Looking back, he knew exactly what he was doing. He either wanted me out of the school so classes were not disrupted or he knew I was having a tough time at home, so was trying to help me out. He was a good bloke and I respected him in my own way.

I was a bit of a prankster at school, but probably sometimes took it too far. I had one teacher, Miss Humphries, who I didn't like. I couldn't tell you what she taught because I didn't listen to a fucking word she said. One particular day I decided to drag the hosepipe into class and soak her with it. It was fucking hilarious at the time. Miss Humphries made the mistake of not liking me and showing it by bullying me. For a while, she got away with it because I respect women.

One day and I'm not proud of it, we had a lesson just before lunch and Miss Humphries left the classroom to get something and said that if the bell rang, we were allowed to leave. I had clocked that she had left her packed lunch on the side so done no more but walk over to it, open her sandwich and gobbed in it. I knew if I got caught out for that I'd be in big trouble, so called Mark over and he did the same. I didn't leave it there, I called every single boy up in the class to do the same. Miss Humphries returned and as she did the bell rang, but prior to that I'd told everyone to stay in their seat. She told us to go to lunch, but I asked her if it was OK if we stayed for a little longer and she said that was fine, but said she must eat as she had marking to do. As she picked up her phlegm sandwich, one by one my classmates were running out of the room and throwing up. I told Miss Humphries I believed there was a bug going round. At the same time, I was heading for the door because I couldn't watch and all the while pissing myself laughing.

In the third year, Rodney moved to the upper school and I was still in the lower. Up the road at the end of old Bethnal Green Road there was another large school, Danford, which for many years was rivals with my school. There would be street fights with large groups of kids from each school. It has now been quiet for a few years, but the hate is still there between the schools. I knew a lot of kids that went to Danford, they wasn't from my estate but mainly from Bethnal Green.

One day I was walking home with my pal, Dominic, who I grew up with on the estate and we came across a boy, the same age as us who was wearing a Danford uniform. Dominic like me loved to have a row so as we were walking towards this boy we looked at each other and knew what each other was thinking. As the boy got close enough, I jumped up and kicked him straight in the mouth. As he stumbled backwards, Dom was on him throwing punches. The boy was dazed and hanging on to a fence and then sprung up and was on his toes and had it away. Me and Dom were laughing and shouting after him that he was a Danford mug.

The following morning at school we were telling our mates what had happened and were still laughing about it. It didn't take long for word to get around the school that Danford were coming to our school at lunchtime and were going to smash up our school and everyone in it because of what me and Dom had done to that boy. Me and Dom didn't give a fuck and were up for it. The teachers got wind of the rumour and locked the school gates.

Lunchtime came and me, Dom and a few other mates were round the back of the school smoking and we heard a load of shouting, so we ran round to the playground. We saw that everyone was huddled together and backing away from the big black school gates. A load of kids from Danford were on the other side of the gates and I knew a few of them and knew they were capable of a row. One of them stepped forward and shouted out 'which one of you lot is Gary Hutton'? I thought nothing of it and pushed my way through to the front of the crowd on my side of the gate and said 'I am, why'? He then told me that

Danford were there to beat the shit out of me so I invited them in. At that point, they all went crazy and some tried to climb the gates. The teachers had obviously called the old bill because I could hear sirens in the background. Danford then said they would get me after school and scarpered.

From then on, St Bernard's and Danford had wars for weeks meeting in a park called Weavers Field between the two schools. At one of the fights one of the kids up the front for Danford was someone I'd known for years, Johnny K from Chicksand, who I later in life became good pals with. We sent Danford running that day because we'd arrived tooled up.

As wrong as it sounds, I had such a good laugh and a great time during my school years as I had my mates' backs and they had mine.

CHAPTER 12

Come Fly with Me

After my first arrest at the age of nine, crime followed crime. Bin saw something in me and it wasn't long before my older peers on the street also noticed I had no fear. My role in my family was to get money and food any which way I could. Bin had uses for me and for the money grabbing pisshead he was, I was gold to him. Say I'd earn £200 for example he would give me a cut of £25, but as I got older, the tables turned and he never knew what I had and I'd be the one giving him his cut. My brothers also would have little earners and give him money now and then as well as kids.

In my teens this had now become my way of life to go out on the rob. I never stooped so low as to rob people's houses that was not my scene or rob some old dear. There were plenty of local factories full of good quality merchandise for the take. They would make clothing and all sorts for all the top major high street stores. The factories were owned by the Jewish who employed cheap labour, mainly from the Bangladeshi community. The older kids on the estate who were now men had started out their criminal careers with the factories but had now moved on to a different level and were getting bigger money. I was 14 or 15 at the time and noticed there was a few quid for the taking, so thought it was now my turn to empty a whole factory and transfer it to my house! Everywhere you looked in my house were leather jackets in all sorts of the latest styles in fashion. You can't beat the smell of new leather and the thought of turning it all into money was like a drug to me. The older blokes who had moved on to bigger and better had taken note of what I was doing and could see I had some bollocks about me, so they started to test me and I'd knock about with them a bit more.

One particular day I was walking around the estate and three young blokes who I had known all my life called me over. They were older than me, always had lots of money and were smartly dressed so I knew they were dodgy as they started out just the way I had. I walked over to the van they were in and they told me to get in so I got in the back. It was a small two-seater van with two of them sitting in the front and one already in the back. One of them told me they wanted me to do something for them which I had no problem with if there was money involved.

They then drove off and told me they'd tell me on the way what they wanted me to do. To tell you the truth I was shitting myself and my mind was racing thinking I can't say stop the van I want to get out. They would have laughed at me and I wasn't having that. The van was heading towards the City and they were very quiet and determined which made me more nervous. We then pulled over and parked on the corner of a backstreet and I noticed a bank opposite which one of them also pointed out to me. The bloke in the passenger seat turned to me and while looking at his watch told me in three minutes a security van would park outside the bank and that a security guard would be emptying sacks of money out of the van and delivering to the bank. I remember thinking this bloke was off his nut and I was in a bad dream and was yet to wake up. He then told me my job was to do whatever I had to do, to get the sacks off the security guard and bring them back to their motor. He also told me the guard knew it was going to happen, but I'd have to make it look good and do a proper job on him, so it looked like a real robbery.

A couple of minutes later, just like he had said a security van pulled over and parked up. This was now happening and a fucking reality not a dream like I'd hoped. My mind was still racing thinking what the fuck am I doing, I'm 14 / 15 years of age. My belly was also racing and jumpy and I felt sick, but the thought of money took main priority in my thought process and that pushed me on. I got out of the van and was walking across the road towards the security van and guard thinking to myself that I'll give him a good dig, two or three if I have to on his jaw to stun him and then take the sacks. Adrenaline was pumping through me which put me on a high and in my head I knew what I had to do and just wanted to get it over with, without thinking too much. I was focussed and getting closer to the guard and only about 20 feet away as he was about to pick up his first sack, so I picked up my pace.

Something had gone wrong because I could hear someone calling my name over and over again and I immediately thought who the fuck is shouting my name at a time like this. It was the three in the van shouting at me to get back in the van and they looked angry which confused me. I mouthed at them 'no I'm doing this' and pointed to say 'look at him I'm going to miss it'. At this point they looked as if they wanted to kill me, so I walked back towards them and the van and climbed back in and asked what was going on. The three of them were looking at me with shocked faces and then one broke the ice by laughing and telling the other two that I had the bollocks of a man not a boy. I was still confused and was told that I had passed their test and we were now going to another place where the real bit of work was and I was going to earn them and me lots of money. Needless to say, I heard those words and was game. Show me the money and I'm more than game.

The bloke in the front passenger seat then said to the one in the back with me not to let me see where we were going and to cover my eyes and ears. I wasn't happy with this because I knew anything was possible with these three as I'd heard stories of what they'd done in the past and what they had got up to. As we were moving, I was trying to peak at where we were and was told it was for my own good that I couldn't see where I was or where we were going to end up but we'd be there in 20 minutes. I did see that we were approaching Tower Bridge and crossing into south London, the only time I had been on that side of the water was when I'd visited my aunt's house in Peckham. We drove over the bridge and every now and then the van would stop and pull over. A little while later we stopped for good and they were talking amongst themselves and I was allowed to see and hear properly again.

I opened my eyes and at first it was a little hard to focus, so I rubbed my eyes and looked out of the window-screen in front of me. We were in a car park and to the right was an office block, but oddly over on the left was a helicopter, so I rubbed my eyes again to make sure. They then told me that we were going to do a bit of work, but they needed the pilot to fly the helicopter! At that point I thought they were fucking nuts and was shitting myself thinking what the fuck had they got me into, so I slapped myself on the back of the head to make sure I was awake. I wanted to hit the 'stop' and 'rewind' button to the point in that day where they called me over to the van and before I climbed in.

I was then told two of them were going to get the pilot from the office block and they'd call me over to the helicopter when they were ready. When they reappeared, they had this bloke with them who was dressed as a pilot including yellow striped lapels on his shoulders and were heading towards the chopper. At first I thought they're kidnapping the cunt and that I couldn't back out and needed to show them I had the bottle, but it was the last place I wanted to be. They then called me and the other bloke over to get in the chopper. We got out of the van and I couldn't feel the floor as it felt like I was floating and in a dream. We reached the helicopter and climbed in.

I was sat in a fucking chopper thinking it was actually happening and was then passed some headphones. The strangest thing happened next and I wasn't prepared, they all turned to me and was looking at me long and hard. I was white with fear at the thought of what we were about to do and shook my head at them as if to say please let's just stop now. My new pal in the front of the helicopter then asked me 'where do you want to go'? I let out a big breath that I'd been holding in for ages and said 'please I just want to go home, take me home please'. He then turned to the pilot and said 'Whitechapel first please mate'. I couldn't believe my ears as we all had headphones on with built in microphones and I could hear the others talking and now they were laughing. They were using the helicopter like a fucking cab.

We took off and headed across London, flying above all the famous landmarks. They were laughing and ribbing me, including the pilot who was in on it and taking the piss out of me saying at one point they thought I was going to cry, but thought I had a lot of bottle because most people my age would have fucked off a lot earlier. As we flew over where we lived, I could see my mates playing football on the green in front of my house which looked so small. We were flying around for about two hours and after that day and after proving myself with the security van they gave me plenty of work. That experience had me hooked on money and tasty clothes and the lifestyle needed feeding. What a great day if you get the chance, it's a must, as the views are out of this world – obviously book it through a proper tour guide and not three mad adrenaline junky money getters!

Following the helicopter incident and me passing their test with flying colours, one of the blokes gave me the rundown on a bit of work he had just come across. He didn't think there was enough money in it for him, but for me in my mid-teens there was, so he offered it to me because he thought I had the bollocks of someone 10 years older than I was and I was game. Sometimes I was so lucky when given a bit of work. I went and had look and it was a huge sports shop that had just taken a big delivery of Reebok trainers. I knew Reebok would sell and fly out of my hands as it was the new big footwear on the street.

The big bales being delivered were six foot high and would have to be broken down, so I knew I couldn't do it on my own and needed help, so called two mates on board and gave them the rundown. We got some tools together and I told them to meet me at 2:00 am as it would be quieter with less old bill knocking about. I knew it was going to take a few hours for us to get our prize and that we'd have to be quiet because at that time of the morning any noise multiplies in sound and can be heard from far away.

The shop front was really secure, but we had a little bit of know-how and managed to stop the alarm from outside. We walked off and waited to see if deactivating the alarm had worked and no old bill or key-holder turned up, so all was sweet. We searched around the place and no-one was about so we got to work to get what we came for. I had a pair of heavy long bolt cutters and with ease cut straight through the chunky big locks on the two sets of roller shutters covering the shop. I was wearing gloves but still wiped the cutters clean and hid them down a manhole so I could leave them behind. If I wanted, I could go back and get them another time. Me and my two pals at that point felt a bit anxious because we knew as soon as we rolled up the shutters they were going to make a shitload of noise, but we didn't have a choice if we wanted to get what we came for. We were used to working during the night and being as quiet as we could so cracked on. Two of us rolled up the shutters while the other one had his eyes peeled and kept watch. The fucking noise from the shutters was unreal.

On the inside of the shutters was a big glass shop front window which we cut through with glass cutters. The window was now out and we were on the move inside. We moved everything we were taking to the front of the shop, so I went out to go get the van so we could start to load up. I stepped outside of the shop and heard a ping of metal hitting metal and then heard it again and again and then something hit me. It was a fucking pellet from a rifle; some cunt was firing at me and shouting that he had phoned the old bill. I threw my hands over my face so I didn't get hit in the eyes and shouted at my mates to get the fuck out of there. As they scarpered, the bastard was still shooting from the roof of a building opposite. It was a fucking night watchman and instead of being a normal security guard and watching telly and falling asleep this prick was patrolling.

We were away on our toes and running through the streets heading back home to Chicksand Street where we knew we could melt away into the flats and be safe on our estate. We could hear old bill sirens everywhere heading in the direction of the sports shop. At that point, it was every man for himself and we split up after agreeing to meet up around the flats later on. I stopped running and started walking as I wasn't too far away from my destination which was just through an alley that came out on to Brick Lane. I was 30 yards from Chicksand Street and just about to turn a corner when an old bill motor pulled up in front of me and there was two plain-clothed old bill in it. They got out of the car and asked me where I had been, so I bluffed and said that I'd just been at some bird's house, I'd fell asleep, just woken up and was on my way home as I would be in trouble if I didn't get home soon. Over their radio, I could hear that my two pals had already been picked up.

By this time it was 4:00 am and they told me I was too young to be out at that time of the morning and said that they wanted me to get in their car and go with them. I told them I was fine as I only lived at the bottom of the street and once there I would be fine but they were having none of it. They took me back to the shop where my two pals were in handcuffs and some fat prick started to shout as I was helped out of the police car. The night watchman said 'that's him, that's the one I was looking at who was in the doorway'. Bollocks is what I thought. I was told I was under arrest and was put in handcuffs and off to Bethnal Green Road nick we went.

They kept me in for 24 hours and I passed the time away by reading the cell walls. Everyone who had had the pleasure of staying in that cell had scratched their names in the walls and funnily enough I knew most of them. Some had written little one liner's that were funny and others just slagged off the old bill. During my interview, I was shown a set of bolt cutters and knew the game was up. I said absolutely nothing, they got nothing out of me, but I was charged with commercial burglary. They then let me go and told me that I had to return to court a month later.

I was still too young to go to court on my own so Bin came with me. The judge wasn't happy and was going mad but not at me, at Bin for allowing someone as young as me to be out at that time of night. I was laughing inside because the judge really slagged him off for being a bad parent. Bin's reply was the usual 'I'm a single parent of 10 kids' trying to get the sympathy vote. The judge didn't ease up at all and really gave it to him. I received a suspended sentence and we were allowed to leave. Bin was so pissed off and called me all the cunts under the sun for getting caught. He said if I ever got caught again he would not attend the court hearing with me – thanks Bin but you wanted the spoils!

Bin didn't give a fuck what I got up to as long as I was lining his pockets with money. When I was younger he used to treat us boys differently compared to my sisters. We all brought Jackie up while dragging ourselves up. This was confusing as a kid because us boys were treated so badly and never shown any love. Not once did I ever receive a birthday card. Every birthday was just the same as every other day. I remember one birthday me, Bin and Kim were talking outside the front of our house and I said 'don't I get anything for my birthday'? Kim looked at me and laughed and I looked at Bin. He turned to Kim and told her to take off a gold keeper ring that she was wearing and told her to give it to me. Kim wasn't happy and refused, so Bin told her he would get her a better ring the following week and he kept that promise to her. This was something I could never under-stand as a kid that my sisters could have anything they wanted including the latest bikes that rich kids had, but I got fuck all apart from a fat lip or a black eye.

Bin bought Kim so much gold. She had loads of it and used to look like Mr T from the A-Team. As she got older she would buy it herself, but as a kid he would buy it for her. She had so much she was once interviewed by a reporter from the Daily Mirror. Kim's words from that interview were "I like to buy gold. I dun-no, why – I just like it. I put down a deposit and buy it by the month. What I've got is worth about a thousand. It's like an in-vestment, innit? Say you're skint, you can just pawn it. Insur-ance? Dunno. Never thought of that." Bin got most of it for her and I never knew the price she paid. I had to go out and get what I wanted and then give it to Bin. I grew up thinking I could go out and get us all what we needed, but my biggest mission in life was getting what I wanted for myself.

As I got a bit older at times I'd lay my hands on a lot more money than £200 and once me and a good pal had it right off. I was roughly 19 at the time and I was in the Queen's pub playing pool and Bin was drinking in the corner. The previous night two blokes had turned up at my house and these two blokes were very well known money getters. They were a bit older than me and would give me bits of work occasionally and they liked to fly around in helicopters for fun! Bin was there when they turned up so knew there was something in it for him. He welcomed them in with a big smile and told them to go upstairs which is where I was. They had come round to see how a bit of work had gone and how much it had come to and now they had come to take the prize and turn it into cash.

I was told to go to the Queen's the following day and stay there, so this is what me and my pal did at 11:00 am, opening time. We got ourselves a drink and started playing pool to pass the time. Every half an hour someone would walk in the pub and give me an envelope full of money, this went on all day and each time the envelope got bigger so more and more money was heading my way. Bin was in the corner with his eyes bulging, loving every minute of it. By now Bin wasn't our carer, not that he ever was, we cared for him and provided him with money for the pub as we always did. Tracey, Kim and Rodney were now working, Darren had just left school and Jackie was still in school so we made sure she had what she needed and then some. Bin was a greedy bastard and now I would only give him what I wanted to; like it or lump it was my motto. My brothers and sisters were working and would spoil him and buy him clothes. He wanted for nothing and lived the life of a spoilt served prince and was waited on hand and foot at all times.

CHAPTER 13

Out and About with Youth on my Side

When I left school, I was getting hold of money and living the life I wanted by being the life and soul of the party in the pubs and clubs and drinking until silly o'clock in the morning. I had money to burn and was spending it as quick as it landed in my hands. It didn't matter because I knew there was plenty more where it came from. I was 17 year's old and well turned out, wearing all the smartest current fashions at the time. I was out every Friday, Saturday and Sunday night without fail. My little sister, Jackie, was being spoilt more than usual and was in charge of looking after my clothes and every Friday she knew she was on a windfall. Is all I wanted to do on a Friday night was have a bath and get out by 7:00 pm.

At the time, a lot of blokes my age were on heroin (smack) but not me. Smack had hit the East End in a big way as well as the rest of London. A lot of my mates who I grew up with are still battling with it today and are in and out of prison getting caught for committing crimes to feed their habit. I'd watched them getting into a right state where they couldn't walk or talk, would projectile vomit and then fall into a deep coma. Smack definitely wasn't for me, so I moved away from those circles. I was a party boy and wanted to have as much fun as possible and being in a coma didn't look much fun. I wasn't completely free of drugs. I would stay out drinking all night and to do this I would take amphetamine which was known as speed at the time. Taking speed stopped me getting drunk and taking it I would be wide awake and on the ball. Sometimes I wouldn't sleep for a whole weekend and you couldn't tell I was speeding out of my nut like many others who were on it. It didn't have the effect on me like it did for those who would be pulling strange faces with their jaw swinging about as they spoke non-stop shit, or chewing gum like a mad person. I managed to control those side effects and didn't let the drug control me as I didn't want to let people see me in that sort of state.

Is all I lived for was the weekend and in the week getting a lot of money to fund it. Me and one of my pals who I had known since being a kid, Johnny K who had been on the frontline during the ruck with Danford while I was at school, were out every Friday. At one point, he had just been released from prison and wanted to stay out of trouble and turn his life around. Just after he got out I told him I was taking him out and put some money in his pocket so he could buy a drink and didn't feel uncomfortable – I did this for quite a while and we used to have such a good laugh. Johnny was a real character and full of life, you knew Johnny was in a place as soon as you walked in and the boy loved to dance.

Years later it was my turn to be released from prison and I bumped into Johnny and he said 'Gal I'm taking you out mate as you done it for me and now it's payback time'. Let me tell you there are not many people like that out there. I asked Johnny if we could do this in a week or so as I'd just got out, so we arranged to go out the following weekend. Shortly after seeing him, I received a phone call that knocked me sideways. Johnny had been in a pub in Stepney and had been stabbed to death. I can honestly say with my hand on my heart I was fucking gutted when I got that news and many people were. R.I.P. Johnny K.

Partying wasn't cheap but as crime was my way of making a living it wasn't a problem. I was addicted to money and it had been inbred in me from an early age that if you wanted something you went out and nicked it. I wasn't the only kid like this from the estate I lived on, there were loads of us like it. When I was roughly 14 year's old one of the older boys who had this 'take what you want' attitude used to give me bits of work and did so for many years. He went on to do a lot of bird at her majesty's pleasure for various crimes he had committed. We would also spend nights out partying together in pubs and clubs even though I was a lot younger than him. We ended up on one of those nights out one evening and went to various pubs all over the East End and then on to a nightclub in Commercial Road. We were having a great night and didn't want it to end when the club came to turn us out so he suggested we go to a blues club, so we jumped in a cab and ended up at such a club in the backstreets of Hackney.

We approached the door to the club which was closed, knocked on it and a big Rasta opened and in his Jamaican accent said 'wat'pon boys'? We paid our fiver to get in and walked through to the club and to say we stuck out like a sore thumb is an understatement. If you have never been to a blues club, you won't find many white blokes in there. The place was dark, the music loud hard-core reggae and there was a thick fog in the air where everyone was puffing. The place was packed and everyone was dancing and enjoying themselves, we ordered our drinks at the bar and started chatting.

Standing next to us were four blokes who were talking and drinking with one of them skinning up. My pal who I was with suddenly out of the blue knocked the rizla paper out of the hands of the bloke who was skinning up just as he was putting his weed in. My initial thought was oh fuck why have you just done that, but he hadn't meant to. I wasn't sure if the bloke had bumped into my pal and that's how it happened, but thought if we do manage to get out of this club alive, we're going to be hurt and in bad shape. The bloke whose spliff it was started to go nuts and his mates followed suit. Me and my pal were just standing there, he was in front of me and I was close on his shoulder just behind him. The music stopped and every bloke in the club was looking at us and I thought we're seriously in a fucked situation.

I was slowly looking around thinking OK where is the first blow going to come from. The bloke who had been rolling the spliff was now ready to sort this out his way and was calling us pussy boys and shouting out to everyone in the club something like 'white youth come here and diss da man who is smoking the herb is getting hurt'. My brain wouldn't work fast enough for an idea to get out of this place alive. My mate done no more than put his hand behind his back in the back of his trousers just below his jacket and in a threatening manner told the bloke we were no pussy boys and if this bloke and the rest of them fucking wanted it, they could have it. I was looking at my mate's back for what he had pulled and also looking at all these blokes in the club thinking I was ready for what they had because we were standing our ground and not fucking going anywhere. The bloke who was shouting and being Bertie Big Bollocks thought we had guns and people behind him were moving back. I looked down again at my mate's hand to see what he had pulled and they were clean, he had fuck all! I tapped my mate and whispered that he was a bluffing cunt and he said to just go with it and we needed get the fuck out of there.

The Rasta, who had let us in at the front door, was now in front of all of his pals and saying everything is sweet boys, let's all just calm down, so I said everything is fine mate. I then turned round to my pal and he'd gone and fucked off so quick it was like he'd just evaporated into thin air! I was in this club on my own, standing at the bar thinking I was bang in trouble and racking my brains trying to think how to get out of there in one piece.

There were no mobile phones back then so I couldn't call anyone. I wasn't sure whether or not it was safe for me to leave, but all I did know was that these blokes were looking at me and must have thought I was nuts to still be standing there looking like I didn't have a care in the world. If I'm honest I felt fear that night, but no way was I running – I wasn't born with the 'walk away' part of the brain. By now it was 6:00 am and low and behold my saviour walked in and fuck me was I pleased to see him. He was an old Jamaican man I knew who everyone called Youth and he appeared to know everyone in the club which was a touch. He walked over to me and said 'little Hutton what are you doing in here'? I told him what had happened and asked him to get me the fuck out of there. He walked me out of the club, to his car and gave me a lift home. Thank you Youth.

One particular night I told my pal Mark to come down to a pub in Whitechapel. He had recently moved to Hackney Road in Shoreditch, so he came to the pub and brought a couple of mates with him. One of his mates became one of my pals over time, but I wish if you could travel back in time I would have gone back and told Mark to meet me on his own. We would be out every weekend having such a laugh. To be honest me and Mark were hooked on speed and would be out every Friday at 7:00 pm. It would start off the same every week by me phoning Mark and telling him I'll be round in a minute and he had better be ready. Mark would then tell me he was only just getting in the bath and I'd tell him to hurry the fuck up and ask him if he had the speed. We couldn't go out without it.

We'd start off our Friday by having a couple of drinks with Mark's dad, Stan, and then go to a couple of pubs and then on to a nightclub. Whenever I was out with Mark I never got into trouble, not once did I end up in a fight. When I was out without him, it was a different story and once I got stabbed seven times by a group of blokes.

I'd been in a pub on Old Bethnal Green Road and it had been a good night out. As the night was ending a fight broke out which was nothing to do with me. It involved four or five blokes who were not from the manor. It eventually all calmed down and the blokes ran off. The pub then shut and I was with a pal sitting on a wall outside and we were drunk. The next thing I knew there was a couple of blokes around my mate, so I jumped up and as one of them came towards me I head-butted him and he went down. What I didn't know at that point was that the blokes who had ran off from the fight earlier inside the pub had now come back with twice the amount of people.

I was surrounded and thought I was being punched. After a little while they stood back, looked at me and then done a runner. I could hear a hissing sound and then noticed blood everywhere. I then noticed that my clothes were in shreds and I looked like a cut up Robinson Crusoe. I could feel my arse was wet, so put my hand down the back of my trousers and when I pulled it out it was covered in blood. I started to walk and could still hear the hissing sound, so lifted up my left arm and could see my elbow bone and blood was pumping out. I put my right hand over it to stop some of the pressure and got myself to the London Hospital.

I was told when I got there that I'd been stabbed many times in the back, legs and my arms. At one point, when I'd been surrounded, I had seen a knife coming towards me and had put my left arm up to cover my chest, if I hadn't that knife would have gone straight through my chest and it could have been a whole different story and maybe not one I'd be able to tell today. Being stabbed doesn't hurt at the time but trust me if you're lucky enough to live and tell the tale, it does fucking hurt afterwards! A few years later I was sitting in a pub and one of the blokes who attacked me that night walked in, I never forget a face.

CHAPTER 14

COD – Slippery as a Fish

One of Mark's pals who he'd introduced me to was a good laugh, but I found him to be slippery as they come because the first time I met him he asked me how I got my money and you just don't do that. He saw me spending money quickly and I felt like he was fishing for information, but I didn't say a word and I didn't tell anyone my business who didn't need to know. After a while, I got close with him and he became a pal of sorts and we'd go out in a group. I was guarded around him to start with but after a while he would talk about bits of work he was doing so I opened up a little. Something would always go wrong around him so I was also very wary.

He was a funny bloke and always cracking jokes but looking back I think he done this because he had a lazy eye which was a big hang up for him. When meeting people for the first time he would keep his eye shut, hold his hand over it, or scratch his forehead to hide his eye. I think making people laugh was his way of hiding his eye. People would ask me what I was doing with the slippery cunt but I'd brush it off. After a while, I would soon come to find out how slippery he was. I had never met anyone like him before and still haven't to this day and I don't fucking want to either.

He would pull some fucking strokes and the cunt didn't give a shit. Once he knocked two blokes for a lot of money who had just come out after a ten in prison. When they caught up with him, he denied it was him and gave these two pissed off blokes the name and address of some poor innocent bloke. I dread to think what happened.

This bloke who I shall name COD didn't give a shit about anyone apart from himself and I used to hear all sorts about the strokes he pulled but I brushed them off. I was always conscious when I had a bit of work and would listen to my gut feeling. If I felt a bit of work wasn't quite right, something inside me would go off like an alarm and I'd walk away. I got this a lot and it helped me from getting nicked over the years.

By then it was the 1990s and me and COD had become involved together in selling fake £50 notes. Back then £50 notes were green in colour and at the time the country and economy was getting hit hard by the fakes knocking about and I suppose I'm part of the reason they are pink today. We kept ourselves low because the less people knew, the better. No-one wants their collar felt by the old bill, so we would mostly only sell to people we knew who would buy in bulk and sell them on. At the time no-one knew there was so much funny money about. Before it was common knowledge to the general public, I'd known teams of men and women who would go out for 12 hours a day hitting cab drivers with a £5 cab ride and getting £45 change and also hitting shops. The old bill knew funny money was about but didn't have a clue where it was coming from or how it was flooding the country.

One day I was in a pub in Whitechapel with COD and sometimes he liked to shout his mouth off to impress whoever was listening or who he thought would be a likely buyer. This particular day a pub landlord, fat Terry, was listening. Fat Terry was a soapy unwashed looking bloke with greasy blonde hair and his nickname Fat Terry says it all really, it's not likely you'll see him running a couple of laps around the local park a few times a week. He would more likely be stuffing his face with some greasy shit. Anyway COD was giving him the rundown on what we had and how much we could get and how much he could have it for. COD was also telling him that the more he ordered, the cheaper it would be. Fat Terry was hooked by COD's sales pitch and told us he knew a bloke who would want some and that he'd invite him down to the pub so we could have a chat.

A while later this bloke walked into the pub and he did not look like someone that was in touch with a few quid and I was right. He was a skinny bloke with a long ponytail, wearing a pair of jeans that had seen better days and a t-shirt that hadn't seen the inside of a washing machine but should see the inside of a bin. He came over to our table, sat down and told us his name was Graham while shaking our hands. COD started to talk and I was thinking to myself, I wasn't sure about it. Graham told us that he knew someone who wanted a lot of £50s and he would introduce us the following day.

The next day we met Graham's contact, Matthew, who was a tall well-built smartly dressed bloke, with grey very tight curly hair and a South African accent. I noticed Matthew seemed a bit shady because he kept watching the door of the pub and I didn't like it, so I walked over to the door, opened it and had a look about and there was a bloke walking up and down outside who wasn't from round the area. I left the door open and returned to the table but didn't say anything about the bloke outside because I could tell he wasn't old bill, but something definitely wasn't right. Matthew told us that he wanted us to meet his partner, Roger, in a couple of days and that he wanted to buy a passport which we could arrange for him. We told him we would need a photo of the person who it was for so we could sort the passport out.

Just before he was about to leave I asked him if he had someone outside which threw him off guard and he asked me why, so I told him I didn't like the way he wouldn't stop looking at the door and he came across that he was uneasy about something and that I'd seen someone walking up and down that I believed to be with him. He smiled at me and told me it was his son so we went to the door and I asked Matthew to call his son over which he did and introduced us, but his son looked scared and his eyes were glued to the floor. I thought this was weird and I wasn't happy with it. We arranged to meet Matthew in a pub in Bethnal Green in a couple of days and then he left. I then invited Graham to stay and have a drink with us. I did this because I wanted to pump him for information and find out more. We started playing pool and chatting small talk, but he was being very cagey and weird and wouldn't accept a drink, but was getting on with COD which looked false to me. I sensed this bloke wasn't right, but Fat Terry had vouched for him so I tried to relax. COD then said he was going to arrange a couple of Arsenal tickets and go and watch the match with Graham as they were both supporters. Graham then managed to escape which was obvious that's all he wanted to do, but said he would be back at the weekend to get the tickets.

The following day Matthew got in touch about meeting his partner, Roger. We were to meet him at the hotel he was staying at; the Marriott in North London. The next day we drove over to the hotel in a stolen car (a ringer) with the number plates of a legit motor. When we arrived at the hotel Matthew was in the car park standing beside a top of the range, brand spanking new Mercedes with another bloke at the wheel. After pleasantries of shaking hands, Matthew told us to get in the car and it turned out the other bloke behind the wheel was Roger, his partner. Roger was a small bloke, a bit overweight, but he was well-dressed in a suit and tie. Roger then went on to introduce himself and told us that he worked for an outfit in the Far East, that had a need for a lot of counterfeit notes. We showed him a sample and he liked what he saw and was impressed with the quality. We knew it was of a high standard because we had already sold vast amounts of it all over the country. Roger then said he wanted £10,000 the next day so he could check them over and that the serial numbers ran differently. COD reassured him that the serial numbers would be as different as possible and would have 20 different numbers in whatever he ordered. Roger then started to ask too many questions for my liking, but COD carried on informing him how the notes were made. I tried to cut all this talk short as Roger didn't need to know how they were made and we eventually arranged to meet the next day and parted company. Me and COD then drove back to the Joiners Arms on Hackney Road in East London where we did all of our business.

When we got back to the Joiners Arms, I asked COD what he thought of Matthew and Roger and all he could see were pound notes dancing before his eyes – legit pound notes! I wasn't sure about this deal and sensed something wasn't right but couldn't put my finger on it. We were talking and COD said he was going to show and sell them traveller's cheques and a passport also. I wasn't happy and said we should just stick with the £50s first and see how that went. The next day we met in a café for some breakfast and carried on our conversation and again I told him I wasn't happy, so COD done his usual and told me I didn't like anyone and called me a paranoid cunt. I'd heard this so many times before, I brushed it off and laughed with him.

After breakfast, we picked up the £10k of £50s, some sample travellers cheques and the passport and made our way back to the Marriott in North London to meet Matthew and Roger. We met them in the bar and as I shook Roger's hand I got a better look at him because when we'd met the day before I couldn't see him properly because we had been in their car. He was a small out of shape man with a blotchy red face, so I assumed the man's gym was a pub and he liked a drink. Again I felt uneasy that something wasn't right because Roger was waffling on about shit and was jumpy and seemed very nervous. He then asked if we had the £10k and said he wanted us all to go to his room because he wanted to check them over. That was fair enough, so we followed him to the lift. In the lift, I could sense that Roger didn't want to talk to me because he was speaking directly to COD. I figured he didn't like me because anything I asked him he swerved answering. Matthew was trying to talk to me, but I cut him short. I was becoming extremely uncomfortable because Roger was asking COD all sorts of things like where in the UK we had been in the last couple of months and COD was fucking telling him. This bloke didn't need to know fuck all of where we had been in the country or anywhere else for that matter.

As we got to the room and Roger opened the door we were about to enter I saw another bloke in the room which shocked me and I asked Roger who the fuck he was. It turned out to be Roger's driver while he was in London. He then made small talk like he was only in town for three days and would be flying out on the Sunday and only had his driver until then. This was now all becoming a bit too much for me so I was pacing around the room while they all sat down. His room was the penthouse suite and was like a fucking greenhouse, not as in hot but fucking windows everywhere. I could see into all of the surrounding buildings which I didn't like because it meant they could see into his suite. I turned round to Roger and said sternly 'oi cunt are you having a fucking laugh, what the fuck is going on? If you think I'm sitting here and doing anything, you're nuts'. Roger jumped up and started flapping telling his driver to shut the curtains and as he did Roger apologised and said he was very sorry for upsetting me. I was seriously pissed off and said no more and sat down.

COD started things off by taking out the £10k of £50s from his jacket and placing it on the table. Both Matthew and Roger picked some of the notes up and were looking at them and running their fingers over the paper and holding them up to the light. At that point, while they were busy, COD told me to calm down and that everything was fine and I should relax. I told him I was sweet and winked at him, but I didn't like anything that was going on. I've been about and I had a gut feeling what was happening in that hotel room wasn't right. If I had been on my own, I would have fucked off because every bone in my body was telling me to get out.

Roger said he was pleased with the product and again asked how they were made so COD went into fucking overdrive telling him. He was telling Roger all sorts of madness and actually talked himself into being the master printer of the operation. Roger was lapping it all up and asking further questions of which COD was more than happy to oblige. I then interrupted and told Roger if he wanted more we could get him more. He then said let's get this deal out of the way and pulled out £2k which we counted and then the deal was complete. Roger then said he wanted to place a large order and asked if we could get him £5m. COD proceeded to tell him that we could get him as much as he wanted as long as he had the money. I told Roger that if he wanted a lump like that then it wouldn't be the same price as what he had just paid for the £10k and the tenner a piece would drop. We were charging them too much from day one as COD had said they had serious money and would pay top whack, so we could afford to drop the price.

COD then told them he had something else he would like them to look at and pulled out a few travellers' cheques and $100 bill. Roger loved this straight away and put in an order for both and we told them we'd have them for him on the Saturday because he reminded us he was flying out to the Far East on the Sunday. Me and COD then left the room with Matthew and in the lift reconfirmed our prior arrangement to meet Matthew on the Friday evening in the Cornwallis a pub in Bethnal Green to give him the passport we were arranging for him. I asked him for the photo and name of the person it was for and it was for himself, so I asked him why he needed it. He was blasé and just said that he was doing something and needed it. He made it sound like he was up to something hooky but I thought no more of it and we arranged to meet at 7:00 pm on the Friday which was the following day.

While me and COD were driving back to the East End, I told him I didn't like one bit of the meeting we'd just had. Again he told me to shut up and that I was paranoid and that we were going to earn so much money out of them in the next couple of months and he didn't give a shit what I liked or didn't. Is all I wanted at that point was a drink, so we went to the Joiners Arms and had quite a few.

CHAPTER 15

Unexpected Meet and Greet

A month or so before our introduction to Matthew and Roger life was going well and we were cracking on selling our goods of £50s and life was one big party. Occasionally I was still doing my own thing and dropping out for a couple of days. At the time, there were no mobiles but I'd always tell COD I was disappearing for a bit and he knew how to get hold of me if I was needed. One particular time I had disappeared for a couple of days and when I got back met a pal in the Joiners one afternoon. It was a lovely summers day and we were soaking it up when along came COD and he had a bag with him, plus a very worried look on his face. I took the piss and asked him if he'd been fucked up the arse because he had a troubled look like he was worried people were going to find out. Me and my pal found this funny but COD didn't find it funny at all and told me I needed to do him a favour. He wanted me to take the bag he was carrying to my house and hide it there. Of course I was curious at what was in the bag, so I asked and he said it was £150k of £50s. I told him he was fucking mad if he thought I was doing that and asked him what he was doing with them because our rule was we only picked up what we needed and never had them around us. He said someone was supposed to pick them up but never showed up. He could tell by my face that I wasn't taking them so asked my pal if he'd take them and put them in his lock up where he worked with his dad. I told my mate not to take them and told COD to take them back to where they came from. He then said his own dad had just been nicked. I said I didn't like this to my pal, but he walked off with the bag and after that I assumed he'd stored it in his lock up.

I used to walk round to my pal's lock up at lunchtimes and have a cuppa with him, his brother and their dad as I'd known them all years. The following day after COD had turned up with the bag, I was on my way to my mate's lock up but as I turned the corner I saw my pal's brother walking towards me and he said I'd better fuck off and turn around as the old bill had raided the lock up and were looking for counterfeit money. I did a U-turn and was on my toes but wasn't going home or anywhere near anyone until I knew what had happened to my pal. He managed to get a message to me to meet him somewhere safe.

I was in complete shock at what had happened and when I met him, he looked terrible and was a white / grey colour. He explained to me that he had been at work and the old bill ran in shouting and screaming and were all over the place and even raided the work space next door. What fucked me off more than anything was the fact that this pal was honest and straight down the line, a real straight goer and it was obvious some cunt had set him up. He then told me that the old bill had found nothing which shocked me again because I'd seen him take the bag from COD. At that point, I thought I was one lucky cunt that I hadn't been there having a cuppa when the old bill had stormed in. The following morning COD told me that he had told some bloke that he had given my pal the bag and where my pal was going to put it so it must have been him who told the old bill. If the old bill had found that bag in my pal's lock up he would have gone away for a very long time, I thank god they never. I also wonder if it was ever there!!

It was now the Friday afternoon following our meeting with Roger and him placing his order to be delivered the following day on the Saturday. Me and COD met and put in place all the arrangements for Roger's order. We then went to meet Matthew in the Cornwallis pub in Bethnal Green, on the corner of Valence

Road and Bethnal Green Road, as we had arranged. As it was a Friday night, we would be out anyway so arranged to meet Mark afterwards at the Joiners at 8:00 pm. When we got to the Cornwallis, Matthew was already sitting at the bar and seemed much more relaxed than he had when we'd met him previously. We sat at a table in the corner and he asked me why everyone was looking at me in the pub and seemed to become uneasy again, so I told him I came from a big family and we all look-a-like so they may think I'm one of my brothers which relaxed him. We gave him the passport and he looked it over and was happy so paid us with £20 notes. He then went on to explain that he wouldn't be at the meeting with Roger the following day and asked us not to tell Roger about the passport we'd arrange for him, which I thought was odd but didn't really bat an eyelid.

After that, we left the pub and phoned Roger from a phone box on Queensbridge Road as we said we would and told him that his order had been arranged and we would see him the next day. He then asked me the strangest fucking question, he asked me if I was connected to the family. I had no idea what he was going on about so asked what family and he said the big family in North London that were running London at the time. I just re-plied you're off your head mate. He then said his reason for ask-ing was because he wanted to know who he was dealing with, so I told him he was dealing with us and no-one else and that he was starting to get on my fucking nerves. He then shut up talk-ing bollocks and we hung up after agreeing a time for the follow-ing day. I walked back to the car fuming and told COD what the prick had just asked me and again said I didn't like the cunt.

Saturday morning came and was a lovely sunny day, I didn't have a hangover because I hadn't drank much the night before and was feeling fresh and good to go. Me and COD didn't have to meet Roger at the hotel until 1:00 pm so COD picked me up and we went for a bit of breakfast. We sorted out what we had to pick up for Roger's parcel. He wanted £50,000 in £50s and £70,000 in travellers' cheques. We popped it all into a case and were ready for our meeting. It was that simple, it was an easy sort of crime because there was no drama. You haven't got to work hard and there are no real victims because you're basically selling a product that can't hurt anyone, no force or violence is involved, it's just a case of drop off, pick up and walk away with a lot of money.

We were ready to make our way to the Marriott Hotel and were driving a ringer which we were planning to sell in a couple of days' time, we'd only had it a week. There was no rush to get to the hotel as we had plenty of time, so we didn't drive too mad and made our way through London at a steady pace. As it was a Saturday, there wasn't a rush hour to deal with and sitting in traffic for hours. We made it to the hotel with time to spare and didn't look out of place when we entered the lobby as we were always smartly dressed. As we walked through I noticed Roger at the bar on the other side of the foyer which was busy with people checking in and out of their rooms. There were nice big couches and plush chairs dotted around with people sitting about and as we were walking across to the bar, I noticed a nice looking blonde bird sitting on one of the couches. She was smartly dressed reading a newspaper and as we got nearer she turned the page and as she did I saw her talk to the cuff of her jacket. I nudged COD and asked him if he saw what I did but he hadn't so I told him what I'd just witnessed. Again he done his usual and called me a paranoid cunt and told me Roger was waiting. We walked past the blonde bird and I looked directly at her, but she didn't look back at me, no eye contact was made so I carried on walking and thinking to myself I must have got it wrong because I was feeling on edge.

We approached Roger and shook hands and he seemed very jumpy, he couldn't stand still and was struggling to get his words out. This was making me fucking mad and as I was look-ing at him, he couldn't make eye contact with me. I was staring at him with a face that would put the fear of god into most peo-ple especially this little fat pisshead that I now knew he was. He invited us to go to his room so we walked over to the lifts and as we were waiting for the lift I didn't saying a word and didn't take my eyes off him. Rolling around in my head was what I had to do, I'd already made my mind up what I wanted to do to him and I hadn't told COD what was about to happen. COD wouldn't have liked it, but I didn't give a shit as this bloke had done my head in the last few days wanting to know the ins and outs of a duck's arse.

The lift arrived, we got in and Roger pressed the button for the floor we were going to and as he did I noticed it wasn't the same floor where we'd previously gone. Now I was fucked off and as the doors closed, in one movement, I spun him round, whacked him with my open palm right across his face and shoved him up against the wall of the lift. I then said something along the lines of 'I think you're old bill you cunt and if you're not old bill you're up to something because you're not right and why did you press a different floor to the one we went to before'. Roger more or less shit himself and I started to search him for a wire or something that would tell me who he was but I found nothing. As I had Roger pinned up against the wall of the lift, COD turned defensive and was trying to stop me and was apologising for me at the same time. Roger had had trouble talking when we'd arrived and now had trouble breathing and had turned grey. COD took hold of Roger and straightened his jacket out for him and told him everything was fine. Roger then spluttered to COD that the hotel had made him move rooms and it wasn't his fault and please stop me as he didn't like violence. I told him, as we were walking to the room, that there was something about him that was making me paranoid and we should just get on with what we came for.

Roger opened the door to his room which was a large suite which had one large window and lots of doors. We all sat down on a nice large plush sofa next to a coffee table and Roger asked us to show him the parcel we had brought for him. COD put the case on the coffee table and opened it as I asked Roger to show us his money. He was on edge and said he had to go and get it. I told him he wasn't going anywhere so he explained that the money was in the next room. The place was like a little flat and he said it would only take him 30 seconds to get it but I wasn't happy. He then got up and walked over to one of the doors, opened it and shut it behind him. COD and me looked at each other and wasn't sure what was going on because it was very quiet, so just sat there and waited for Roger to return.

All of a sudden all hell broke loose and every single door flew open with lots of people running towards us shouting. I looked around the room and over to my right there were three blokes running towards COD so I jumped up and as I did noticed four blokes running towards me. These blokes were massive and I spotted they had dark brown objects in their hands and they were screaming at the tops of their voices. I had no idea what they were shouting and noticed light fading and darkness descending over me as they were getting nearer because they were so big. Grabbing me they put me face down on the floor and the shouting stopped. They were all over me and tied my hands behind my back, not with handcuffs but with quick strap ties.

At that point, I started to shout back to take what they fucking wanted but warned them within 24 hours I would know who they were and would be doing the same to them. I thought we were being robbed and the cunt Roger was part of some low life outfit that go around robbing people because it wasn't unheard of that people get robbed at such meetings like the one we were having. This was what was racing through my mind, I thought that we were being tied up and were going to be left there. I remember telling the blokes around me that I didn't give a shit what they took but to remember my face as they would see it again because people that pop into my life always pop back especially if they've crossed me.

I was still face and belly down on the floor and one of the blokes bent down to me, turned my head towards him and said 'oi mate I don't know who you think we are, but we're Scotland Yard and your nicked' and then pushed his badge into my face. My reply was 'thank fuck for that I thought I was going to end up in the boot of a car' and I started laughing which was probably relief.

CHAPTER 16

Weekend Away

I could hear photos were being taken and was then pulled to my feet and the old bill shouted to each other that the rooms were safe and clear. They then swapped the ties on both me and COD for real solid cuffs and walked us over to the couch and sat us down.

As we sat down I told COD to not say fuck all from there on in. We both knew the score and from that point onwards I would not be saying a word to anyone. While sitting there some tall skinny bloke with brown hair in a side parting came over. His hair was not short and also not long, but it made his head look square so he looked odd. He was also very pale, not smart look-ing at all and was wearing a leather jacket, white shirt and a cream pair of trousers, an outfit that I wouldn't have been seen dead in. He stood on the other side of the coffee table directly in front of us and said his name was DCI Dave Taylor of the Scot-land Yard Regional Crime Squad and that we were under arrest for the possession of counterfeit currency. He told us that we did not have to say anything (I thought too fucking right we don't), unless we wished to do so but anything we did say would be written down and held against us in a court of law. As I looked up at him, I felt like I had the wind knocked out of me. Standing next to him was none other than the fucking blonde bird who had spoken to her wrist while reading the newspaper in the lob-by. My chin hit my chest and the words COD had used rang in my ears – you're paranoid!

All the old bill were kissing each other's arses and congratulat-ing each other on how well they'd done. I had one of the giants sitting next to me and as I looked down at his hands, I saw that he was holding a dark brown wooden truncheon. When they'd burst in the room earlier, I thought they were holding handguns which is why I thought we were being robbed. He was trying to be my pal by trying to talk to me and asking if I wanted a drink or if the cuffs were too tight. I just kept thinking fuck off dickhead, I'm not talking so fuck off.

The next thing I knew a bloke ran in the room with a large camera and started clicking taking photos. He went so far as to move the suitcase containing the merchandise out of the way so he could take a photo of me and COD in the same shot and moving the case in again to get everything and everyone in the photo. I tried desperately to bury my face in my chest so he couldn't get a clear photo but it was difficult and my hands were still cuffed behind my back. I had no idea why this bloke was taking photos and I didn't like it. We were then helped to our feet and told we were being taken to a police station and would be leaving the hotel the same way we had come in. We were warned not to try anything and told that we wouldn't have a chance to escape because outside of the hotel it was mobbed with old bill. They again asked me my name, but I ignored them and thought if they didn't know who I was yet and I got a chance to get free I'd be on my toes like a shot. I knew deep down that if what they said about the hotel being surrounded by old bill was true I wouldn't have a chance of getting away but you can't blame a bloke for thinking it! My head was doing overtime thinking about the last few days and everything that had happened. My mind was racing on who was who and who the fuck was to blame for this set up because some cunt had obviously grassed us up. I was so pissed off with myself and beating myself up inside because all the signs were there, but I didn't listen to my gut instinct. Fucking COD had kept shooting me down calling me paranoid and I'd listened to him rather than my gut feeling which had done me proud through my life until that point.

We were escorted to the lift by a few massive coppers and they stayed close. One of them had a broken nose and had his hair gelled back and was wearing a t-shirt which he looked ready to burst out of because he was so big. I resigned myself to the fact that I wouldn't be escaping anywhere so didn't bother trying. He kept asking if I was OK and asked us not to make a scene and to get to the police station without any fuss. I was thinking fuck it they haven't got anything on me apart from walking into a hotel suite with a suitcase and if I say nothing what can they do to me, lock me up for a couple of days and then let me go? I could live with that.

We arrived at the lobby of the hotel and as we were walking through people were staring and the poxy photographer was back on the scene snapping away. As we left the hotel uniformed old bill were everywhere plus vans, cars, dogs, it was the full works. I was put in the back of an unmarked undercover police car and flanked by two of the biggest blokes I'd ever seen. There were also two coppers in the front of the motor and they told me we were going to Hampstead police station as their governor had arranged it and then they carried on talking amongst them-selves. One copper in the front turned to me and said 'you're not saying much, we were told you were the one we had to watch out for because you were more likely to kick off', he then laughed and they all joined in. I was so angry and was thinking you cunts, if it was one or two of you without the cuffs it might be a different story but four of you, no thanks. I wasn't giving them what they wanted so they could beat the shit out of me.

After a little drive we arrived at the old bill station, drove through gates and into the car park round the back. I was taken out of the car and walked into the big old Victorian style building and was delivered to the large front desk, the custody desk. The police sergeant at the desk who was in charge of the station told me my rights while I was in custody and gave me the rundown of what I was entitled to. He asked me my name and I knew as soon as they took my fingerprints they'd find out who I was and the game would be up so I told him. The CID who nicked me wrote my name down and then radioed it through to Scotland Yard. DCI Dave Taylor then walked through the door with COD. They removed my handcuffs and I was taken to a cell and left alone. I laid on the bed and my head started to race again, I was going over everything that had happened. This was giving me the fucking hump and I couldn't calm myself down.

Roughly 30 minutes passed and the cell door was opened and two CID were standing there with some handcuffs and told me we were going on a trip. I stood up, they put the handcuffs back on me and I was back in the car park. I could hear them talking amongst themselves and heard them say they had an address for me and that's where we needed to go right then, before anyone found out I had been nicked. We then set off with a car behind and a car in front of the one I was in and was going straight through traffic lights making our way through London. We arrived at the address they had for me and they asked me who would be in. I didn't say fuck all and they kicked the door off its hinges and went in and had a look around. They came back out and were fucked off because it was apparent I didn't live there. Again I said fuck all and was rushed back into the car and back to the police station.

There was a panic at the police station now because they couldn't work out why they had an incorrect address. I thought to myself that if they assumed I was going to tell them my real address they'd have more chance of Miss World walking into the police station naked in all her glory. I was then put back in a cell and told them I wanted to phone my solicitor but was told I wasn't allowed just yet. That pissed me off because I knew my rights so I demanded to see the custody sergeant. I was then allowed to make my one phone call and phoned my solicitor who told me to say nothing and that he'd be with me within the hour. I then had time to think again and my mind was back racing, I was thinking how fucked I was and I wouldn't be getting out of the station anytime soon because they didn't know where I lived and there was no fucking way I was going to tell them. I was also trying to work out who the fuck Roger, Matthew and Graham were and was there anything that gave a hint in the last few days that one of them was a grass. I hadn't seen Roger be nicked. All I did know was that fat Terry had a lot to fucking answer for and if he wasn't going to be answering me in person anytime soon, it would be someone else paying him a visit.

When you're in a police cell, the best thing you can do is sleep because there is nothing else to do unless you want to read the bill of rights which is a government booklet which tells you your rights while you being held. While you're locked up if you want a drink, you have to ring the buzzer which goes through to the custody desk. Sometimes you can ring that buzzer for hours before someone will come and answer you so I'm always in favour of getting my head down. This time I couldn't get my head down and was pacing up and down thinking and thinking some more. I thought I'd worked out that I was right that Roger and Matthew must have been old bill. I couldn't work out if Matthew had been putting on a South African accent and playing a part. I thought Graham must have been working undercover also and that his part of dressing like an unwashed tramp was all part of the set up. Is all I knew for a fact was that I was in a cell and I had to wait and watch the facts unfold. I laid down on the mattress with an old blanket and pillow that was provided. The mattress was very thin and made of something that looked like leather and could be wiped clean easily, the blanket was itchy and the pillow was made of the same material as the mattress. These items are standard in every police cell. I tried my best to sleep but couldn't.

I was laying there for a few hours and then the cell door opened and a familiar face, my brief Mr O'Leary, walked in. He looked smart in a three-piece suit, polished shoes and he had some paperwork tucked under his arm. I jumped up and he put his hand up as if to say wait before you say anything then turned to the police officer who had let him in and said 'could you please leave us and it is fine to lock the door and leave us alone, I will ring the buzzer when I'm finished with my client', so the officer did as he was told. I was desperate to find out what he knew. Once we were alone he relaxed and sighed and asked me what I was going to be saying to which I said I'll be saying fuck all, I've said fuck all so far, I know nothing, I've seen nothing and I don't know anyone. Mr O'Leary then wanted to move on very quickly because we didn't have much time before I went in for questioning.

Mr O'Leary told me that all the old bill had on me was that I was walking into a hotel with a lot of counterfeit money. He said that they wouldn't tell him too much and were not giving much away which he said was standard but he felt like they were being over the top in my case and he wasn't sure why. I confirmed to him that I would not be saying anything apart from 'no comment' and the only thing I had told them was my name and that's all they'd be getting from me. Mr O'Leary was happy with this and said we could work on things when they released me. I told him that I was pleased to hear that because that was the only plan I wanted to work with. He then got his papers together and told me he was going to tell the officer in charge, DCI Taylor, that I was ready to be interviewed. He then pressed the buzzer and started to fix his tie and asked me once more if I was sure I was ready to say nothing when being interviewed. I just said I didn't have a fucking clue what was going on and I wouldn't be saying fuck all. He was happy that I was happy with that plan and the door opened and he left.

CHAPTER 17
No Comment and Famous

Five minutes after Mr O'Leary left my cell he was back with DCI Taylor and the big copper who had been sitting next to me while I was handcuffed at the hotel. DCI Taylor put out his hand and said 'hi Gary, I'm DCI Taylor and I'm heading this investigation'. I did shake his hand but didn't say a word as I was led to the interview room. I sat at the table with my brief next to me and the two coppers on the opposite side. They proceeded to go through the legal jargon of how they would be taping the interview etc. and again I was read my rights. As they were getting the tape ready they tried to make small talk, but I just sat blankly not saying a word. Once they were ready they asked Mr O'Leary if we were ready to begin and he turned to me, so I nodded. They started by saying their names and it was then that I found out the big copper's name was DC Bradshaw. I was asked my name which I did disclose and then the conversation went something like as follows:

Taylor / Bradshaw: How did your day start?

Me: No comment.

Taylor / Bradshaw: How did you get to the hotel in North London?

Me: No comment.

Taylor / Bradshaw: How do you know COD?

Me: No comment.

Taylor / Bradshaw: Tell us about the counterfeit money?

Me: No comment.

Taylor / Bradshaw: Who is Matthew and Graham?

Me: No comment.

DCI Taylor then looked at me and told me they had me bang to rights and I should help myself by helping them and tell them all I knew. Again, he got 'no comment'. DC Bradshaw then piped up and started to tell me I was going away for a long time and if I helped them they could make my time away a little shorter. I just thought to myself what will be will be. He then went on and asked me to tell them the full story in my own words and if they could help me they would. I sounded like a stuck record, but I didn't give a shit and gave them another 'no comment'. I could see they were getting pissed off with me but that was fine, I could have sat there all day saying the same thing to every question they asked. They asked me loads and I was bored but was on autopilot. A couple of hours passed and I didn't care because I would have only been sitting in a cell with my mind driving me nuts anyway so was thinking you crack on mister.

I was told I wasn't helping myself, but all I cared about was not helping them. They then said to me that the interview wasn't going anywhere and asked me to tell them who Roger was. I was thinking it would be nice if someone would tell me who the fuck everyone was but again said no comment. They told Mr O'Leary they were finished interviewing me for the time being, stated the time of the end of interview and pressed the stop button on the tape recorder. Bradshaw then told me to stand up and follow him as he was taking me back to my cell but first would be taking my fingerprints and mugshot. Mr O'Leary told me he would come and see me in my cell shortly, we shook hands and I followed Bradshaw.

Bradshaw in his thought process must have thought bad cop wasn't working with me so tried good cop and wanted to be my pal. He was talking a load of bollocks and doing his best to get me to talk, but I wouldn't have any of it and just ignored him. He took my fingerprints and photos for their file, I washed my hands to remove the ink and then we made our way back towards my cell. As we were walking back, he stopped, turned to me and said here is my card and handed me a business card which I took and looked at and asked him what it was for? He told me that if I ever felt like talking to give him a call. I was thinking what a prick but said thank you and that once my family found out I'd been nicked they wouldn't want to talk to me and I'd have no-one to talk to so I thanked him and told him he was very kind and it would be a great help for me to have someone to talk to when I was sent to prison. He looked at me with confusion written all over his face and then realised I was taking the piss, so shouted at me to give him his fucking card back and pushed me in my cell. I couldn't help myself and said to him completely straight-faced 'don't you want to talk to me anymore?' He shouted he didn't want to be my fucking counsellor and called me a backward cunt! He slammed the cell door shut and left me cracking up laughing as I'd got exactly the reaction I wanted - reel him in and then piss him off!

After a little while Mr O'Leary returned to my cell and told me they were going to charge me, were refusing me bail and were going to keep me until Monday when I would have to appear in court. I said OK and that we could ask for bail at court and he agreed with me. He said that they were not fucking about and this whole sting had been very well thought out and they did not want me back out on the street. They had taken me to

Hampstead police station because it had a magistrate's court built into it and it was very secure. Mr O'Leary said they wanted to find further evidence. He then told me that they wanted me now so we went to the custody desk where the custody sergeant was sat behind the desk. DCI Taylor stood next to me and I was charged with possession of counterfeit currency and I was asked if I had anything to say so I replied my usual 'no comment'.

I was then returned to my new home for the weekend and asked if I wanted anything to eat. I was starving at that point so said yes. I had a result because they said it would have to be take away because it was now late and there was no food at the station. The copper then brought me a coke and a burger, touch! It was now late on a Saturday night and I was still trying to work out in my head what the fuck had gone on, but then just thought fuck it, go to sleep. I was so tired, I managed to drift off.

The following morning I was woken up by the cell door being opened. There was a uniformed copper standing there with a newspaper in his hand. I looked up at him and he chucked the paper on the floor and said 'you might want to read that sunshine' and then he left. I was half asleep and looked down at the paper and on the front page, in big bold capitals, was the heading 'WE SMASH £5M FAKE RACKET'. I just thought to myself it was fuck all to do with me and I didn't like the News of the World because it was full of shit, so I turned over and went back to sleep.

A bit later I was woken up again but this time by a voice calling my name. I was unsure who it was because it was coming through the wall and was a bit muffled. I took no notice and had a piss. The person calling my name was getting louder and louder and shouting read the paper Gal. I walked over and picked the paper up from the floor and flicked through the pages and low and behold, staring up at me, was a photo of me. I closed the paper in shock not reading one word and put it back down. I was so confused. The voice shouting at me was asking if I'd read it yet and then I realised it was COD, I shouted back no. COD has been aptly named for this book because he was my co-defendant. He then started to shout 'read it Gal, it's about us, we're famous, we're famous Gal'! I picked up the paper again and started to read it and then the penny dropped. Roger was a reporter for the News of the World. I couldn't read another word and put the paper down as now I knew I was fucked and up shit creek without a paddle. Now everything started to fall into place.

This was some sort of sting and I had been stung by the queen fucking bee. I felt like my life was heading towards a curb of shit, a curb I couldn't jump off of like the one I jumped on and off of when I was a young boy and had ran away from the children's home and was free and happy. I was sitting in a cell in the same clothes I'd been wearing for well over 24 hours. I asked the custody sergeant if it was possible to get someone to bring me some fresh clothes and food as I was starving and he agreed. I'd already told Mr O'Leary to ring a couple of people for me so they knew what had happened and could be at court on the Monday morning. The custody sergeant asked me if I wanted COD to be put in my cell as apparently he was requesting this. The custody sergeant said that now we had both been charged he couldn't see a problem with COD's request, I could, but wanted to know if he knew anything more than I did. I no longer trusted him and memories of people asking what I was doing with the slippery cunt started to float back in my mind, but I couldn't let COD know that. I was worried about what he was going to say when questioned and whether it would come back to haunt me over the next few days or even months.

He walked into my cell and was carrying his mattress, blanket, pillow and a copy of the News of the World. He asked me to read it to him as he hadn't read it because he didn't have his glasses and couldn't see it. That day was the only time I read that story in the paper until 15 years later. While I was reading it to COD, I was fuming and effing and blinding. I found it hard to read because at the time my reading wasn't great. I was so angry I wanted the floor to open up and take me. We then started to talk and I asked him what he had told the old bill and he said nothing and then asked me why. I told him that I'd said no comment throughout the interview and it hadn't lasted long because they'd gotten bored. He then said he had done the same thing and that we were going to be alright. He said this a lot over the next few months, but I'd say that I knew something wasn't quite right with the case and again he would call me a paranoid cunt. He also apologised and said he should have listened to me with regard to the deal with Roger. It was too late for apologies seeing as we were both sitting in a cell and had been charged for possession of counterfeit currency. We were both brought fresh clothes, trainers and hot food by our families and after a while fell asleep. The next morning we were up early, washed and dressed and were ready to be taken to court. We waited all day and later in the afternoon were finally taken up to court.

We entered the court through some steps that led to the dock. It was an old looking court with lots of dark polished wood. I saw some friendly faces that I was really pleased to see, family members were there and mouthed to me asking if I had seen the paper. I nodded to say yes and they replied 'you're fucked', as if I didn't know that already. The judge walked into the courtroom and it began. DCI Taylor had a part to play and stood up and told the court that Scotland Yard were working hard to gather evidence and were opposing bail. He went on to say that the two men in the dock were the main players in the underworld of counterfeit currency and had flooded the country over the last few months and Scotland Yard wanted us kept off of the streets until they had completed gathering their evidence. I knew then that we had no chance of being granted bail. The judge then looked down at his diary and said we were to be put on remand and would return before him in two weeks. We were then returned to our cell.

Well, that was an interesting outing. I was being held on remand because the old bill thought I was a major player in a counterfeit ring – what the fuck was that all about? We were told that we were being transferred to HMP Pentonville prison situated in North London and we'd be on our way as soon as the police van was ready to take us. It was roughly 6:00 pm and we were handcuffed and led to the prison van which are also known as sweatboxes. They are big lorry type carriers and inside have ten small cells which are 2ft by 2ft which are so small that you can only sit down in them. Each cell has a small window that you can see out of but no-one can see in. While cuffed in these small cells you sweat like a pig because there is no air hence the nickname sweatbox. We were strapped in and off we set to Pentonville my new home for the foreseeable future.

CHAPTER 18

Pentonville Pisshole

After a drive, we arrived at Pentonville and when we came to a stop, we were led to a holding room with other inmates and our handcuffs were removed. One by one we were called and searched and our belongings were taken from us. We were then processed, given a prison number, asked what religion we were and whether we were a vegetarian or vegan. We were then given a set of prison towels and some soap and told to strip off to shower and then doused in some flee powder shit. I was then asked to bend over so a prison officer, also known as a screw, could look up my arse. I was also asked to pull the skin back on my cock so it could be checked. I bet screws when they were young boys never dreamt for their career they'd be asking grown men to bend over so they could check arseholes and checking men pulling their foreskins back! No wonder they're miserable bastards most of the time. After that degradation, I was told to get dressed back into my own clothes which I was allowed to wear while on remand. I was then seen by a doctor who asked my medical history and if I had any medical issues.

It was by then getting late and after a mad couple of days I was tired and just wanted to get my head down and have a good night's sleep. I asked the screw when we would be taken to our cells because I was knackered and at that point I could have slept just about anywhere. We were told that shortly we would be taken to the remand wing of the prison. All London prisons have a remand wing and two or three convicted wings. At the time, Pentonville really was a rundown shithole or I should say piss-hole. It's an old prison built in 1842 where people were once hanged for the crimes they had committed and had not had the

60 Minute Makeover team in to give it a once over since it was built!

I wasn't ready for what happened next, the screw led us through the prison and we reached the biggest thickest door I'd ever seen in my life. He told us that beyond the door was the prison's remand wing, A wing. He put the key in the door, turned it and struggled to pull it open. When he did manage to pull the door open, I was hit by a smell I will never forget in my life. I struggled to breathe and my eyes watered, the smell was so pungent I wanted to throw up. I asked the screw what the fuck it was and he laughed and told me I'd get used to it soon enough. I told him I doubted that very much and could only describe the smell as evil. I put my hands over my mouth as I didn't want to breathe it in, but it was so overpowering. The screw walked passed me and said to follow him up some old steep metal stairs which led to the first landing. As I was looking around, there were cell doors everywhere and we climbed some stairs until we came to the fifth landing. Again, I asked the screw what the smell was as it was choking me and he replied plain as day, its piss and you'll get used to it. Of course I had smelt piss before, but this was on a different level. The piss I'd smelt before that day was like roses compared to this stench.

We walked along the landing and stopped at the end cell which me and COD were told we would be sharing. It was quite late and it appeared that the other inmates were asleep. I walked in the cell and the screw banged the door shut. Is all I wanted to do was sleep so I told COD that I was having the top bunk of the metal framed bunk-beds. Before I settled down I needed to take a piss so looked around the cell and saw a bucket which had a lid on it in the corner. Is all I could think was where is the fucking toilet? I thought sod the bucket I'm not going in that and I'll wait until the morning. I got my head down as best I could but

129

was driving myself nuts with my mind racing. Something wasn't right and I was annoyed with myself for not listening to my gut instinct. I was now in prison and had no idea how long I was going to be there for. It's an awful feeling thinking you could be there for years before getting out. I finally managed to drift off to sleep on my first night.

The next thing I knew there was a lot of noise of doors being opened on all the landings. I could hear voices shouting out orders 'open the ones' and once that was done 'open the twos' and so on until all the landings' cells were open. By now I was bursting for the toilet. When my cell door opened I ran on to the landing to find the toilet and oh my god, there were three to four hundred men all carrying buckets. They were carrying buckets of their own piss to be emptied into a special kind of sink and the smell was un-fucking-believable. I wanted to be sick and heaved at the stench staining the landings so ran back into my cell to the window and sucked in fresh air through the bars from the window. As I was sucking the fresh air into my lungs I was thinking I'll never get used to this and me and COD will not be using that bucket to piss and shit in, we have to have a rule for that if we're going to carry on sharing a cell. How can anyone just sit there while their cellmate takes a dump in a bucket and then casually leave it sitting there all night? I may have been banged up, but I wasn't an animal and thought I won't be treated or behave like one.

Each landing, in turn, was called down to the 'ones' (ground floor) and to the hot plate which was where breakfast was served. We were called to the hot plate three times a day and served by other inmates also on remand. The food was shit and made by convicted prisoners from the other wings. For the first few days, I couldn't eat what was served, but after that I had no choice and after a while it was OK and I'd eat it.

130

As I walked around the prison, I started bumping into lots of people that I knew and they seemed pleased to see me and I was pleased to see them. They were all saying the same thing that they had seen the story in the News of the World and telling me that things didn't look good for me. I was upbeat and laughed it off by saying things like yes I know, I wanted them to get a photo of my better side. During the quiet times, I was still beating myself up trying to work out who was who. I didn't trust anyone and didn't really talk to anyone as some weird shit was happening.

One day my cousin Johnny visited and told me that fat Terry was shitting himself and that Graham had turned up on the Saturday morning for the Arsenal tickets. I thought to myself what a cheeky cunt. Apparently fat Terry had been trying to get hold of Graham since it had come out that I'd been nicked but had had no luck. I told Johnny to tell fat Terry that his name hadn't been mentioned but that I wanted answers and he had better deliver them to me. I wanted to know who was who because he had vouched that Graham was his pal and now I was sitting in a prison cell looking at a lot of bird and it was down to him so he had better find out as soon as possible.

While you're on remand you are allowed a visit every day and I had a lot of people who wanted to come and see me, so the two weeks went by quickly and it was time to go back to court. I'd arranged that I would be applying for bail and put up a large sum of money to ensure that it was granted. I had a good friend who was going to be in court and help me get bail and had the means to get me out. We were at court and I got my brief Mr O'Leary to put my case forward to the judge. Mr O'Leary put forward that I was willing to abide by any rules that the judge set, that there was someone in court willing to offer £75,000 as surety for my bail, but the judge turned me down flat. I couldn't fucking believe it, I was staying in prison. COD didn't even apply for bail, he said he knew we wouldn't get it so what was the point. With bail you only get three chances to apply, then after that if you've been knocked back, you stay in prison until your trial.

After that knock back, we were taken back to Pentonville. I was thinking oh well I'm not getting out of here, but silly bollocks COD, in my eyes, didn't seem bothered about it at all which I thought was odd. Following my bail knock back, I spent my time in prison chatting to other people I knew in their cells, playing cards, or getting drunk on Hooch that we used to make. Prison life is so fucking boring so anything to break up the day is welcome. You're woken up early and locked up for 22 hours of the day, so the time you're allowed out of your cell you make the most of. Some inmates like to break up the day by fighting each other and fallouts happen a lot, but that wasn't for me and I didn't get involved.

Is all I was interested in was what was going on in my world, what was happening to me and the shit that I was in. COD was acting weird, scared even, he wouldn't leave the cell and the only time he did would be at meal times or to chat to one or two other inmates. This unnerved me because he wasn't right and I didn't trust him as far as I could throw him. I was playing everything very close to my chest and keeping him sweet until I knew what the outcome of my future was, which wasn't going to be good either way.

The weeks were passing slowly and I was going through the motions of the daily routine which at times was so fucking boring. There was absolutely nothing to do but think and think and think some more. I was sending and receiving letters and this was my contact with the outside world unless I could blag a screw to let me use the phone in his office, which I did quite a few times. I've been blagging from a very young age and can blag for England.

One of the screws, who I blagged for a few phone calls, was an alright bloke called Mr Churchill and was in charge of the landing. He was ex-Forces, like many of them are, and he liked to think he was running the show. I let him think that so it occasionally got me what I wanted. My cell was at the end of the landing and when Mr Churchill would open up the cell doors and get to near my cell he would shout 'so how is celebrity corner this morning'. He liked the fact that he had someone in the newspaper on his landing, but I didn't take any notice of him. I suppose it was something he could go home and tell his family. A few years after I was released from prison I bumped into him and he had become a van driver and was delivering parcels for one of the big courier firms. He was a bit shocked when he saw me and it was obvious he didn't want to talk to me, but I made a point of talking to him to bring him down a peg or two because he walked around that prison like he owned it.

Another person who was in 'celebrity corner' and in a cell next to mine was Charles James Spencer-Churchill, Marquess of Blandford, known as Jamie Blandford. He is a distant relative of both Sir Winston Churchill and Diana, Princess of Wales. I'm not sure what he was inside for, but he had a bad smack habit and sold his Rolex for £10 to an inmate when he arrived. I've recently read that after all these years of having a naughty past, he has now been clean for five years, so good luck to the fella and the estate, Blenheim Palace, which he stands to inherit.

It was then time for another bail hearing so off to court I went again. COD didn't bother applying yet again and I started to wonder what the fuck he knew that I didn't. He was adamant that we would get bail in a couple of months and that's why he wasn't applying early on. I was given another knock back even though I offered the surety again. Friends I knew would stand to lose a lot of money if I had got bail and done a bunk which I wouldn't have dreamt of. Three months went by and I resigned myself to the fact that I was on remand in prison until the trial. I thought to myself that being on remand was better than being on the convicted wing because I was allowed visits every day. Once convicted and moved to that wing, you're only allowed one visit every two weeks.

Time came for my final bail plea and COD also applied this time round. We were both granted bail, I couldn't believe it. We were given our bail terms and told that we must turn up and sign in at Bethnal Green Police Station every day and £5k must be put up each as surety. At that point, I was fucked because I'd told the person who was willing to put up the £75k for my bail security not to come to court because I wouldn't be applying. The only person there for me that day in court was my brother Rodney. I asked him to sign the papers and told him that he didn't have to have the £5k on him there and then, but if I did a bunk he would have to pay up. Rodney signed the papers and I was on my way home. The first thing I wanted to do was have a good bath and get the smell of Pentonville pisshole off of me.

CHAPTER 19

You Just Don't Do That Where I'm From

I was finally home and all anyone wanted to talk to me about was the News of the World story. I was absolutely sick of it and didn't give a shit where they were when they read it. All I wanted to do was find out information and pay fat Terry a visit for some of that information. I walked into his pub and he was standing behind the bar, he looked very pale and like he'd lost a few pounds since I last saw him. He offered me a drink and we went and sat at the corner of the bar. He couldn't apologise enough. I told him I wanted him to tell me exactly what he knew from day one. He said he knew Graham from one of his pubs in Hackney. He informed me that Graham drinks in there and was seeing one of the barmaids who worked for him, so I thought this was a good start. I then asked him who Matthew was and he said he didn't have a clue and had never clapped eyes on him until he walked into the pub with Graham that day when I'd met him. I said I wanted to meet with and speak to Graham, so needed contact details. What he said next, I could have punched him straight in the head. Apparently since I'd been arrested he had tried to get hold of Graham but hadn't had any luck plus his girlfriend the barmaid had disappeared and not been back to work since. The last time fat Terry had seen him was when he'd popped in the pub on the Saturday morning and had asked if COD had left the Arsenal tickets behind the bar.

My faced turned and my shoulders tensed up, there and then I didn't know whether to beat the shit out of fat Terry or spit in his face. This fat useless prick had vouched for Graham and now didn't know where he was. Fat Terry must have noticed my face had changed because he was nearly crying swearing that he'd done everything he could to find Graham, but hadn't had any joy. I told him he'd better find some joy and find fucking Graham at the same time. I knew fat Terry had nothing to do with it, but I'd been set up and it had started with Graham, so he'd better come up with either Graham or an address. Eventually, Terry did come up with an address but when I got there it was an empty flat. The people next door told me the people who had occupied the flat had moved out a few months ago and hadn't been seen since. Fucking marvellous.

The very first weekend after my release Mark had arranged for us to go out because people wanted to see me. He turned up at my flat with COD and it was just like old times with us three going out on a Friday night but this time was different. As we left my flat and were walking towards Mark's car, I noticed two plain-clothed coppers sitting in an unmarked car. As we got in Mark's car, I asked them why they'd brought the old bill with them. They both looked across the road and COD said not to worry about them and that they'd soon get bored and let's carry on, go out and have a great night. We went out, but I was a little wary, couldn't relax as I didn't want to be out and couldn't enjoy myself.

The following morning COD asked me to meet him for pie 'n' mash, the only one I'll go to is Kelly's on the Bethnal Green Road at the top of Valence Road. I was up nice and early and decided to take a nice walk and meet COD there. It was nice to take a long walk after being on remand so off I set on my own. Well, I thought I was on my own until I started to notice some faces around me that looked like old bill. I tried to ignore it but as I got to one end of Bethnal Green Road, at the Cambridge Heath Road junction, and made my way to get to the other end to where the pie 'n' mash shop was, I noticed cars with plain-clothed old bill in them and people talking into their hands. I recalled what Mr O'Leary had said to me and knew he was right in that the old bill wanted to know more and wanted me to lead them somewhere. I assumed this was probably why I had been granted bail.

I arrived at the pie 'n' mash shop where COD was already waiting, we ordered two and two each and tucked in. After I'd left a clean plate, I told him that I'd been followed the whole way and asked if he had. He said he didn't think he had, but to be honest he wouldn't have had a clue if he had. We left the shop and as we walked along I pointed out the old bill to COD, they were all over us. We got about half way up the Bethnal Green Road and I'd had enough and suggested we try and give them the slip, keep them on their toes and give them something to do.

I waved down a black cab and we jumped in and asked the driver to take us to Whitechapel Road. As I looked out the back of the cab, I could see people jumping into cars, so they were on their toes! I said to COD that once we got to Whitechapel Road we'd get to Chicksand and run into someone's house, so by the time they caught up with us we'd be gone. As I looked at the front of the cab, I took note of the driver and fuck me I couldn't believe who I was looking at. I told COD that the driver was old bill and he asked me how I knew. It was the first copper to nick me at the age of nine! COD weren't having none of it so I asked him to watch.

I asked the driver how long he'd been driving a cab and he said about 10 years. I then said 'so the police force didn't work out then mate'? He started to waffle on, but I knew I was right so said to him 'you don't remember me do you'? He looked at me and I went on to tell him that he nicked me at the age of nine and that I never forget a face. He then folded and said that he used to be a copper, but gave it up and started driving a cab. I told him to pull the fucking cab over which he did half way down Valence Road, just before the railway arch. The cheeky bastard then asked us as we walked away if we were going to pay what was on his meter. I turned back and said 'sorry mate I've only got a fifty pound note' and walked away pissing myself laughing. He must have moved up in the force since nicking a little street urchin nearly 20 years beforehand!

As time went on, I distanced myself from COD and kept my head down. I was signing in at Bethnal Green nick every day as part of my bail conditions. If I hadn't signed in they could have sent me back to prison and that was the last thing I needed as I needed to be on the outside, sorting things out and be prepared for the trial once the date was fixed. I was constantly thinking to myself I'm not guilty and that's what I was sticking with. I had explained this to my brief and he was looking into a barrister who would help me fight it. Meanwhile COD, my fucking co-defendant, was pleading guilty. Obviously this was doing me no favours but at the time I thought bollocks I'm still going to fight this because it had felt like one big set up right from the start. My brief had told me we'd know more once the crown prosecution had served him with the papers on what they truly had against me and would let me know immediately once he had them.

Life was going by and I was keeping myself to myself not really wanting anything to do with anyone. COD was still cracking on and I thought up to no good but I didn't want any part of it. I didn't know if or what he was up to, so kept away from him as best I could. I was still going out occasionally having a few drinks but playing no part in any crime and just keeping my head down. I would have been such an idiot if I had because I was still being followed and was under surveillance.

One night I was in the Joiners Arms on Hackney Road and me and COD had used this pub all the time like an office plus you'd always catch us and Mark in there on a Friday night without fail. This particular night was a weeknight, it was about 8:00 pm and I was sitting in the corner of the bar on my own. COD was at the other end of the pub sitting at a table with some blokes I didn't know. They were doing something I think was dodgy involving some sort of money making scam but as I'd dropped out I didn't know exactly what. Even if I hadn't dropped out COD would have been the last person I'd have wanted to make any money with. It's an unwritten rule that once you've been nicked the game is up and over, you take what is coming to you and deal with it. You do not carry on playing, you shut your mouth and say fuck all. I had my suspicions about COD and was worried that he would make something up about me to save his own skin as I'd witnessed him do to others beforehand. I'm not ashamed to admit that I was scared he would put me in the shit, so was still keeping him sweet but from a distance. I didn't know what he was capable of because I felt like I didn't know him anymore and something in my gut was telling me something wasn't right.

I was still sitting at the bar minding my own business when I saw something that put the fear of god in me. I wanted to be anywhere but where I was sitting at that moment in time. The doors of the pub opened and in walked two blokes, so I looked up and I could not believe my own eyes. I went into shock, my mouth dropped open and the rest of me sat rigid, frozen on the stool I was sitting on. I could not take my eyes off of the two blokes who had walked in. They walked across the pub and over to COD's table. COD told the blokes already at his table to leave him for a minute while he had a chat with the two who had just walked in. They sat down and all greeted each other like they were old pals who hadn't seen each other in a long time.

The barmaid actually asked me if I was OK because apparently I looked like I'd seen a ghost. I told the barmaid that the jacket over the chair at the table next to me (that I'd put there before the two blokes arrived) was not mine and that I was leaving the pub. The jacket was mine, but I had a tool in the pocket that I was carrying around at the time and it could have got me nicked. As I looked over COD said to the guests at his table 'look Gary is over there', they looked at me and raised their arms and smiled like we were old pals. I was looking in disbelief. I turned to the barmaid and told her that the two blokes at COD's table were the old bill that had nicked us. It was none other than DCI Dave Taylor and DC Bradshaw. I walked out of the pub and my head was in bits. I couldn't for the life of me think why he would be meeting them in a pub. What sort of interview technique was that?

At that point, I was more than worried about what COD was up to and could only assume that he was all about saving his own skin. I had to do the same but no fucking way would I ever even think about going down the route I thought he had chosen. I was in a real bad place and this was some heavy shit I could do without and I knew it would only get worse. I only ever told one person what I'd seen that day and that was my pal who had been raided and who COD had given the bag full of counterfeit money to, to hide in his lock-up. I confided in my pal what I thought and what I'd seen and that I was worried that COD would get me put away for a very long time.

We kept this to ourselves and even now I don't feel right talking about COD in that light, but you will understand why I have not named names. From that moment, I kept away from him and my reckoning was that if I hadn't known you all of my life I would have nothing to do with you and I still stick by that plan to this day. Don't get me wrong if I'm ever introduced to new people I am polite, I'm not a rude person, but I won't involve myself with more than a hello and polite chit chat. In my eyes, it's the safest way to be.

* * *

I was still signing in at the police station every day and not seeing anyone apart from Mark, but one day when I left the police station on Bethnal Green Road, COD pulled up with two other blokes in the car. I knew one of the fellas but not the other one. COD jumped out of the car and was acting all happy to see me, asking me how I was and asked me to wait a minute as he wanted to talk to me. He ran in the station to sign in, I said hello to the bloke I knew in the car and walked off. I got about 25 yards and then heard my name being called, it was COD shouting 'Gal, Gal I want you'. I shouted back 'another time, I've got to get home', but he wouldn't have none of it and kept shouting so I walked back to him. He said he was on his way to Watford to see a bloke we were in prison with and asked me to go with him. This bloke was the only person COD would talk to while we were inside. I said I didn't have time to go with him, but he wouldn't let it drop, so I unwisely got in the car. The bloke I didn't know in the car was a cab driver and the other bloke was a big harmless lump, Bill, a nice fella but had a major gambling habit.

It was all small talk on the way there and as we were nearing Watford, I heard the real reason why they were on their way there. The car was full of fake £50s. I couldn't believe what I fucking heard and thought thanks a fucking lot for putting me in such a situation. I told COD that I wanted no part in what he was up to and that I was fucked off he hadn't told me before I got in the car because no way would I have got in.

141

COD made a couple of phone calls to someone, I don't know who. We pulled up about 800 yards from three houses on a country lane which were on my right and over to my left was a white van at about the same distance. I could see that there was a bloke in the van. COD told Bill to get out and go over to the middle house and drop off a package and to collect some money. As Bill was about to get out of the car, the white van started to move towards us and picked up speed. It didn't look right so I said to Bill not to get out of the car as I thought the white van was old bill and as it got nearer it slowed just enough so that I could see there were more people in the back of it. The white van carried on and drove by the car we were in.

Now I was seriously fucking angry and said 100% they were old bill and yet again COD called me paranoid. Bill was then told to stay in the motor and the cab driver was told to go for a drive as the person who was meant to be in the house wasn't in yet. We drove around for a while and I was busting to go to the toilet so asked the driver to pull over, but COD told him to carry on as we were near the house we had left. All the country lanes looked the same to me as one bush is no different to another. I was still bursting for a piss and I couldn't hold myself so asked to stop again but again was told we were almost there. We pulled over in a country lane and it was a little darker outside, but I could see the three houses from earlier, so knew we were in the same place we had parked an hour earlier.

Bill got out of the motor and walked towards the house and I jumped out and ran towards the bushes for a piss. I unzipped myself and started to piss which had been causing me severe pain and started to feel relief and much happier. I looked over to my left and Bill was walking back to the car, so I started to shake my manhood dry and as I did, I heard cars skidding and people shouting. There were men jumping out of the bushes and the whole place lit up like someone had just uncovered the sun in a split second. My only thought was oh fuck this has got to be a joke.

As I turned around, there were two blokes running towards me with their police badges being displayed. I was told I was under arrest for possession of counterfeit currency, so I told them the only thing I was in possession of was my cock, because I was still shaking it off. They allowed me to sort myself out and then put me in handcuffs. I was told they were South East Regional Crime Squad and I was being taken to Watford police station. We were all put into separate cars. I was looking around and it was obvious someone knew they were coming. I'd been drawn into this circus as an innocent party and again it felt like another set up. As we slowly drove off I noticed the white van from earlier with six happy plain-clothed officers all congratulating each other on a job well done. I'm paranoid am I?

All the way on route to the police station I was asked questions but I said fuck all. I was thinking it was fuck all to do with me, I'd only gone along for the ride and thought I was visiting a pal from prison. Even if I had told them I was only along for the ride they would have never believed me because I was on bail and had been on the front of a national newspaper for the same thing I'd just been picked up for. I was basically fucked and felt like I'd have to just suffer whatever the outcome would be.

They got me out of the car and walked me into the station. We were walking towards the custody desk and I could see COD with his back to me so he wasn't aware I was approaching. I was less than 10 yards from him, he seemed really annoyed and what he said next has stuck in my head like a tumour since that day. I heard him say the words 'why have you nicked me, you were told not to, as I work for Dave Taylor of the Regional Crime

Squad Scotland Yard'? As those words stung my ears like a swarm of wasps I took in a massive gulp of air and as I exhaled, the words ooooh shit escaped my mouth. The custody desk officer leaned forward, pointed at me and shouted at the officer by my side, 'get him out of here and put him in a fucking cell'. I was then dragged off to a cell. I was numb and in shock. Even with what had been suggested to me and what I'd suspected I still couldn't quite believe COD was a grass. I had now heard it directly from the horse's mouth and it hit me like a freight train.

CHAPTER 20

Court and My Last Resort

I was taken to a cell and was in complete shock at what I'd just heard. I think it must have been obvious that I had taken it as a blow because the officer who put me in the cell said to me 'if I was you mate, I'd wake up and tell us what we want to know because it's not as if we don't know already. You're in shit now and you can thank your so called mate for that.' He locked the cell behind him and my head turned to mush and I started to pace around the cell. I couldn't sit still and was panicking about what COD's role would be in my future. I had no idea what this man had already said, what he was capable of or his limits (if he had any) and I didn't have a clue if I was being dragged into something against my will. If you're a grass, you're capable of any sort of low life action and him saving his own skin by any means possible worried me.

All through the night I tried to get my nut down but it was impossible as my mind was racing and is all I could hear was COD calling me. I just ignored him and kept quiet. He was shouting all sorts like 'I'll get you out of here with no charges' and 'trust me Gal, I'll get you out of here'. Him shouting things like that was further confirmation to me that he was a grass, not that I needed any more persuading. I was concerned even more so that he now knew that I knew for sure that he was an informant for the old bill.

I kept thinking how fucked I was and all of a sudden he was silent. I don't know what possessed me to do what I did next, but I put my head to the cell door and shouted at the top of my voice 'I know no-one in this police station' and repeated it a couple of

145

times. I'm not sure why I shouted it but it felt right at the time and I thought to myself I would be taped, so didn't want to incriminate myself further by saying anything different.

After a while, I was taken to an interview room. I had asked for a brief and one had arrived; a proper dopey prat. I told her I knew nothing, it was nothing to do with me and that I wanted her to get me out of the station as soon as possible. Her response to what I'd said was 'tell the old bill that it's nothing to do with you' – thanks for the great advice! I told her I would be saying 'no comment' to all questions that they asked. I did just that during the interview, apart from telling them that the driver was just a cab driver, and was taken back to my cell. After a while, a copper came to my cell and told me I was being released without charge. I looked at the copper and told him I was going nowhere until my brief told me I could go and I would only leave the station with her. I trusted no-one and had no idea why the fuck I was being released. I was passed a phone and my brief told me I was free to leave with no charges.

As I left the station, I was met by COD and Bill. Bill had been charged and told me he was bailed to return to court and then left me and COD alone. COD then turned to me and said something like 'see, I told you I'd get you out with no charges'. He then took a big wad of money out of his pocket and tried to give me some. I walked off saying I was going home, didn't want to talk to anyone and that I was staying indoors until it was time for me to go to court and be sentenced.

I found out after a while that poor Bill got two and a half years and I believe that he was part of the bait in some sort of deal that had been drawn up. I had no part in any deal but I'm sure COD did. I have no idea what else he had done and who else he had grassed up. I was on edge and kept thinking to myself that I couldn't tell anyone what I knew and I had to play this knowledge very close to my chest. I had to be very smart with any move I made as I had no idea what the bloke was capable of.

My brief, Mr O'Leary, had now been served with the papers so we knew what was going on with my case. We were working together to have the best possible chance for when the trial started. Our plan was to fight it all the way. My brief found me the best possible barrister who wanted to fight my case because he wanted to change the laws on entrapment in the country, so my case was just what he was looking for which was a result for me. I visited his chambers for a meeting which were opposite the high court on the Strand. He was very well-dressed, had the silver fox look and was a good looking bloke in his 50s who was so well turned out he looked like some sort of Lord. He was full of fight which I really liked and spoke so well, unlike myself! For the life of me, I can't remember his name but his fighting spirit was just what I wanted in my corner.

I walked into his office and was blown away by this man's presence, he was very inspiring. The first thing he said to me was that he wanted me to know that he really wanted to fight my case. There was one problem, he had a very big case that could erupt at the same time as my case. His other case, he had been working on for years and was committed and if it did kick off at the same time as mine he would not be able to represent me.

I was gutted by this blow and he could see that. I asked why I was in his office because this was my life on the line and I couldn't bank on half promises. He said he really wanted my case and told me how we should fight it. He had a way with words that was too much for me, but I got the gist of what he was talking about and we came to an understanding and agreed the way forward.

We agreed that I would happily say in court that I would have no doubt probably been taking part in some crime the day I was nicked, but I would not have been taking part in the particular crime I was arrested and charged for if it had not been for the News of the World setting up the crime and making it happen by arranging the meetings. In an American court of law that would have been entrapment and against the law. Me and my barrister agreed we would fight in this manner and would change the law, easy!

It sounded so plain sailing but this was my life we were talking about and nothing is ever that easy or straightforward. We were ready for my big day and the case my barrister had been working on for years came up two weeks before mine – how's my fucking luck. I was now fucked and running around trying to find a barrister to represent me but could not find one who wanted to fight my case and to be honest I didn't blame them. The evidence was completely against me.

A pre-hearing was booked and I managed to find a barrister to defend me, not fight for me. At the pre-hearing, we heard for the first time the evidence stacked up against me. We found out that Roger was a crime reporter for the News of the World. In that newspaper, they advertised weekly for people to contact them if they had a story to sell which they could investigate. That was where Graham and Matthew came in. My defence pushed for the prosecution to tell the judge how much the News of the World had paid Graham and Matthew to be introduced to me and COD. This was something they were against disclosing and fought not to, but the judge ordered that the information be available and put before the court. The prosecution played dumb that they didn't know and asked the News of the World for the information who in turn duly flapped around and delayed court proceedings. Eventually, they found it and everyone in the court was on tenterhooks. The prosecutor then, in his quietest voice as if trying to sell something broken, said that the News of the World had the public's best interests at heart and were doing a duty to protect the public by paying such a vast sum. They waffled on for quite a while and further delayed proceedings. I was thinking just get on with it, just fucking tell the court the figure and stop fart arsing about. He then said that they were paid £40k. The whole court was in shock. The prosecutor was then asked to repeat the figure because he had said it too quietly. He was then asked by my team who the large sum of money was paid to so again he buried his head in his papers to delay time further.

My team then asked him if this was a normal amount to pay someone for this kind of story and were told no it wasn't. It was the largest sum that had ever been paid for a story. My team then asked the best question yet and asked the prosecution to tell the court what the sales figures for the News of the World had been the week before and the week after they published the story on me with the front page headline 'WE SMASH £5M FAKE RACKET'. It turned out they had sold millions of extra copies. In fact, they'd sold 4,724,042 copies and at 50p a copy they'd made nearly £2.5m that week. My team then told the court that it was all driven by greed of paper sales.

Now I know I said I would have probably been somewhere else taking part in a crime, but it wouldn't have been that crime. We now know today what the News of the World was capable of to get a story as it has been closed down for wrong doing. In my eyes, they created the crime and all to sell papers and line their own pockets. Roger had been paid a bonus because his work had made the front page, so he was also driven by greed. The prosecution were then asked who was paid the large sum of money of £40k and it turned out it was Matthew so they were asked to ex-

149

plain who Matthew was. The prosecution said that they would need a break because they would need to ask the News of the World. They did not want to give up this information because if there was going to be a full trial, Matthew would have to be a witness. The court was then told that Matthew was an informant and that they did not have any further information. They wasn't sure if Matthew was even his real name.

I was pissed off because it was all bollocks and the judge was happy with it all. He then said we had to move on to the evidence against us, the accused. The prosecution rolled out their lot and had tape recordings of us talking with Roger and film taken from the rooms in the hotel. I was watching all this and worked out that the lens of the camera must have been in a tiny plant on a side table in the room. We were bang to rights and fucked. The day didn't get any better and they had enough evidence to get us 10 – 12 years.

COD was oddly still upbeat and seemed to be watching a different court to me because he kept telling me we were going to be fine. I was thinking to myself that he must have made some sort of deal and if I pleaded the same as him, they couldn't give me a longer sentence. I didn't know what was going on, but I knew I'd seen and heard enough over the last few months to plead guilty the same as him. I also thought that in one of our meetings he had put himself up as the master printer so I couldn't get a longer sentence than him unless I fight it and lose. I'm not that silly so pleaded guilty at the next hearing.

Now we are where we started this story. If you think it finishes here, think again. Let me tell you, if it can happen it will happen in my life because what happens to me doesn't happen to others.

CHAPTER 21

Prison Life and a Different Kind of Currency

I was now in a holding cell at Wood Green Crown Court and had been sentenced, but I had no clue as to how long for and my head was all over the place. COD then entered the holding cell and looked gutted by what had just happened. His face was as long as Mile End Road. I don't think his part of the deal had come through.

I was called out of the room because my barrister wanted to talk to me alone. I was shown in to another room and sat down in front of a six inch thick window with a vent so me and my barrister could hear each other. He looked upbeat and very pleased with himself which made me angry so I shouted at him and asked what the fuck had just happened in the court because I was confused. He told me he thought that my luck had changed and that I had received a seven and a half year sentence. I honestly thought he was taking the piss and told him so, as I paced up and down the room shouting and cursing. He then raised his voice at me and said that he hadn't finished speaking yet, so I told him I didn't want him to finish because if there was more I didn't want to hear it and he could fuck off. In my head, I was trying to work out how old I would be when I was released and it didn't feel good.

I managed to calm myself down and started to listen to what he had to say. He went on to tell me that it wasn't all that bad and I had honestly been very lucky and that I had been given just over two and a half years for each offence which totalled seven and a half years, but the judge had said that I would only have to serve two and a half years. I couldn't believe my ears and my mood changed in a split second. I shouted out 'get in there' and could now understand why the screw had told me I'd had a result. I was now buzzing and so happy.

He then carried on speaking and told me that with time already spent on remand my sentence wasn't too bad. I thanked him and his team for everything they had done for me and he said they hadn't really done anything. Afterwards, I agreed with his last comment because I believe the sentence was already sorted beforehand and they just played a role in the day's events. He went on to tell me that we would appeal the sentence and in time we would hear more. I was so overjoyed and full of beans.

I was taken back to the holding cell and COD was not a happy boy, but I was surfing on cloud nine. As I was laughing I told him to cheer up as it may never happen. He told me that the sentencing was bollocks, we should never have been sentenced for that long and should not have to serve the length we had been given. I told him what's done is done and we should just get on with it. I can't tell you how happy I was that I had changed my plea to guilty because I had received the same sentence as COD. I was also thinking whatever he had done I had had nothing to do with and over time I would wean him out of my life. One thing that did and has stuck in my mind is we were never charged with the ringer or the passport, they were never mentioned. The keys for the ringer and the ID were found on COD and it's my assumption that that could be how the old bill got him to turn over, it's just a guess and I'll never know for sure. One thing they didn't find when we were arrested and searched was a gram of the naughty powder I was carrying. I flushed it away as soon as I was put in the cell. I was in enough trouble and didn't fancy a party for one in a cell.

We were taken to Pentonville prison, processed and given a prison number. Mine was NWO 627 and this would stay with me until the end of my sentence. We were also told to take a shower, given some prison clothes, put in front of the doctor and taken to the wing. We were staying on the B-wing, the convicted wing not the cushy remand wing I'd known. At the time, it was the longest prison wing in Europe and my god it was a shithole. We were shown to a double cell we were to share and settled in. At first it was strange but it didn't take me long to adapt and get used to it, I didn't have much of a choice.

I had a cell next to the kitchen because I was working on the hotplate serving food to the inmates. Working on the hotplate meant I could be out of my cell a lot more, which meant I had a lot more freedom and had more room to work at getting what I needed. The place was that much of a shithole, the cell I was in was running alive with cockroaches. At night time when it was lights out, you could see the floor move where it was covered with the bastards. You couldn't step out of bed. To stop my bed being run alive with them, I had to put four large empty baked bean tins, filled with water, under each leg of my bed to stop them climbing up. I'll be fucked if I'm spooning cockroaches! If they were in my cell next to the kitchen, you can imagine what the kitchen was like.

There are two worlds that run alongside each other, one is the outside world that I now live in today and the other is prison world. In the outside world, we try and get by and most of the time get by with what we have no matter how little. In prison it is the survival of the fittest. If you show any sign of weakness in prison, there are people waiting to pounce and take whatever you have. They will take whatever and I mean whatever you have and take it any way they can as they have nothing to lose. As we all know prisons are dangerous places, full of dangerous

153

people. It is called a prison for a reason and to keep dangerous people away from the *normal* public. It's full of all types, murderers, rapists, armed robbers, nonce cases, child killers, junkies, you name it they are in there. What can you do to someone who is already imprisoned doing a long term stretch who has nothing to lose? In answer to that there is nothing you can do because no-one cares what you get up to in prison. What happens in prison, stays in prison. For me, I was ready to survive and do whatever it took to get what I needed and wanted to make my stay as easy as possible, it was my mission.

There are things you need in prison and to get these things you pay with currency like phone cards etc., not the hooky £50s type currency! Currency in prison has a higher value than on the streets of the real world. New phones had been introduced that could be used with special prison issue phone cards which you could buy for either £2 or £4. These could be bought with your wages from your prison job. There were various jobs you could do like cleaning or working in the kitchen cooking meals. You could buy these cards once a week out of your private cash if you had any and could also buy toiletries, snacks, chocolates, biscuits, crisps and soft drinks. All this plus tobacco is currency, but the biggest currency of them all is drugs.

My first task when I got in there was to get brand new prison issue clothing because the ones I had been given had been worn many times before they got to me, and that didn't sit right with me. So firstly I found out who was working in laundry and got myself brand new shirts, t-shirts, jeans, jumpers, pants and socks. I had the right currency so it was easy and I didn't plan on going without anything throughout my sentence.

COD was very withdrawn at this time and was constantly on edge. I felt sorry for him as he was under a lot of stress because he knew I knew what he had done and if it would have got out his life wouldn't have been worth living. He no doubt would have got a daily good hiding, but I couldn't do that to him because I felt sorry for him. He wouldn't have lasted five minutes on his own. I made a decision that I would never say a word in prison about what he had done and I would share with him what I had. Right or wrong on my part I needed to do that for my own peace of mind.

The canteen opened once a week and everyone got what they needed to pay back the currency they owed. I had it all. At night if I fancied a munch I could because my cell looked like a tuck shop. For people who didn't pay their debts one of two things happened. The first would be they'd go on the 'numbers' which is rule 43 of the prison code. This is part of the prison where people go to be protected. Say, for example, a low life had committed a crime that is not acceptable to the human race, they are asked as soon as they walk into a prison if they want to go into protection, or the normal population. The numbers is the last resort, but most of those sort of people choose to go into protection rather than take a beating every day. Secondly, for those who didn't pay their debts they got a good hiding.

At any one time you were only allowed three phone cards in your possession. Not me, I had the nickname BT because I was always on the phone. Being on the phone was a way of taking away the boredom and knowing what was going on in the outside world. Prison can be so boring and it was nice to talk to my outside pals and family about the normal things in life and not just about crime with my inside mates because that's all inmates talk about.

If you're serving a short term sentence and are sentenced in London, you will stay in a London prison. All major cities have these short-term prisons and they are called dispersals, but if you are sentenced to a longer term you will be shipped out to a long term prison. It is all down to the crime you have committed where you will end up. In a short term prison, you will serve no longer than a few months unless on remand. The turnover of people in a London prison is daily, someone is always being released and there is always someone to take their place. While I was in prison, mates would always come and go and someone I knew would always turn up which was good because it broke up the time. I can honestly say I had some of the best laughs I've ever had in prison, but I'm not promoting it because I also had some of the worst times.

One bloke I knew, Murphy, had a job down the block as a cleaner. He was from North London and was a big bloke who loved the gym. The block is a part of the prison where you are sent if you're being punished for something like fighting or causing any sort of trouble. In the block, rule 43 (numbers as it's called by inmates) cannot protect you and people who have been in protection fear for their life if they are sent there. The block, in any prison in the country, is underneath the prison with no windows or natural daylight. Murphy came up to me one day and wanted to speak to me in my cell for privacy. We sat down in my cell and he told me that a bloke in the block was asking about me. This prisoner had only arrived a week beforehand and had asked to be put in the block straight away as he didn't want to come into the prison or join any wing and didn't want to leave his cell to wash or get food so everything was being delivered to him.

Murphy told me he started speaking to this bloke because he wanted to know what the score was with him and why he wasn't mixing with anyone. I obviously questioned Murphy about him and the strange thing was this bloke's name wasn't listed anywhere. He had asked Murphy about the prison and who was in there and had specifically asked if I was in there. Murphy tried to pump him to get information on why he was asking, but he wouldn't say the reason. I asked Murphy to describe this bloke which he did and straight away I knew who it was. I told Murphy he had to get me to the block, but he said he couldn't. The only way I'd get there was if I kicked off and caused some bother. This wasn't a good idea because if I did get myself sent to the block I wouldn't have been able to get to him anyway, but fuck me did I want to get hold of him.

Murphy had described the way he looked but as soon as he said he spoke with a South African accent I knew it was Matthew. Apparently he had been caught trying to get out of the country and would you fucking believe he'd tried with a dodgy passport! Now was payback time and payback is a fucking bitch. I told Murphy when he went back down to the block I wanted him to tell Matthew that wherever he was and whatever prison he ended up in someone would know me and he would get what was coming to him, the dirty grass cunt. Murphy did what I asked the very next morning and when I saw him later that day he told me that Matthew had shit himself and had started crying and screaming. Apparently he was making so much noise a screw had to try and calm him down.

Matthew was only in Pentonville for a week, but that week I made his life hell even though I couldn't get to him. The low life was moved out of Pentonville and no record could be traced of where he had been moved to. Trust me I spoke to everyone and tried my hardest to find him but in the end I thought what goes around comes around.

It was now my turn to move prisons and I was told I was going to Camp Hill on the Isle of Wight, which fucked me right off. I went to see one of the screws in his office and told him I wasn't going anywhere near the Isle of Wight and sarcastically asked him if he knew how fucking far away it was. He told me yes he did know and I would be moved the following week. I insisted that I should be moved to an open prison because my crime was a white-collar crime and I shouldn't be treated like a hardened criminal. The arsehole told me I would not be going to any open prison anytime soon because it wasn't right for me. He also said I was running around the place like no-one he'd ever seen and he knew I was into everything that went on. I just said 'let's see who gets transferred shall we' and left his office.

I went back to my cell to think it over. COD had also been told he was going to Camp Hill and wasn't happy and was scared about being moved. The only reason I didn't want to be moved was because it was too far for anyone to travel and visit me and I didn't want people travelling that far. I was fuming I was being moved and that my visitors would have to get a train, boat and a fucking bus, it just wasn't on. As for me being into all sorts that went on, them moving me wasn't going to change that. Being in prison was survival and if you can't catch me, I'll carry on.

Eventually, I drove the screws mad and got my own way. I was told there had been a change of plan and I was going to Bullingdon in Oxfordshire. At the time, I had never heard of it and nor had anyone I knew. I was told it was a brand new prison and I'd be one of the first prisoners to be housed there. I was happy about this because it wasn't too far from London and was OK for people to get to so I didn't create any further fuss.

CHAPTER 22

B Cat - BULLingdon

I was told I would be moved within one week and I was ready. I was happy to get away from Pentonville because it was a Victorian built shithole. I packed all my belongings which consisted of a stereo, prison clothes, my personal letters from my family and friends and court records of my case, and the time came for me and COD to be transferred. We were taken to the main reception and processed and as we were the only two that were being transferred that day, it didn't take long. The transfer also wouldn't take long so we wouldn't be sitting in the sweatboxes dropping off and waiting for others who were being moved. We met the screw who was going to be our escort and as he walked in the office he was all full of himself and had a big smile on his face. We shook hands, said hello and he told us he would be taking us to Bullingdon and said he hoped to not have any trouble out of me. I laughed at this. I was happy to see him because I knew him and he was a nice bloke who used to be a bouncer in a club called Benjys on Mile End Road and he was also on the wing when I was on remand.

We set off and the journey was due to take about an hour and half. Sitting in a sweatbox for that long without taking a piss was a long time and I needed to go so told the screw. He warned me that if we stopped off that I shouldn't try anything. I promised him I wouldn't and he said he would sort out a cold drink as well. We pulled in to a police station which made me piss myself laughing and so did the screw and he said to me 'you didn't think I was going to stop at a McDonalds did you'? He put the cuffs on us and took us off the sweatbox and to the toilets.

We carried on our journey and as we got nearer the prison he told me there was someone I knew who was already at the prison and he would sort it out that I'd be put on the same wing for which I thanked him because life inside is always a little easier when you know someone.

We arrived at Bullingdon which was in the middle of nowhere and surrounded by fields. We were taken off the sweatbox and lead in our cuffs to the reception where we were searched and processed. All the while I was looking about thinking what the fuck is this place.

In the prison system there are categories of prisons and prisoners. The categories are as follows:

AA cat

A cat

B cat

C cat

D cat

The category you are placed in, deciding on what prison you will be sent to, depends on your crime and sentence term. AA is for very dangerous men like terrorists, mass murderers etc. and from there it works its way down. The longer you serve and behave yourself, over time you can drop down through categories / prisons. For the crime I was sentenced with, I shouldn't have been where I was standing. As I was looking around checking the place out I could see that this was some high security shit and I wasn't happy.

The screw who had escorted us told me that he was going to have a word with the Senior Officer (S.O.) to see if he could get me put on the same wing as Tom, the bloke I knew. Tom was in for armed robbery on a security van and was serving eight years. There was an inmate cleaning nearby so I asked him what sort of place it was. He told me that it was a B Cat prison and I wasn't going to like it. It pissed me off because I I'd been stitched up good and proper. If it was a B Cat then there was going to be some fucked up and dangerous inmates and I'd just been put in amongst them. The screw came back and told me he had sorted it and he had also sorted for himself to take me to the wing because he would like to see Tom for a chat.

As I was walking through the prison, there were very long and enclosed walkways with no access to the outside grounds. We arrived at the wing and it was like nothing I'd ever seen before. It had its own high-tech central control office where the screws sat and controlled every movement of every inmate. The wing I was standing on had three wings running off of it which were separated by three big gates. As I walked through one of the big gates on to the wing, I was greeted with the only smile I'd seen since arriving, Tom. He told me that he had an empty cell next to his and he was going to have a word to get me in there, which he did so in I moved.

I went to unpack my stuff and while I did the screw who had transferred me was having a chat with Tom. Once I was unpacked and the screw had left Tom made a cuppa tea and we caught up. He gave me the rundown of the place but had only been there three weeks himself. Tom then showed me around the place and said that there were a couple of people in there that I knew which I thought was a result. I settled into my new home and thought to myself prison was prison so I'd better crack on and make the best of it.

There were still a few empty cells on my wing so people were turning up all the time and cells were soon filled. They were lovely little cells with little en suite toilets and sinks, which were all freshly painted and clean because everything was brand new. There was a pool table, table tennis, TV room and a fully loaded wet room with showers and a bath. I loved this and spent hours soaking in the bath, but only if COD or Tom stood at the door. That way you could totally relax and enjoy it with no-one walking in uninvited. I'd also do the same for them.

There were a lot of inmates from all over the place: Wales, Liverpool, Manchester, the Midlands who I call country folk. There were only a handful of Londoners and only one person from Brick Lane; John Ling. As kids, like me, he was always up to something. His family moved out to Essex when he was about 12 years' old and I hadn't seen him for years. He had been in and out of prison for years and had a heroin habit, but when I met him in prison, he was clean. He had been at Bullingdon since it had opened. John looked like he was having a rough time, so I told him I'd help him out to get him on his feet. I said he could work for me and I'd see him alright. I told him I wanted phone cards and tobacco to start with, gave him the currency and sent him on his way.

It wasn't long before I was up and running and John was getting me a steady flow of phone cards and tobacco. After a couple of weeks, I came in to my own and me and COD started running the prison gambling book. It had started out as a bit of fun on our wing on a Saturday morning taking football bets. For example, if someone wanted to bet West Ham beat Spurs, they would put their currency down of half an ounce of tobacco, or a £2 or £4 phone card and then if they won they would get double their currency back. The more people that bet, the more chance me and COD didn't have a chance of losing. Some people didn't smoke so they would bet chocolate and food. I didn't care what they gambled as it was just another way of getting what I needed to keep me comfortable while inside.

It wasn't long before word got out all over the prison and we were taking bets on horseracing and all sorts. Even some of the screws on my wing were getting involved and having a bet. I had different types of income of currency. I had a carrier bag full of tobacco that would last me a year and what I would loan to people. If you borrowed some tobacco, you would pay me back double. On canteen days, I would get it all paid back and if it wasn't tobacco I'd ask for packets of biscuits or bottles of soft drinks as payment. I had all I needed and me and COD were sorted.

John was running around getting me a good steady flow of phone cards. I loved being on the phone to the outside world. John was also getting me tobacco from around the prison because he also had a prison job in another part of the prison. In Bullingdon everyone was required to work or take part in education. I was the wing cleaner because I'd sweetened up the wing Senior Officer. If I was the wing cleaner, I didn't have to leave the wing. We had church to go to on Sundays which is where a lot of deals were done and if you wanted to have a chat with someone from another wing, you met at church.

John was doing well, but I started to get suspicious that he was up to something, so I pulled him up. If I hadn't known him all of my life I would have just beaten the shit out of him, but as I had known him all my life I gave him a bit of respect. I called him into my cell and told him to push the door ajar, not shut but just ajar so no-one could see inside. I then told John with my fucked off face and a raised voice that I'd heard he was back on the gear and I was fucked off that I'd been helping pay for his shitty habit

163

and it wasn't going to carry on. He basically shit himself and swore to me that he hadn't turned me over or taken from me. I told him to go and get the currency that he had which belonged to me. He then told me he would go and get it but first he had to quickly sign for a recorded letter which had arrived for him. I agreed he could go and do that but he was to return straight back to me. What did the silly cunt go and do? He walked straight into the control office and put himself on the numbers (rule 43, protection). When you put yourself on the numbers for a prison debt, you have to declare who you owe and what you owe. The cunt broke all the rules of prison life and life in general. I didn't give a fuck as it was him who would have to live with all the lowlifes, nonces and rapists. I would have rather been beaten up or died than have to live in the same breathing space as that scum. I forgot about John and just moved on. It was no big deal and just proved to me again that you couldn't trust anyone in prison.

We had some good laughs in Bullingdon and used to have little parties in each other's cells. We'd make Hooch and get drunk. It broke the time up which was good because most of the time it dragged. Some of the screws weren't too bad in there, there were a few women screws, but mostly men. They would just let us get on by not bothering us and they'd actually be quite helpful if you needed it. I used to play my music really loud and rarely would they ask me to turn it down.

One female screw didn't mind my loud music and used to have a little sing along which made me laugh. At one time the song of the moment was Dreams by Gabrielle (the bird who wore an eye patch), it was a real summer tune. I would play that song over and over again on my CD player – CDs had just come out at that time. Before then I'd play Mary J Blige – her first album was my favourite. This female screw told me she was going to Spain on holiday for a couple of weeks, so I told her to have a good time and think of us being banged up and she laughed. Two weeks went by and she was back. She walked onto the wing in a white shirt and her tan was unbelievable. We were all pale and a pasty grey colour because we didn't get out much. Even when we did get out in the exercise yard it was covered in netting. The female screw walked towards me and her face changed from a smile to stern looking and she said 'oi you Hutton, you spoilt my holiday'. I laughed and said I'd been in prison the whole time she was away so how did she work that one out. She said that every bar and club she visited while in Spain had been playing the song Dreams and every time she heard it she thought of me. I laughed and told her she must be in love with me and it wasn't my fault. Her face changed back to a smile and she walked off.

CHAPTER 23

Who is Living in my Home?

At bang up time COD was finding it hard and for the first two months, every night, he had panic attacks. He would jump out of bed and start banging on the cell door screaming and shouting. Of course this woke me up and most of the wing. He would be shouting 'gov, gov, gov' to get the attention of the night guard. He would say he needed tablets and wanted the night screw to get them for him. They would come and give him some paracetamol, I'm not sure what he thought they were. He'd be deathly pale and breathing heavily and getting himself in a right old state. After he would take the tablets and I'd calm him, he would settle down. I'd have to talk him through whatever he was feeling just to try and get a bit of peace and quiet. I was a fucking doctor to him as well as everything else.

Until you live with someone in such close proximity, you don't really know them. I found COD to be very weak and there was no way on God's earth he would have got as far as he did without me, he would have had nothing. Everything I knew about him made me feel sorry for him, stupid on my part? I'll let you come to your own judgement. He wasn't someone who should have ever been involved in crime, he just wasn't cut out for it. After getting to know him in that cell, he came across to me as a real mummy and daddy's boy. Given my time again, I would have never have got involved with him. Hindsight is a marvellous thing!

After a while, prison becomes the norm and it might be prison, but it is an inmate's home. It would be like being on the outside at home, for example if you ran out of sugar you would pop to your neighbours to borrow some, or nip round to a family member's house for a cup of tea. That's what we did in prison. I was out of my cell most of the time because I was wing cleaner, which meant I did as little as possible. I had to have a job though because my long term goal was to get out of prison and working was part of your ticket to get out, so I thought being wing cleaner would help me. Unbeknown to me in Pentonville I had been assessed and deemed to be unsuitable for an open prison. For the crime I had been sentenced for, I should not have been in a B Cat prison. B Cat was full of some naughty people who wouldn't think twice about opening you up.

One day I was walking along the landing and I heard a screw telling a new bloke to get the fuck out of his office, not to ask him for nothing and to get back to his cell and stay there. The tone the screw used was one of hate. As the bloke left the screw's office, I had a good look at him, he was a weird looking bloke and didn't make eye contact with me as he walked by me. On my wing there were four landings with 10 cells on each landing, some being single cells and others double, so there were a lot of inmates and I knew most of them if not directly through another inmate. If I didn't know someone, I had nothing to do with them. After hearing the screw shout, I didn't think it sounded right so I walked into his office and asked him what it was about. He told me nothing but I could tell by his face it was something not nothing.

After that little episode, I started to pay more attention to who was around me and who was on my wing and started to become uncomfortable with what I saw. I spoke to six blokes who were the only people I had anything to do with; I either knew them on the outside, someone I knew on the outside knew who they were, or I had met them through someone inside. I had met Tom in Pentonville through someone I knew. Me and Tom became very close over time, but I always sensed even he was hiding something from me. Bang, 10 years later I found out what it was he was hiding and it shocked me to my very core, but I'll come on to that.

One morning, like most mornings, a screw would go round to all the cells and deliver mail while everyone was at work. I would still be on the wing because I was wing cleaner and I'd be pottering about mopping the floor or such like. I had it sweet because I made sure everyone kept the wing clean, so my job was easy. I was sitting in my cell waiting for Tom and making a cuppa for me and him. Tom's job was to clean the screws' office and control room. Tom was running late this particular morning, probably because we were having a cuppa and a chat! A screw walked into my cell with a letter in his hands and looked worried and told me the letter was for me. I jumped up and told him I'd worked that one out for myself because he was standing in my cell doorway. The look on his face wasn't right and I knew he had read it because all mail is read by the screws before being delivered. Because of the worried look on his face I had all sorts running through my head like something had happened to my family or someone had died. I told him to give me the letter and he said he'd let me read it on my own and that he'd be just outside. That statement sent me into panic overdrive. I was thinking please God don't let this be happening. As I took the letter out of the envelope, I noticed it was prison issue writing paper so I knew it was from another prisoner in another prison. The writing was hard to read and was that bad I couldn't understand it but after a while I worked out what it was about and who it was from.

I finished reading it and walked out of my cell and asked the screw why he had acted like someone had died because it had put me in a right fucking state. He said he was sorry and that he didn't know I knew the person who had written the letter. I reminded him he knew fuck all about me and fuck all about who I knew. The letter was from a major underworld figure who I don't want to name because this book is not a guide of who's who and who knows who in the underworld. The letter had obviously shaken the screw a bit and I used that to my advantage while in prison because this screw would come in handy.

While I was in prison I started to have a puff, I'd never smoked it before because I didn't like it, but being inside it gave you a good night's sleep. I'd tried it as a kid, but it wasn't for me because I didn't like the smell or the effect it had on me, it turned me into a zombie. At the time, in prison, it was well smoked by many inmates. One day while all the other inmates on my wing were at work I was laying on my bed in my cell puffing and a screw booted open my cell door, walked in and shouted at me asking what the fuck did I think I was doing. I jumped up and told him he had just burst into my home and asked why he had kicked my fucking door in and would he be happy if I did that at his home. I told him to go back outside and start again by knocking! As soon as I said it I thought oh fuck I'm going to be nicked for that and have days added to my sentence. Well, I couldn't believe my eyes, he turned around, walked out and closed the door behind him. I quickly put the joint out and opened both the windows. The screw then knocked on the cell door. I was pissing myself laughing inside and thinking you never just did that Hutton! I shouted out for him to come in and thought I'm going to milk this for all I can. Like I said earlier if you show weakness in prison a screw or inmate are ready to pounce and you'll get taken. He said he'd only come for a chat so I asked him again why he'd kicked my door open. He didn't answer that and said I shouldn't be smoking puff to which I responded I'll do what the fuck I like in my own home. I then walked off.

I looked at it like this. In prison he was a screw with power but not so much to me. To me he was a country bumpkin and I was going to show him just how smart a street urchin just like me can be. I told everyone that I spoke to on the wing not to speak to him because he'd given me the hump by kicking my door and invading my personal space. They spread the word around and over the next two days no-one talked to him. Even when the screw asked an inmate a question no-one replied or acknowledged his existence. Two days went by and he came up to me and asked to have a word. We went to my cell and I invited him in. As God is my judge, he told me that I was making his work life a misery. He was upset that no-one was talking to him and it was making him feel like a nonce case – what a fucking statement! In his head, he was now an inmate and didn't want to be treated as an outcast. I remember saying to him 'look you're not a bad bloke and I'll tell everyone to talk to you and everything will get back to normal' and put out my hand to shake his. As he put out his hand I grabbed it tight, stared him straight in the eyes and said 'if I do this for you, you have to do something for me'. He looked at me and I stared straight back at him, not blinking and deadly silent. He agreed with me, said he would and thanked me. I then told him I would go and tell everyone he was a good bloke. He came in very useful to me.

As I said earlier, I'd started to pay attention as to who was around me. I was looking at the people on the wing and didn't like what I saw. A lot of the inmates didn't look right so I started to dig deeper. I wasn't happy that Bullingdon, my home, was taking lots of inmates from other prisons all over the country to fill up the empty cells. Basically, other prisons were spitting out the rubbish they didn't want and they were ending up at my home. This was bollocks in my eyes because no-one knew anyone and the only person who knew for a fact what you were inside for was the screws. I started to ask people how do you know so and so and if they said they didn't know so and so I'd ask why the fuck they were talking to them.

There was one particular Indian bloke I got the feeling that he was not right, so I did a little digging. I found out that he used to kickbox and was from the Hemel Hempstead area. He had probably never kickboxed in his life and just said it so people stayed away from him. He wasn't on my wing but had the job of dustman so would go around all the wings and empty the bins on the landings. Each inmate who had a little bin in their cell would empty it every morning into a bigger bin on their landing and he would empty the bigger bins.

There was a bloke I knew that used to talk to him so I asked him what he was inside for and he told me that he was coming to the end of an 11 year term. I thought wow that's a long fucking bird and asked what the hell he had done. He told me that he had almost done nine of the 11 years and had come to Bullingdon because it was close to his home and it wouldn't be long before he was released. I told him that wasn't what I asked and he said he didn't want to tell me because he knew what I was like and that it was all a big mistake and binman hadn't committed the crime and it was a long story.

I told him I wasn't going anywhere so he went on to tell me that binman was going out with a bird and her dad was a racist and didn't like anyone who wasn't white, so she wasn't allowed to see him, but binman would climb up into her window at night, she would let him in and they'd do their business. I thought this was odd because that doesn't get you 11 years in prison and 11 years is a weird sentence. As you get to know people in prison, you get to learn what people get for different crimes and judges most of the time tend to give out the same sentence for the same crime and his sentence wasn't right.

171

The bloke I was talking to then told me this was where it got a bit fucked up. One night he had climbed up to his girlfriend's window and had sex with her 11 year old sister. Well my belly turned over, I felt sick and was completely in shock. After he told me that I turned to him and said 'and you talk to this cunt who has raped an 11 year old kid you cunt'. He was regretful and said he knew he shouldn't have told me, so I told him it would be the last thing he ever told me because I'd never talk to the cunt again. I didn't know him well anyway and was only being nice so I could find out information which I did.

Hearing that fucked me as I seriously fucking despise paedophiles and rapists and while I was in prison, I didn't want to be anywhere near anyone like that. The first thing I did that evening, while everyone was out of their cells either on the phone, watching telly or playing pool or table tennis, was go to my cell and find my court papers that showed the crime I was in there for and I knew everyone else had their own set of papers. I walked to the TV room, opened the door so everyone could hear me and told everyone that what I had in my hands were the court papers from my trial and I was going to put them on the pool table so anyone could read them. Some people were looking confused and worried as I was shouting for all to hear. I then said that as my papers were out I wanted to read each inmates' papers in return. I also said tell everyone that if they didn't bring their papers tomorrow, I would come to their cell and read them anyway because I didn't want any fucking nonces, rapists or child killers breathing the same air as me. A flow started and a few people I knew went to get their papers and put them on the pool table.

It came to bang up time and we were all locked in for the night and all through the night I could hear cell doors being opened and closed. I was lying in bed wondering what was happening because it wasn't right for cell doors to be opened during the night. In the morning, we were let out of our cells and I asked Tom what was happening the previous night with doors opening and closing. Tom said he thought that people had put themselves on the numbers. As I walked around the wing there were lots of empty cells and Tom had been right. Is all I could think was dirty lowlifes, but I was really happy because I didn't want to live with animals like that. Later that day I walked around to the cells who still had people in them and looked at their paperwork and everyone who was still there was OK and I wanted to keep it that way.

CHAPTER 24

My Survival Mission

After finding out who was who I felt more peaceful that the wing was clear of vermin, but that peacefulness didn't last long. I still had to look at the Indian kickboxing binman who was occasionally on the wing emptying bins and it was winding me up. How can anyone rape an 11 year old kid? Is all I could then and can now think about is that poor baby. It makes me physically want to be sick and makes my blood boil and at the time I couldn't believe no-one had already sorted the cunt out.

In my head, I was thinking that if some sick bastard did that to a member of my family I would certainly want someone to seriously beat the cunt if they had the opportunity. I decided that that was my mission and that's what I was going to do for the victims and their families. I was going to give these fucking animals a taste of the pain that they'd inflicted on their victims and their poor families. I cannot put into words and describe just how much I hate this kind of filth, it sickens me that they have the right to breathe the same air as the rest of us. My hatred for this kind of scum has been with me since I was a kid, long before I was sent to prison. I had hate and still do have hate for anyone that commits such an atrocity and when in prison I had a chance to do something about it.

I told COD what I was going to do and he said he was going to education, as he did every morning. I remember thinking to myself, thanks mate but also thinking why I should expect any different. This particular morning I walked out of my cell and did my little bit of mopping of the wing and watched everyone leave the wing to go about their jobs. I walked back into my cell, got two prison issue socks and placed one inside the other. Everything in a cell is run off of big batteries and I had two which were in my CD player. I put the two batteries inside the socks and doubled it up into a knot as I didn't want the batteries falling out of the sock.

A good 45 minutes had passed since everyone had left the wing and I knew the Indian binman would be along shortly, so I walked out of my cell and stood on the landing. He collected all the other wings' bins first and my wing last. After a bit, he walked through the gate onto my wing. I was on the ones (ground floor) and as he walked towards me, I said good morning mate with a big smile on my face. I'd never spoken to him before, so didn't know what he made of me that morning when I did speak to him. He walked passed me and took the bin on my landing to be emptied.

As he was emptying the bin I casually walked back in my cell, grabbed the sock and wrapped it around my hand and stood outside my cell door. Again he walked passed me and up to the twos (first floor) to empty that bin and as he did I smiled again and asked if he was OK. He nodded and carried on walking. I was standing there with one hand behind my back and with the other smoking a fag. Off he went to the threes to empty that bin.

I then put my fag out as I could see him coming back. As he came back towards my cell, with my hand wrapped in the sock, I smacked him with full force right in the centre of his forehead. Stunned, he went down like a sack of shit and as he did I hit him again and again and again. There was claret everywhere. He was crawling along the floor screaming like a pig being slaughtered and trying to get to the stairs which led to the screws' office. All the time I didn't let up and as I was hammering him, I shouted you raped an 11 year old girl you fucking animal. I was hitting

175

and hitting him and could hear his bones cracking every time I connected with him. He was now at the bottom of the stairs on all fours still as I was not letting the bastard up. He looked up at me and I could see that his head was split wide open and there was blood everywhere. I could see white flesh deep inside the open cut and I aimed for it again and again and the force of the blows was making a deep thudding noise which was joined by his screams of agony. I then told him if I had had longer with him he would be leaving the prison with no bollocks and as I said it, I smashed the sock into his groin.

By then people were starting to come back on the wing so I ran and got my mop and cleaned all the blood away from my cell and off the stairs as best as I could. COD walked past the binman and knew exactly what had happened and grabbed a mop to help clear up and as he did the alarm went off. When the alarm goes off that means, within two minutes, 20 screws will be swarming the wing looking for where the trouble is coming from and the prison will go on lock down. What I didn't know at the time was that the screw on watch had remained in his office on the twos and had shut the door. There had been no-one in the centre control room so no-one had seen anything. After a couple of hours, the word had got about that I wasn't having any nonc-es on the wing and that I was hell-bent on finding who they were.

My next move was to stop these animals moving into the empty cells on my wing. One day I had been outside thinking and had done a few laps walking around the yard. I walked back onto my wing, into the wing office, shut the door behind me and sat opposite the screw who I believed now owed me a favour. I thought I'd try my luck and told him that I wanted to call in the favour he owed me. His face said everything, I could see he was thinking; oh fuuuck. I told him that I wanted him to tell me who was a nonce, rapist or any other form of low life. I told him I wanted him to look up everyone's details on the wing because I didn't want any animals near me. Without blinking an eye, he point blank refused so I asked him that if I thought someone was a wrong'un would he look them up for me. He neither said yes or no so I took that for what it was.

Following that chat, I was on the lookout and on full alert for who I thought was a wrong'un. I went down to Tom's cell and he was making a cup of tea so I sat down. As we were chatting, he told me about a bloke who was on the opposite wing, who was apparently telling everyone he was inside for rape and he didn't care who knew or found out because no-one could do fuck all to him. I said to Tom we'd soon see about that and asked who it was. Tom said he would show me later when we were in association which is when everyone was out of their cells. We could see the opposite wing but we couldn't walk on to it.

There was an area of about 20 foot square where the wing control office was. It was a sterile area between the three wings and where the control office could view all three wings. Later that day me and Tom were standing by the gates looking across to the other wing trying to see if we could see this bloke for Tom to point out. He then appeared and Tom told me it was a bloke in a tight blue t-shirt who was walking towards the gate. I was looking at this bloke and he was a white fella who was a mountain of a man. I was thinking wow no wonder he is telling everyone that no-one can do fuck all to him. Me and Tom went back to my cell and I told him that when everyone went to work the next morning I was going to walk off the wing and front this cunt out and see what he was about.

The next morning I was up nice and early and had some breakfast. Me, Tom and COD sat down and were having a cuppa and

I told them I wasn't taking a tool because I just wanted to put it on him and suss him out. When breakfast was finished, everyone was ready to leave the wing. I walked up to the gates just like everyone else, including the other wings. I was looking across and could see the white-mountain. All the gates were opened and everyone was walking through including me even though I was the wing cleaner and don't normally leave the wing. Now all the inmates from all the wings were in a holding area and being counted by a screw. As the screw was doing the headcount, I knew I didn't have long because there would have been one head too many (mine)!

I was stood right next to white-mountain, looked up at him and said you alright mate. He looked at me, nodded and said cool bruv. Everyone in prison calls each other bruv. My face changed and with the face of someone who wanted to kill him, said to him I'm not your bruv and is that right no-one can do fuck all to you in here and is it right you're a fucking rapist? I was right in front of him and not going anywhere. He moved back and so did all the other inmates and he said yeah that's right and what are you going to do? I said to him you'll see what I'm going to do cunt. As he said that a screw walked over and put his hand on his shoulder and moved him away and said come on Hutton, you're not meant to be here. Now the bloke had got louder, so then I knew he was a shitcunt as well as a beast. As I walked away, I told him I'd show him no-one could touch him and that someone should have sorted him out a long time ago. I was taken back to the wing and was in a rage thinking how can all these inmates just let these people live amongst them especially one who was saying that no-one could do fuck all to him. Shame on anyone who has been in prison and knew someone was a nonce or rapist and didn't do anything about it.

I knew I couldn't get to this beast to give him a good beating because he was on a different wing, so I came up with the next best thing. I put together a plan that I would have to pay for, but I had all manner of currency and would happily pay so this wasn't a problem. One bloke I knew was in art class so I asked him to make a banner with the words in big bold letters and 'fuck off rapist'. I got another bloke to get a highly inflammable polish and a glass bottle. When these two are put together, you have a cocktail recipe to cause mayhem! I asked a favour of another junkie bloke who always needed currency and was moving from white-mountain's wing onto my wing. I asked him, as he was moving that day, to light the inflammable bottle and launch it into white-mountain's cell. As the junkie threw the lit bottle into his cell, we put up the banner. White-mountain came running out of his cell onto the landing shouting the odds. I was standing at the gate telling him that I told him I would sort him out and was laughing at him. The alarms then went off and we were all put back in our cells. The fire brigade were called, but it was fine because it was only white-mountain who caught on fire. He was taken off the wing and never to be seen again. It was 2-0 to me so happy days.

By now some of the empty cells on the wing were being filled up, but with normal people. They were filling with people who had lived an honest life of crime and when I say that I mean not sick bastards who have mentally scarred innocent people, or even worse. Everything was good and full of laughter on my wing, but one day on walked a bloke who was going to fucking break that. I was playing pool and blowing my own trumpet I'm a fucking good player along with table tennis. They call it a misspent youth I believe! Inmates still wanted to try and beat me, so this day we were playing pool for currency and in walked this bloke carrying all of his stuff. A screw was showing him to his cell. I was sizing him up as he walked by and I didn't like what I saw, so was wondering whether he belonged on the wing. I put down my pool cue and went back to my cell to have a think and sat there for a few minutes. This bloke looked roughly 35 years' old, had mousey greasy hair, a scar down his right cheek and looked like a soapy looking tramp. To me he looked like a fucking nonce.

I walked over to his cell and nice and calmly put my head in his door and said welcome mate. He replied hello and sounded American, but the tone of his voice sounded slow like he was some sort of inbred like the hillbillies you hear in films. I asked him what prison he had just come from and he told me he'd just come from court. Wrong answer, hillbilly was a lying bastard, so I asked what he was in for. In his slow inbred tone, he said burglary. I wish you could hear me say it the way I heard it, buurglaaryyy. At that point, I couldn't help myself so told him to fuck off and he didn't look like he could break into his own house if he was locked out. I then walked off because I'd heard enough and went back to the pool table. My mission list had now grown.

CHAPTER 25

Different Mind-sets and Mentalities

During visits you get to see who is visiting who and quite a few times I'd seen Tom's missus visit him. She was a bit older than me the same as Tom was, and she was a very attractive woman. One particular day she had visited Tom and on our way back to the wing I wound him up and while laughing said to him that his missus was being looked after (by another man) and was enjoying him being away. He turned to me and it was like someone had pressed a switch in his head because he completely changed and said to me in a cold tone, completely deadpan and with no emotion, that the first day he was released he was going to take her over to Epping Forest, dig a hole, put her in it and he was convinced that she'd soon tell him if she had been with another man and then he laughed it off. I was a bit taken aback and was looking at him thinking to myself that those were not the thoughts of a normal person. In my head he wasn't well if he was thinking that, let alone saying it.

I couldn't get what he'd said out of my head so the next day I pulled him up on it and asked him if he was being serious. He said that what he'd said the day before was exactly what he would be doing on the day of his release. I was again shocked and just walked away from him. That sick comment or threat stuck with me for a very long time.

Just before bang up I made some enquiries as to who hillbilly was. I wanted to know if he was a nonce case or not and I would have laid money on it he was. I was told by someone who owed me a favour I'd know in the morning. That night I didn't sleep too well because I'm like the rest of the world, I want information fast.

The next morning I was up nice and early, washed and dressed and ready for another day in paradise. My cell door opened and my information walked in. My suspicions were confirmed and I had been right hillbilly was a nonce. The person's face who was telling me said a thousand words and to narrow them down, what he had read, I could see, had made him feel sick. He went on to tell me that hillbilly had been convicted for buggary on two little kids. I felt sick. I had a picture in my head of two little kids I knew who were close to me in my life at the time and it made me want to cry.

My head then came back on and all I could think was the sick bastard had to leave the wing and by any means possible. I thanked the person who gave me the information and left my cell to go for breakfast. Thankfully I didn't see hillbilly at breakfast and worked out in my head what I needed to do. I told a bloke who worked in the laundry that I needed him to get me three sets of prison overalls, three jumpers and three pairs of boots. Later that day he brought these items to my cell. I told COD my plan, but he didn't want to help – no change there. I also told two other blokes and they wanted to have it as well.

During the evening while everyone was playing pool or watching the telly we met in my cell. I gave both of them a set of clothing and boots each. I took my jumper and cut one of the arms off and cut eyeholes out and now I had a balaclava, so put it on and the other two did the same. We had table legs as tools and had a bloke at the ready for when we'd finished so he could destroy our clothes because I knew it was going to be messy.

We were good to go, but I needed COD to do one thing for me and told him that once we went in to hillbilly's cell that he had to make sure that the door didn't shut and he must keep it open which he said he would do. We then opened my cell door and ran to hillbilly's cell. I was the first one in and he was writing a letter, so I shouted 'write about this in your fucking letter' and hit him square in the face as he looked up at me in total shock. He fell off his chair and onto the floor. We beat him and beat him and beat him some more and gave him everything we had. It was the beating of his life and his cell walls were red. When we'd finished, we ran out of his cell and pulled the door shut and it locked. We then went to my cell, quickly changed, walked out of my cell like nothing had happened and went to play pool. At bang up he was found and taken to hospital.

That night hillbilly's cell was closed off and the old bill came and taped it off as a crime scene. I didn't give a shit what shape he was in because in my eyes if you do what he'd done you should get that every day of your life and more. I had a good night's sleep that night. I found out the next day that hillbilly was in a real bad way. I still didn't give a shit and remembered what I'd been told about the two poor kids who had to live through every day with what that cunt had done to them.

Over the next week, I beat myself up with my thoughts. I started to think that I was going to end up staying in the prison system for the rest of my life if I carried on with the mission I'd given myself. I also thought that if I carried on someone would end up being killed and I didn't want to spend the rest of my days in a place like that. On the flipside, I was also thinking that these people deserved everything coming to them. During that week, I asked a screw a few times whether hillbilly was coming back to the wing but he said no. At times I was a bit worried and hoped he wasn't dead and other times I didn't care what had happened to him, but My main thought was I had to get out of Bullingdon and the sooner, the better.

My focus changed and shifted on getting out of Bullingdon as I'd been in the shithole for six months and it was sending me stir crazy. I hadn't been out in fresh air for so long because the place had enclosed walkways, so when you walked to a different part of the prison you didn't get to go outside into the grounds. That was something I really missed. I missed being able to walk where I wanted to at any time so I started to put a plan together. Hillbilly the nonce who had been given a good hiding was now out of hospital and on the numbers. I could see him in the numbers yard as I looked out of a cell window. He had broken bones and was on crutches.

Some people may read this and think I'm out of order and that it's one criminal attacking another criminal and that two wrongs don't make a right. Others will read this and think what I did was absolutely right and that Binman, White-mountain and Hillbilly got exactly what was coming to them and just what they deserved. Everyone is entitled to their own opinion. My personal opinion is that anyone who harms children or women physically for their own sick sexual gratification needs fucking sorting out.

In 1999 I found something out that completely done my nut in and chilled me to my very core. As you know, I had become quite close with Tom. When I'd got to know him, he had been imprisoned for armed robbery. We were pals in prison and I thought I knew most things about him, but always felt he was hiding something from me and what he'd said about digging a grave for his missus didn't ring right with me. They were the words of a mentally unstable person. I found out years after I was released that Tom had been charged on three counts of rape and given three life sentences. His crimes made the papers and he had been given a nickname which I will not disclose because it's unnecessary to cause any more pain for his victims. According to reports, he had attacked his first victim early in 1992 shortly before I was sentenced and also shortly before he was sentenced for armed robbery. After his release, he had carried on these sick attacks. What shocks me to my very core is the fact that Tom committed these vile acts against those poor victims, but he was more than happy with the beatings that had been given to those mentioned above. In my eyes, they're both the scum of the earth.

A month went by and I was close to being transferred from Bullingdon to an open prison where you're almost free. It wasn't an easy ride and I had to jump through hoops to get there. I'd been told on the quiet by a screw that for me to get out of Bullingdon I'd have to apply for a D Cat, stop all of my activities and keep my head down. In prison, they are watching everything you do all of the time and to a certain extent know exactly what you're up to. I decided that I would play their game and do what I had to do to get out of there. I had enough tobacco to last a very long time and didn't need anything else apart from my phone cards being replaced when they ran out so I decided to drop everything out and play the screw's game.

After a while of behaving myself, I applied for a D Cat and had to sit in front of a panel which consisted of the wing Governor, Senior Officer (S.O.) and a screw from my wing. It was their job to assess whether or not I was high risk and fit to be in an open prison. Up to that point I'd been deemed to be unfit which was why I stuck in Bullingdon. I was interviewed by the panel which was part of the process and I thought I did well. Two weeks passed and I finally got a letter which gave good and bad news. They'd granted me to D Cat, but said that I wasn't ready to be sent to an open prison. What a load of bollocks, so I was a D Cat prisoner in a B Cat prison. What fucking good was that? I was told that I could apply for an open prison transfer in a few months' time and if accepted, I would be on my way. I remember thinking yeah right, like that's going to happen.

A couple of weeks after receiving the knock back I went to the central control office and there was a S.O. sitting there by himself. I said to him that I knew he could get me out of there just by tapping my name into the computer. He looked at me and told me I was right. He also told me that Bullingdon had been in contact with a D Cat prison called Spring Hill and they had spaces that needed filling but I wasn't going anywhere. I then asked him why I had a D Cat and he said he still didn't think I was ready for a D Cat prison. After some light banter and a little know how, I left the central control office with my name on the transfer list and with the promise I'd be moving the following Saturday.

COD was also a D Cat prisoner and in my deal to get out of there, I got his name on the list for Spring Hill as well. I made some phone calls and found out from a good pal of mine that a few people I knew, who were coming to the end of long stretches for armed robberies, were at Spring Hill. Time to leave soon came and I was all packed and ready to go. I could not wait to get the fuck out of Bullingdon and was buzzing at the thought.

We were handcuffed and put on to the sweatbox with a few other blokes. As we left the prison through a set of big gates, I looked back at the shithole and promised myself I would never go back there again. To be fair, I should never have been there in the first place because I'm not a bad bloke. Regardless of where I'm put I'll always survive the best way I know how, it's what I'd been doing all my life.

CHAPTER 26

There's No Place Like Home

We reached Spring Hill and drove up a little winding road and arrived at a red and white lifting barrier which we went through. The prison looked like an old stately country house with large brown bricks. There were lots of fields and open spaces surrounding it which was new to me. We were taken off the sweat-box, had our handcuffs removed and told to stay put and that someone would be collecting us to show us where we would be staying. I lit a fag and just stood there looking at my surroundings thinking was this really happening and thanking my lucky stars. There were inmates just idly walking around doing what they liked. It all felt a bit weird and surreal.

There was another big building over to the side of the stately manor that looked like an old Victorian prison. I'd heard about this place called HMP Grendon Underwood. This is where sex offenders are treated and given therapy and where the bad of the bad are. Looking at it, it looked like the sort of place where no-one was leaving anytime soon.

Someone came to collect us and we were shown to what I can only describe as a dosshouse. I found out afterwards that Spring Hill had been some sort of base for the secret service during World War II and home to some brave men who I respect enormously. They had slept in metal polytunnel type subways and let me just say these didn't look like they had been touched since and they stunk. I walked in to take a look and there were 10 beds lined up on each side of the room. It looked like something out of an old black and white film and I couldn't help but think what the fuck is this place. I was thinking about 20 blokes that don't wash and I was expected to sleep in a bed next to them. I had no idea who I'd be sleeping alongside or what they were in prison for. I didn't like this one bit and was not happy. I was that pissed off I was close to asking to be taken back to Bullingdon.

A few minutes later two blokes who I knew from Bullingdon walked in. Darren and Pat were two lovely blokes from Camden Town and we had mutual pals on the outside. When we were in Bullingdon together, we'd pop to each other's cells for a cuppa and a chat and had many good laughs.

A few years after being released I met Pat on the outside and he told me that Darren had been out drinking one night in Kentish Town and had been kicked out of a pub. He had been drunk and the landlord had given him a good kick in. Darren had gone home, got a shotgun, walked back to the pub, walked in and shot the landlord dead. Darren was one of the quietest blokes I'd ever met, spoke so softly and had a very mild manner. When we'd been in prison together we had occasionally drank hooch that we'd made and Darren would always say he would not drink hooch with me because it changed him as a person and he didn't fancy his chances with me. We would all laugh this off, but he was telling the truth, alcohol changed him in a big way.

Pat and Darren gave me a tour of Spring Hill and a rundown on the place and I couldn't believe what I was seeing. There was a full sized swimming pool and tennis courts! We got back to the war hut and I was still having second thoughts about the place like when I was first shown the stinking sleeping tunnel. I went for a walk, COD followed and I found myself walking around a field and it was just what I wanted to do and I was able to do it. There was no having to ask a screw for permission, no gates opening and closing and no cell doors. I'd only been there two hours and I really liked the place, but the place I had to sleep was a big no.

As me and COD walked back towards the war hut, I saw an old face I knew and he called me over. He was standing outside what looked like a row of brand new little bungalows. We both greeted each other with big smiles and a good strong handshake. He told me he'd heard I was being transferred and he'd gone to the trouble of getting me a room of my own to sleep in. He showed me and COD to the room and it was the bollocks and we couldn't believe our luck. He went on to tell me that Spring Hill was a great place and they had pizza and Chinese takeaways every night. He said I would fit right in with everyone and there was a good bunch of people there and I wouldn't have to sleep in the war hut with the other 20 inmates.

I loved what I was hearing and as we left the bungalow he pulled me to one side and told me something that would fuck up everything I had just heard. He told me that the offer of the room was only for me and that the no good cunt COD was to remain in the war hut. I looked at him and told him that for my own reasons that I couldn't go in to, I could not leave COD behind. He told me that COD was known for being no good and that I should fuck him off. I couldn't fuck him off because I knew he was a dangerous liar and could have made up so much shit about me to the old bill. I was looking at my pal thinking that he didn't know COD was a grass or what he was capable of. Looking back now, I wasn't thinking straight and I should have fucked the no good cunt right off there and then.

I walked back to the hut and COD knew what had happened and that he wasn't welcome, but we didn't talk about it. I told him I wasn't staying there and put things in motion. I made a phone call and told that person to meet me in Aylesbury at the

McDonalds, which I'd spotted on the drive there. That was where I needed to get to and nothing was going to stop me.

I made a couple more phone calls and it was all set for the following night that I was off. I told Darren and Pat to look after my stuff and that they could keep my CD player. All I wanted was my personal letters and I asked them to bring them out one weekend when they were on home leave and I'd arrange to meet them in London to pick them up. I spent one night in that stinking war hut and it was one night too many. The people in there stunk, were snoring from one end of the tunnel to the other and I didn't get one wink of sleep. I couldn't handle it and was up and about as soon as the sun came up.

I went for a walk and again had second thoughts about whether I should stay and ummed and arred about whether I'd made the right decision to get out of there. I was thinking about whether I should have taken the single room in the bungalow from my pal where they were having takeaways every night. I decided that I'd made my choice and throughout my life I had made choices both good and bad, but I'd always seen my choices through to the end.

It got to about 5:30 pm in the afternoon and I was ready to go. I asked COD whether he was staying or going with me. That was his choice and I told him I would be gone within the hour because I had someone picking me up. When it came to crunch time and me leaving it was only then that COD told me that he was coming with me. The only possession I took with me was a Sony Walkman and a set of headphones.

We left the hut and walked straight across a field. When we got to the edge of the field, we had to climb over a six foot fence. We had roughly three hours before the screws would do a headcount and realise we'd had it away on our toes. Once we had climbed over the fence, we ran across another field and kept running. I was aiming in the direction that the sweatbox had arrived in, but there were fucking fields and more fucking fields that were never ending and all looked the same. We finally saw a tiny little village and decided to go through it to see where we were because we didn't have a fucking clue. We were approaching the village and cars were passing us. We thought about stopping one of the cars, but thought better of it.

We arrived at the village which was an old and quaint little place with a post office shop, a butchers, a pub that looked like something off of a postcard and had rows of little thatched houses. As we were walking through there were little old ladies looking at us and quite obviously talking about us. The penny then dropped that we were wearing prison clothes and stood out like a sore thumb. I told COD we needed to get out of the village and back in the fields sharpish before someone phoned the old bill. At the end of the village, we saw a signpost which indicated that Aylesbury was 10 miles away. We needed to get there because my lift was waiting.

We were running through the fields for some time and then broke between walking and running. Time was passing and I had no clue how long we had been moving but the sun had started to go down and it was getting dark. Within no time at all it was pitch black out and we couldn't see fuck all and were lost. My hearing is second to none so I told COD to stop. I closed my eyes, not that I could see anyway, controlled my breathing to slow it down and as I did this I could hear someone talking. We started to walk towards the voice, stopped so I could listen again and now I could just make out what was being said. I told COD what I heard and he pissed himself laughing. I could hear someone saying 'come on, come on you, that's the way'. COD was still laughing and I walked towards the voice I could hear and saw a light. We climbed through a hedge and it was a farm with stables.

The voice was a little girl who was probably 10 or 11 years' old and was getting her horse ready to put in the stables for the night. As she was brushing her horse, I walked over to her, said hello and told her she had a lovely horse. She told me that the horse was four years' old. I asked her if she liked music which she did so I asked her to put my headphones on so she could listen to my music. I asked her if she could take me to her dad and she was happy to. She put her horse in the stable and walked towards the house. On the way across the yard, I took her by the hand and we spoke about music.

We knocked on the door and her dad answered so I said 'hello mate' as you do! He was obviously quite shocked and pulled his young girl's hand free of mine. His face was showing terror and I didn't blame the poor guy. I was standing there holding his daughter's hand in full prison clobber. I couldn't imagine what was going through his head, but he looked scared because for all he knew I was a complete nutter. I told him all I wanted was a favour and had done nothing but ask his daughter to take me to him. I pointed out the Walkman I had given her and she said through a smile 'look daddy it plays music'. The bloke thanked me. I told him I wasn't a bad person and wasn't in prison for anything he should be worried about and I just needed a favour because I'd had enough of prison and needed to get home and needed a lift to Aylesbury. He told me to hang on and he'd just get his keys – result! As we got in his car, I did think is this bloke going to drive us straight to the old bill so I was on edge. He didn't know I was on edge though because I was making small talk and having a chat. He asked what I was in prison for and when I told him, he said he remembered reading something like that in the paper. As we pulled over at the McDonalds, I thanked him and told him to wait one minute. I walked over to the car that was waiting for me to give me my lift back to London and asked the gent waiting for me to give me some money. I walked back to the farmer's car and gave him £100. He told me that I was the nicest escaped prisoner he'd ever met and we both laughed. I thanked him again and jumped into the waiting car and was on my way home.

I couldn't wait to get there and the whole drive home I was buzzing. I couldn't wait to change out of my prison clothes and as we drove off, I started to strip off. The person who had picked me up had brought fresh clothes for me. We stopped off on the drive, got rid of the prison clothes and had something to eat. All I wanted at that point was a soft bed and a good night's sleep and that's what was waiting for me, so London bound it was.

CHAPTER 27

All Time Low

I was now back in London and it felt good to be home. I wasn't exactly home but near enough and not where the old bill would find me and they had tried. I was living in North London and was sorted. Being on the run was a different ballgame altogether. I couldn't drive, get the train or a bus because these modes of transport can be stopped and ID needs to be produced. One of two things could have happened if I was pulled over in a car, I could have stopped, or not. If I had been in a car on my own and pulled over, there was no way on God's planet I would have stopped, so walking everywhere was my best option. I had a name and date of birth I could give if stopped in the street, but if I kept my nut down that was unlikely to happen.

The first night I got back, it was late. It was strange for me because I wasn't used to being up so late, my body clock had changed from being inside. As soon as I got my head down I was out like a light and the next morning was up bright and early and on my way to the East End. I wanted to see my little sister Jackie and she knew I was coming and I couldn't wait to see her. Jackie, Tracey and Kim had been very good to me while I was away and wrote to me all the time and did anything I asked of them. I walked into the house I'd grown up in and we had a big cuddle. I'd missed Jackie so much because she was the apple of my eye even though she could be a little bitch at times I loved her deeply.

We went and sat in the front room. Bin was there but didn't say a word and stayed in the kitchen. I don't know what I expected from him but some sort of acknowledgement wouldn't have gone amiss. I had a pouch of tobacco, some rizla papers and a lump of puff with me and as me and Jackie were talking I started building a spliff. I told Jackie that I had to get out of prison and told her all about Bullingdon and what a fucked up place it was and that it was full of nonce cases. I also told her in great detail about the beatings I'd handed out and I knew I had to get out of there because otherwise I'd be spending the rest of my life in there. At that point, Bin walked in and gave me a dirty look which I thought was because I was skinning up. Jackie told him to leave me alone and that I'd only been doing it while I was away and that he should carry on about his business, which he did. He was acting strange and it was like he was on edge, but I put it down to him not liking drugs. Me and Jackie talked and talked and spent a few hours together. I felt so much joy and love that day and it was just what I needed. I felt normal once again.

My first weekend out I went to a pub in North London and was really taken aback by the kindness I received. The pub I went to was a pub used by ex-cons and old school money getters. Some people would call these men gangsters, but I don't know any gangsters, I know people like me that have a love affair with money and the type of people that had had a rough upbringing and followed a certain path in life. As I entered the pub, it was known that I was on the run and I was greeted with smiles and drinks put in my hand. These gentlemen were also putting money in my pockets which were becoming full with £20s and £50s. I couldn't say no because this would cause offence and these were proud men. I accepted their kindness but didn't feel right taking it. I understood why they did it because I've done it myself for others in my predicament.

I needed to get back in the game, get a few quid and get on my feet because that was my life. Months went by and I was doing

OK. I still wasn't ready to go back to prison to finish my sentence. In two months it was Christmas and I told myself that I would give myself up after then and finish off the bollocks time I had left. As much as I loved being out, I still wasn't free. Being on the run wasn't a nice way to live because I was always looking over my shoulder and planning everything I did in enormous detail. I had pre-planned mapped out routes if I needed to get away quickly. My brain was working 24/7.

A month went by so it was now one month to Christmas and my sister, Jackie, called me. She told me that Bin had tried to top himself and was in hospital. What the fuck? I told her I would get to the hospital as soon as I could. I put the phone down and called my brother Michael who lived just around the corner from Bin with his wife and kids and asked him what the fuck was going on. He told me he wasn't sure exactly what had gone on with Bin but also told me that our sister Kim had been nicked for cutting an Asian bloke's throat. Apparently this bloke had just been walking by the house and she'd attacked him for no reason. I said to Michael that there must have been a reason and he must have done something to her because you don't just attack someone for nothing. Kim had always had a temper but had never flared up without a reason. By then she was a youth worker and working with young kids and was doing very well.

I asked Michael if the old bill were involved with Bin's suicide bid and they wasn't, but he told me that Kim had been detained at St Clement's on Mile End Road, which was a mental health hospital. I was taking a risk, but I told my brother I'd meet him at the London Hospital. I couldn't go and see Kim because St Clement's was a secure hospital and you couldn't just walk in but at the London Hospital I could.

I made my way there and met three of my brothers outside; Jimmy, Michael and Terry. We were all very worried and couldn't believe what had happened. We couldn't understand why Bin had done what he'd done because he wanted for nothing and was waited on hand and foot. He had his clothes bought for him and money given to him all the time to go to the pub. Even after everything he had done while we were growing up we still worshipped him and felt like we owed him something. I can honestly say, hand on heart, I put that man on a pedestal with Jesus Christ even after every beating he'd given me and the mental torture, I still loved him. Where we grew up people showed him a lot of respect and in their eyes he deserved this because they saw him bringing up a load of kids on his own.

Me and my brothers walked into the hospital and on to the ward where Bin was and me and Michael approached a nurse sitting at the desk while my other brothers Jimmy and Terry stood back. I asked the nurse where we could find Mr Hutton and explained that we were his sons. The nurse stood up and loudly said 'you don't want to worry about him, it's your sister you should be worried about'. The nurse had hate written all over her face and after announcing that, she just walked off. Me and Michael looked at each other and I said something like what the fuck was that all about, nurses don't talk like that. I was completely confused by what she'd said. I turned around to Jimmy and Terry and Rodney came walking out of a room and called us over.

The room he had walked out of was Bin's room and we walked into it. Rodney was now sitting on a chair beside Bin and holding his hand. The rest of us were standing around the bed and puzzled I asked Bin what had gone on and why he'd tried to kill himself. I was concerned and despite all of his faults, I cared for this man and didn't want him to die. He looked at me and had fear in his face and what he said to me next would change my life forever. With terror in his voice, he said 'you will kill me'. He was looking at me like he'd met his maker and he started to cry. I had never seen this man cry or show any emotion. I asked him why he thought I'd do that and one of my brothers went into panic mode and went on to tell us all that he'd taken tablets and didn't know what he was talking about. I said I understood that but again asked why he thought I would kill him. Bin then looked up, directly at me and said the words 'all I did was touch her tits'.

My body immediately became rigid, every muscle in me jumped to attention and I asked everyone in the room what the fuck he was talking about. My brother then again jumped in and said he didn't know what he was talking about and the drugs he'd taken were making him say crazy shit. I told Bin to tell me what he was talking about. He was sobbing now and told me that is all he'd done was touch Kim's tits. Now he was right, I wanted to fucking kill him.

Things then started to get heated and I'm not sure how, but we all ended up outside the room. Me, Jimmy, Michael, Terry and Rodney were standing outside of Bin's room after what he'd just told us and one of them started to talk and said that what we'd just heard in that room we never speak of again. He then put his hand out and the other three followed suit. It was now my turn and they were all looking at me waiting for me to put my hand on theirs like some sort of brotherly pact. No fucking way was I putting my hand on top. My cunt of a dad had just told me that he'd touched my sister in the most disgusting way and she had been sectioned in a mental hospital. I asked who was with Kim, told them to get fucked and walked out of the London Hospital.

I was fucked. My head was spinning. I didn't know where I was walking to but I was fucking wired and adrenaline was rushing through me like a fucking tidal wave. What Bin had said was racing through my head over and over and over again. His terrorised face was imprinted in my memory like someone was repeatedly stamping on my head. I don't know how I got there, but I got back to where I was staying in North London. I just sat there, numb and unable to think straight. I didn't tell the person I was staying with what had just happened and just sat on my own.

The next day I phoned St Clement's where Kim was and spoke to a nurse on the ward. She told me that Kim had been sedated and was scheduled to be assessed by a doctor. The nurse said Kim was having some sort of breakdown but that was all she knew. I found out later that day that Kim had been arguing with Bin and in the heat of the moment had told him she was going to kill him. She had ran out of the front door with a knife in her hand and the Asian bloke had been the first person walking by so she had grabbed him and cut the poor man's neck. Thankfully, it wasn't a deep cut. Kim then screamed at Bin that it should have been his neck. Shortly afterwards she was arrested but because she was in such a state, she was sectioned under the Mental Health Act and taken to St Clement's where she was to be assessed to see if she was mentally ill. She wasn't allowed to leave until the doctors deemed her fit to leave. I was worried that it could have been years and I couldn't do a fucking thing to help her. It was killing me thinking of her sedated in a place like that.

I wanted to kill Bin but I still didn't know for a fact if it was all madness and the drugs had made him say what he'd said. I didn't know if Kim had just lost the plot and gone crazy. I was the most confused I've ever been in my life and my brain was in complete chaos.

It was now two weeks before Christmas and COD had been caught and taken back to Pentonville. He called me and was asking me to give myself up. I was listening to him but couldn't talk because all calls in prison are taped. I was in no fit state to go back to prison after what I'd just learnt. I got the person who was standing with me to tell COD that I was going to give myself up after Christmas. I then heard COD say that he needed me because he was in trouble and some blokes were putting it on him, bullying him and he couldn't deal with it himself. He was told that I'd be back in two weeks and would sort it. Within 24 hours of that phone call, I was back in Pentonville.

I was sound asleep in the place I was staying at in North London and the old bill came through the door. I like to be one step ahead and that time was no different. Before they'd booted the door in I was hiding under the bath. I'd previously taken the bath panel off for such an occasion. They had searched for me around the flat for a bit with no luck, but then they let the dogs in so I was fucked! After a night in a police cell in Islington, I was taken back to my suite in Pentonville.

CHAPTER 28

Merry Christmas and a New Year's Resolution

I arrived at Pentonville and had to go through the bollocks of seeing the doctor and being issued with prison clothing. For my break from prison, I was given loss of earnings and an extra 42 days but I didn't care and just thought add it to the rest. Things had changed at Pentonville and I didn't go straight back on to the main wing. I was put on a holding wing for 24 hours and then sent back to the main population. Those 24 hours in the holding cell were interesting! I was given a single cell which I was happy about because it meant I didn't have to listen to someone snoring or talking for England. I got myself some hot water for a cuppa just before bang up time. As I was getting my hot water there were another, say, 20 blokes milling around but one stood out. There was one little Chinese bloke running around asking anyone and everyone if they had any smack (heroin). He was clucking (withdrawing) and needed a fix. He came up to me and in his best pigeon English asked 'you got any gear mate'? I said no, I didn't touch the shit and fucked him off.

I walked back to my cell with my cuppa and could see the little Chinese fella walk into the cell next to mine. I walked into my cell, kicked the door shut, sat down and rolled a fag. After an hour, I could hear the little Chinese fella in the cell next to me screaming out in pain. He must have been in so much pain because the noise he was making sounded bad. I knew this was going to last all night because he was going cold turkey and withdrawing from the smack. The racket the cunt was making was driving me insane. I couldn't think straight anyway because all I could think about was my poor sister Kim and what she was going through. I felt helpless because I couldn't do anything for her or comfort her because I was stuck in Pentonville poxy piss-hole.

Hours were passing and I couldn't sleep. My head wouldn't let me and what with the junkie writhing around in agony next door it just wasn't going to happen. I then thought of a plan to get some sleep. I banged on the wall and shouted at the Chinese fella so he could hear me and told him to go to the window so he could hear me more clearly. I was thinking this was going to be hard work, but I had to give it a go just to try as I just wanted to nut out. I told him I had some smack and I would give him some to help him through the night, but he would have to pay me back double when he laid his hands on some. The noise this bloke was making he would have ripped out one of his kidneys there and then if I'd asked so of course he said yes in his broken English. He didn't have a clue that I was the bloke who'd fucked him off earlier.

I told him that he needed to make a line which is made out of bed sheets. In prison, lines are used to pass things from one cell to another during the night. Anything can be passed on a line i.e. matches, rizla papers, drugs, anything. The Chinese bloke didn't have a clue what I was talking about, so I had to slowly talk him through cutting up bed sheets in to strips and tying a cup to the end of it. This took him about an hour to work out. While he was doing that, I was laying down and trying to get some sleep. The good thing was it was taking his mind off the pain he'd been in and he was focussing on getting the drugs he needed, or should I say the drugs he thought he was getting! Once the line was made I told him he had to hang it out of his cell window and swing it to my window, so I could catch it and put the gear in it for him. He did this a few times, but I told him that it was too short and he needed to make it longer. As he was making the line longer with more bed sheet strips, I had more peace. All night long he was throwing that line to my cell. I'd fell asleep so my job was done.

The next morning I woke up and he was still throwing that fucking line. I was pissing myself laughing. It was now breakfast time and the cells were opened. I walked into his cell and gave him a roll up and told him he must go to the doctor and get something to help him. I also told him that I didn't have any smack. He actually thanked me and called me a kind man for helping him get through the night. I only wanted some fucking kip but if he wants to call me a kind man, I'll take it.

After breakfast, I was told I was being taken to the main wing and I was ready to get there because I couldn't do another night on the holding wing. I walked on to the wing and was met by COD, who looked pleased to see me. I asked him who the blokes were that were giving him grief, and the reason I would be spending Christmas in Pentonville, and he told me it was all sorted because one of them had been moved off the wing. I asked him who the other blokes were and he took me to a little weasel junkie. I looked at the weasel, looked at COD and told him to give the weasel a dig. COD shit himself and said no-no it's now all sorted. I just walked away and thought fuck him.

As I walked away two blokes stopped COD and I heard them say 'is that your mate who you got nicked with, the one you said was a grass'. I heard COD say in a panicky voice 'yeah, yeah but he's not a grass, I was just saying that'. I then reconfirmed in my own mind what I already knew, COD was a top class cunt and could not be left on his own. I didn't say anything at that point and just carried on walking. I walked to the cell that I'd been given as I just wanted to be on my own with my own thoughts. What I'd heard didn't bother me because I can look after myself and the two blokes looked like two bob shitcunts anyway. I said nothing and thought COD was being COD and had let his mouth run away again and was talking bollocks – no change there then.

While I was sitting with my thoughts in my cell, a bloke walked in and told me that we were sharing. He introduced himself and sat down. He was an Irish traveller. I don't mind travellers as they are good people and like me they are shown from a very young age ways of getting what you need in life to survive. My new cellmate wanted to talk and fuck me this bloke could talk the ears off a donkey. We went to get some dinner just before we were banged up for the night and took it back to the cell. He then went off on one again talking and talking. I don't like to be rude but after a little while I had to tell him I didn't want to talk anymore and that I just wanted to get my head down.

I told him to take the top bunk and I'd give him two spliffs if he'd smoke them and go to sleep. I'd switched and I wasn't asking him, I was telling him. I was tired and didn't want to be around anyone as my head was elsewhere. He did as I asked but was looking at me like I was some sort of madman and asked me what I was in for. I laughed because I knew he was thinking was I a nutcase and he wasn't sure if he was sharing a cell with a murderer.

The following morning I woke up, got washed and dressed and walked to the landing office and asked for a single cell. I was told there wasn't any so I went to COD's cell and told him that the traveller was taking his single cell and he was moving in with me into the double cell. I told everyone who needed to know what was happening and that's what happened.

I soon settled back into prison life and the day to day bullshit and the brain dead bollocks of people talking about crime and more crime. I hated it. I was phoning my family regularly but knew what they were saying to me on the phone wasn't the whole truth of what was happening on the outside. I arranged with the S.O. a private phone call to Kim in St Clement's hospital. The S.O. was very understanding and arranged for me to use the phone in his office and locked me in so I wasn't disturbed.

Kim sounded heavily drugged up which pulled at my heart. I didn't ask her too much just simple questions like was she OK, did she have everything she needed and were people visiting her. She told me that Bin was visiting her every day and stayed with her until she went to sleep. Kim telling me that made my head feel like it was splitting in two. Hearing that Bin was doing this was a total head fuck and I couldn't work out what the fuck was going on. I told Kim that I would arrange for someone to bring her some cigarettes so she had plenty and that I would phone her again very soon. She asked me if I was in prison and was that the reason I hadn't been to see her, so I told her yes. She then carried on talking, but she wasn't making much sense. I told her that I loved her and when I was out of prison I would do everything within my power to get her better. Our short conversation then ended.

All the time I was in Pentonville I came across a few people that I had a feeling were nonces, but I just kept away from them. How could I do something to them knowing that one of my own had done so much worse and I hadn't done anything? My head was in no fit state to dish out any kind of punishment for these people, I do believe I would have seriously lost it and would never have left prison. I felt like I should have done something but until I had sorted out what the fuck was going on in my own family, I just kept my head down and struggled through the day to day rigmarole of prison life.

There was one bloke that I met who did make me sit up and listen to him and to this day I still can't work him out. He was an older bloke from the East End and I started talking to him because he seemed a nice fella. He was on Judges Remand (JR) pending reports and being on JR means you are automatically sent to the convicted wing of a prison. After a while, we got on to the subject of what he was in for and he asked me one day if I knew anyone in Brixton prison. I thought about it for a minute and said yes I do and asked him why. He told me that he was being transferred there and he'd never been in prison in his life until that point so didn't know anyone there. He asked me if I could have a word with someone so he could hook up with them. I asked why he was being sent there and he told me it was a long story and for mental health reports, so I asked him what for?

This is what he told me in a roundabout way. He said his wife would always go out every Sunday afternoon for a drink with her pals and he told me the name of the pub which I knew, but I didn't say anything and just listened. He said she'd get all done up by doing her hair, wearing new dresses and shoes, the lot and it had been going on every Sunday for months and she'd come home at all hours. He said he'd found out she was seeing some bloke and told me the name of the fella and I fucking knew him but still I didn't say anything. He went on to tell me that one Sunday she was getting ready in the bathroom putting her slap on and going the whole nine yards.

At that point, for the life of me, I couldn't see where the story was going and he was talking to me like I was an old pal and we were having a catch up. He said he told her that she was not going out that particular week and she replied that she was and it went on like that. He said he would be going to see her new fella and again told her that she wasn't going out and again she replied she fucking was and he couldn't stop her. He then told me that he done no more and went and got his handgun out of the bedside drawer, walked into the bathroom and shot her twice in the head. I was speechless and looked at him and thought oh my god, you're not well mate. He also told me he couldn't wait to get hold of the bloke and then asked me what sentence I thought he would get after the reports had been done. I was shocked and just told him to tell the doctors exactly what he'd told me and in the way he'd just told me and he'd get nutted off for 10 to 15 years, but it was OK because he really wasn't well. We both laughed our bollocks off! I never did find out what happened to him in the end, but he must have got nutted off for sure!

It was now a couple of days before Christmas and a tree was put up. Christmas cards had started to arrive in the post, but it didn't feel like Christmas at all. I had never felt that shit in all of my life. In a London prison you are banged up for 22 to 23 hours a day and the days are always the same and very short. You get up, eat breakfast, get banged up again, then you have exercise so walk around the yard, eat lunch, then banged up again, eat dinner and then you're banged up again, then you're let out for hot water. This takes you up to about 6:00 pm and then you're banged up again until the morning. On bank holidays you're banged up for even longer. The screws obviously take time off over Christmas, so there are cutbacks on the times you're let out of your cell. You're literally only allowed out for food, so that Christmas I was over-thinking and had far too much time to myself

My thoughts started to turn to madness and I had to keep all of this in because I couldn't be seen to be having a rough time. All I could do to stop myself going mad was numb my thoughts and the way to do that was puffing. I started puffing more than I ever had and it helped. When I was behind closed doors, my head was running away with me and puffing stopped that. Days and nights were all rolling into one. One morning I was let out of my cell for breakfast and heard a band playing Christmas carols, this shocked me. I looked over the landing and there in the centre was the Salvation Army in all their clobber with a brass band singing their fucking hearts out. As everyone was walking to breakfast, there were long faces everywhere and no-one was talking. Everyone wanted to be anywhere but right there right then. This was the saddest place I'd ever been in my life. Every-one was down in the dumps and the Salvation Army were a re-minder of everything we were missing. We wouldn't have the love, kindness and laughter with the people that meant the world to us. That Christmas we were in two different worlds. Christmas lunch was served and I swore to myself I would never spend another Christmas like that ever again. Christmas day was one day that didn't last long and the following day everything was taken down. I started to look at my calendar and was work-ing out when I'd be released. After New Year my mood was a little better as we were let out of the cell a bit more.

In the New Year me and COD were moved to the B-wing which had been given a makeover and had been cut into two smaller wings. I had started to get back in survival mode and was back on track getting what I needed; phone cards, tobacco and food. I was doing fine, but it was all a front. Inside I was slowly dying and my head was fucked. I knew I could flip out at any time and was only just holding myself together. I was making daily phone calls to Kim and trying to help her as best as I could. There was so much I wanted to ask her but couldn't. Without seeing her face to face, I wouldn't ask her too much. This was too much for me and at night my head sounded like a car engine ticking over and getting faster and faster. This was all going on in my head and there were no brakes or keys to turn it off and each night it was getting worse.

I was told that I was going to be moved to another prison in a few weeks' time and they wanted to send me to Camp Hill on the Isle of Wight again which was the prison I'd previously managed to avoid. I was not fucking happy and no way was I going as I had more reason than ever not to go there as my family and world was in turmoil. I was told I wouldn't be able to get out of it and was called to the wing office. The S.O. told me that the date had been set and he told me to be ready. I told him that I couldn't go to Camp Hill because I had too much going on in my life and needed to be close to London. He wanted to know why but I couldn't bring myself to tell him as I hadn't told anyone. He came across as an alright bloke, but I wasn't telling him fuck all, so thanked him and left his office.

I started to concentrate and focus on getting out of being sent to Camp Hill and came up with a plan. I found out that if you're on hunger strike for 24 hours before being transferred, they can't move you. One week before my scheduled transfer I announced to the S.O. that I was on hunger strike and I wanted him to record it in the incident book. He did this because he had no choice and before I left his office, he told me that I'd still be going to Camp Hill, hunger strike or not.

From that point, I could not be seen to be eating meals and occasionally only be seen to be drinking water. Two days went by and the S.O. walked into my cell and told me to stop all my nonsense as it would not get me anywhere. I replied 'oh is that right, well it's certainly not going to get me to Camp Hill, that's for sure'. He told me I was going about it the wrong way by being on hunger strike but that he would help me sort something out. I said I would stop the hunger strike if he helped me and he agreed. Little did the screws know that I was eating better than anyone but obviously I never left any evidence of food in my cell. Where the screws eat is just on the outer limits of the prison and trusted inmates are given the job to cook for them. I knew two of the blokes who prepared their food and had sorted them with the right currency and they were getting me all I needed. They were delivering my food every night just before bang up and it was much better than what inmates were eating that's for sure! It was a bit of a game to me, a game of Hutton vs Prison Authorities.

I had finally decided I needed to get away from COD. I needed to be on my own and get my head straight and I was done with him hanging around and me having to baby him. It was time for him to man up and get on with it. It felt to me like it was my chance to get him out of my life once and for all. I knew he was dangerous on his own and would tell people all sorts of shit about me, but I also thought that the old bill didn't have a use for him anymore and he couldn't make stuff up about me to get me nicked and my sentence extended. It was now time to part company on good terms if that was possible. I'd finished playing games with him. I didn't have the energy for a hanger-on as I had enough on my plate with my family. After some time, he was moved to HMP High Down and I was told that I was moving to a C Cat prison called HMP The Mount in Hertfordshire. I found out that The Mount was the first prison in the country to be running a trial where inmates were allowed TVs in their cells. I remember thinking 'oi, oi that sounds like a bit of me'. I only had a week to wait and it couldn't come sooner.

CHAPTER 29

Old School Gent

I was transferred to The Mount in the usual way, in a sweatbox. The journey wasn't too long, about an hour or so from London. The Mount is on the outskirts of Bovingdon Village near Hemel Hempstead. I went through the usual rigmarole of seeing a doctor and being processed and was then taken to the prison wing I was staying on. I was taken to my cell which was a single and suited me down to the ground. I unpacked my stuff, settled in and thought the place didn't seem too bad because I had walked to my cell through the prison grounds, which meant fresh air rather than everything enclosed like Bullingdon. It still had a 40 foot wall all the way round it. On my way through the grounds I had spotted a football pitch and gardens and it looked very nice.

I had a wander round the wing and bumped into a few faces that I knew and they showed me round the place. It wasn't like Bullingdon at all as there were three wing blocks and on each block there were two floors which were all connected to a central building. In the central building, on the ground floor, there was a dining hall and a big kitchen. On the second floor were the screws' offices, a small kitchen where inmates cooked their own food, plus another room where you could store your own food in freezers and a phone room where you could use your phone cards.

As I was being taken round I was told that inmates were allowed on each other's wings and that everyone was doing long birds and kept themselves to themselves. Being able to walk on other wings was strange to me but I'd only been there an hour at that point so didn't think too much of it.

After a while, I went back to my cell to chill out and have a little sleep. Even though I was free to walk around, my body was used to being banged up 22 to 23 hours a day so I tended to sleep a lot to pass the time. Time for the last meal of the day arrived and I'd only eaten breakfast so went to get some food and saw more people I knew. One bloke I knew told me that he had a spare cell on his landing and he'd get me in there which he did the following morning.

I settled in quite quickly and found The Mount to be a very relaxed place. I was told that if I behaved and kept my nut down I would be granted home leave in six months' time. I was now in the last year of my sentence so decided I would do just that and keep my head down. I was phoning Kim at St Clement's every day and keeping in touch with other members of my family but not once did I speak to Bin. When I spoke to Jackie or Tracey, I was very guarded with what I said because I didn't know what they knew, if anything, about what had happened. They did tell me that Bin was going to St Clement's first thing every morning and was staying with Kim all day until the evening. I couldn't get my head around this, I found it so strange and in my head so much was swimming around as to why he was doing that. After some time, I was informed that Kim wasn't going to be charged with cutting the Asian man's throat, but she would be detained under the mental health act and would have to stay at the secure unit in the hospital. This was good news because she was clearly unwell. When I spoke to her, she was telling me that she was also in prison and that she was sometimes allowed out into the garden but that it had a big wall surrounding it. My heart went out to her, I felt so sorry for her and I can't begin to imagine the stuff that was going through her mind.

In my own mind I had to concentrate on the prison that I was in and the need to stay strong for Kim. I started to get the things I needed and phone cards were more important than ever because Kim was top of my list to phone every single day.

The landing I was on was full of people who had done long bird, had a couple of years left and were working their way to a D Cat open prison. They cooked their own food and were a very close-knit unit. They did everything together including working out in the gym and walking around the prison grounds. I fitted in and got myself a job. I didn't want to do fuck all but the job I had meant I was on the wing so I could move about and get what I needed and that's what I did.

One bloke I met was a very nice man. He was a lot older than me, he was 50 and I was 26, but we still clicked and had a bond because we were similar people regardless of the age difference. He was from West London and was an old school gent. I was in the cell next to his and we spent a lot of time together talking, walking and getting on with the time. Like me, Gent had currency, but unlike me he didn't keep control of his own. He was doing what I'd done in the past and was dropping it on someone else who worked for him. I was puffing more than ever when I met him. We'd have a puff during the day and always at night so a good night's sleep was had. Of a night, I had a telly in my cell, a full flask of hot water and tea bags so I was comfortable. I had the paper delivered every morning with my letters and once a week I had my local rag the East London Advertiser delivered also.

One night Gent asked me to build him a spliff because he couldn't do it. Of course I said yes and because he didn't have his on him, I said that I'd build it with my gear. The bloke that did have his gear normally rolled his joints for him every night but this night he asked me. At bang up I sat down as I did every night and built two spliffs plus an extra one for Gent. I passed it to him on a line and settled myself down with my choice of TV programmes. I sat back, lit my first spliff and chilled out and let the night pass.

The following morning I did my usual and ticked another day off of the calendar and walked out of my cell for breakfast. As I left my cell Gent told me he'd had the best night's sleep he'd ever had in prison. Looking at him, it looked like he'd had a good night's sleep too. I said to him that he must have dropped off early because he hadn't called out to me all night. Normally he would shout out if he found something funny on the telly and while laughing would call out to me asking if I was watching the same programme.

Gent went on to tell me that he wanted me to do something for him and as he said it he had a concentrated puzzled look on his face. I told him to tell me a bit later what he wanted done and that I'd sort it and then we went to get some breakfast. After a couple of slices of toast we went back to my cell, made a cuppa and sat down for a chat. He told me that he thought he was being ripped off and asked me how much puff I'd put in the spliff for him the night before. I told him I'd put the same amount in his as I always put in my own. He went on to tell me that he normally had three or four spliffs a night but had never slept as well as he had the night before. Gent then said he wanted me to build him a spliff that night again with my puff. He also said he wanted me to take the spliffs that the bloke who worked for him would give to him and open them up and look through them. I knew what he was getting at and said I would.

That night at bang up he gave me the three spliffs to look through and some of his puff to build him one. Like me, he didn't smoke tobacco in prison, only puff to get a good night's sleep. I rolled him a spliff and sent it through on the line, he smoked it and told me that it was the same as the night before and that he was happy. With the three spliffs he'd given me, I cut them open, moved the tobacco to one side and the puff to another. In each spliff there was only puff at the end of the joint so when he was lighting them he could smell it but there was hardly anything in all three. I told him I'd done what he'd asked and would speak to him the next morning.

The next morning he walked into my cell full of beans, smiling and said he'd had another great night's sleep. I made a cuppa and we sat down and I showed him what I'd found. I told him how they were built and that in the three spliffs he'd given me to open up there was probably not quite enough gear for one. He then told me that the cunt who was working for him had been ripping him off for the last six months. Gent wasn't fucking happy. I said to him I knew it was none of my business but asked who it was and when he told me I was shocked. The bloke who was working for him was a junkie and on smack. Gent said he knew the bloke on the outside and he knew he'd be in trouble. I offered to help sort the junkie out, but Gent said I was a good bloke and had done what he'd asked and that was enough.

I knew Gent was old school, no fucking mug and was a very well respected man in West London. He walked out of my cell, straight into the junkie's cell and shut the door behind him. While he was in there, I stood outside on the landing. Three or four minutes later Gent came out and we sat back in my cell. As we sat there talking, I could hear a big commotion going on outside. The screws were running around and we were put on lock down. Gent turned to me and said 'one more thing and I know I don't have to ask you this, but I haven't left this cell, you good with that?' Of course he didn't have to ask me and we never spoke about what he'd done in that junkie's cell. I did find out what had happened and it wasn't nice. The junkie was never seen again and apparently was on the numbers in another prison with a gift for life on his face.

That is how prison is, it's all done behind closed doors. If you want to give it mouth and fight out in the open, you're not serious because it is going be broken up within no time at all by the screws. Behind closed doors, it's on, and someone is getting hurt.

There were a lot of people in The Mount that I knew or knew of me and it was OK for a little while, but I was counting down the days for home leave. I wanted to leave these people behind and be with the people who meant the world to me. I had been at The Mount for four months so applied for home leave and the date I wanted was 4 June, my birthday. I couldn't think of a better time to be out for a weekend. I then had to wait.

I was still on the phone at every opportunity and this wasn't liked by the other inmates. Some used to make snide comments in jest, but I knew it was meant. They saw me as some young bloke who was doing better than them and had all he needed. Some of them had nothing and started to get jealous. I'd give some of these so-called London faces a hand up and sort them out until they found their feet and did this for a couple of blokes, but after a little while this was seen as me being a flash cunt. I wasn't being flash, I was being helpful.

One day out of the blue I received a letter from my brief about an appeal I'd put to the High Court about the length of my sentence. I had finally received a date. I was buzzing and thought to myself I could be getting out. If the High Court found my sentence to be too long, then I had a chance they would reduce it. I was thinking that if there wasn't a chance in hell of this happening then why would I be given a date to appear in court.

I was out running every day. I'd run laps of the prison twice a day and was fit, had a great tan and was eating really well, so was looking and feeling healthy. The running during the day helped me take my mind off of Kim. I was still talking to her every day, but one day I phoned and was told that she'd escaped from the hospital and no-one knew where she was. She had climbed over the big wall in the garden and took off. This brought my world crashing down, I was worried sick and felt so helpless. I didn't like the idea of her in the hospital, but at least I knew she was safe and being looked after.

Now she was on the loose and unwell. My head was racing 10 to the dozen and my heart was breaking at the same time. While she was in the hospital and I knew she was safe, I'd found a way to suppress my thoughts and get through the day but Kim being out there fucked me mentally.

I really wanted to help the hospital with information that may help find her, but couldn't. I was unable to tell anyone because in prison if there is something major going on in your life that's upsetting, it can jeopardise your chance of home leave. I thought about asking a priest to make some phone calls for me to the hospital, but it would have all been logged and again wouldn't have been good for my application for home leave. To the outside world I was fine but inside I wasn't coping.

My court appearance was one week away and I was called into the S.O.'s office and told that a prisoner from another prison had put in a request for an inter-prison phone call and it would happen that evening. I was baffled and asked who the prisoner was. The name stung my ears, it was COD.

CHAPTER 30

You too Son

I hadn't had contact with COD since being transferred from Pentonville and that was just the way I liked it, so why the fuck was he phoning me? The S.O. told me to go back to his office at 7:00 pm because that's what time the call was scheduled for. I did just that and the phone rang right on time. I'd decided I was going to cut COD short of anything he wanted to talk about because I wasn't having the cunt put me in any more bother on a taped call. The S.O. answered the phone and confirmed I was with him to the screw on the other end and then passed me the phone. He then left me on my own and waited outside. He must have thought I was fucking stupid, I knew he'd listen to the taped conversation later.

I took the receiver and said hello and COD's voice came through trying to make small talk. I cut him short and asked why he was phoning. He said it was about our High Court appearance and he'd been told he could phone me so we could talk about the case. I told him there was nothing to talk about and we were just going to court to see if our sentences had been cut, he said he knew that but thought he'd use the call anyway. Is all I could think was that he was a slippery little cunt, so just told him I'd see him at court.

Then the real reason came as to why he was calling me. He told me he had something to tell me and asked me if I knew a bloke called Robert Rockman. I thought for a couple of seconds because I knew Robert very well, he was like family. I've known Robert all of my life, he's older than me and also lived in Spelman House so was always in my house. He's a lovely bloke and when I was very small (Robert would tell all this) the first word I ever learnt to say was his name. He is a good man, was good to me when I was growing up and someone I trust.

I told COD I knew him but left it at that. I didn't want him knowing anything about my friendship with Robert. COD then went on to tell me that Robert was telling everyone at High Down prison that I was a grass. This made me angry because I would have put my life on it that Robert would say no such thing. Firstly he had no reason to and secondly if Robert had something to say to me he would say it to my face. I told COD I wasn't carrying on the conversation, I'd see him in court and then put the phone down.

I walked out of the S.O.'s office, straight to the prison phones and made a phone call to someone who would get a message to Robert for me. The message was to ask Robert what the fuck was going on in High Down and tell him what I'd just been told. Like me, the person I called knew it was all bollocks. What with everything else going on in my life, I really didn't need this added shit. I knew COD was full of shit and I also knew within a week this would be confirmed.

The time had now come for me to go to the High Court in the Strand in Central London. I'd been sent one of my summer suits, so got myself smartened up and was looking and feeling good. As I arrived at the High Court, I was blown away by the building. I'd passed it thousands of times, but had never been inside and it was impressive. I was taken off of the sweatbox and taken to a holding cell and as I walked in, COD was sitting there. He was still wearing his prison clothes, was very pale and looked rough as shit. He looked at me, mouth wide open, and asked me where the fuck I'd been on holiday? At the time I was tanned from all the running, had a fresh haircut and was wearing a good whistle. He was sitting there with another Herbert from the same nick as him. They both looked like a couple of down and outs. I knew COD would end up like that when left on his own.

We were called into the courtroom and I was taken aback at how grand it was. There were three High Court judges. We were sitting in the dock which was up in sky because we were looking down on what was going on. Earlier on, in a short but sweet conversation with my barrister, I'd been told that I wouldn't be asked anything. I was told that they would just read out their findings and they had already looked over the sentence and would have already made their minds up.

One of the judges started to talk and I could barely hear him but got the gist of what he was saying. It was clear that they'd found the sentence that we'd been given a fair one and said we had been lucky to be given such a short term. I wasn't too fussed and thought oh well back to prison I go. We were taken back to the holding cell and COD asked me what I thought about Robert Rockman. I told him that I'd be speaking to Robert soon and as I did COD's face dropped and I could almost see the colour drain from his face. I also told him it wouldn't be a nice outcome. I knew Robert hadn't said fuck all because the previous night I had spoken to someone on the phone who had told Robert what COD had said about him calling me a grass. Robert hadn't been happy on hearing this and I knew when COD got back to that prison that night that he would be in for a little bit of Robert.

I heard later exactly what had happened when COD had returned to High Down and my source had heard this from Robert's mouth. There had been six or seven blokes sitting about and COD was talking and had said that the bloke he'd been nicked with (i.e. me) was a grass. Robert had asked COD where he was from and what he'd been nicked for, so COD went on to tell him. Robert had asked COD if the mate he'd been nicked with was Gary Hutton and COD had said yes. Robert then told COD that he was talking out of his arse because he knew me and there is no way I was a grass. After that COD shut his fucking mouth. Robert had told COD he wanted to see him on his own but COD didn't want this so had got three blokes to protect him who wouldn't leave his side. I could so see this about the little weasel.

When I was inside, as well as the lows, I really did have some of the best laughs and saw all sorts of madness. I'm not saying try prison because it's no walk in the park and no place to end up, but I met some real good characters, plus, of course, some odd balls. One bloke I spoke to a few times was called Sasha, that wasn't his real name. Sasha was as gay as they come and the campest person I have ever met. He told me of some of the prisons he had been to and of some of the men he'd been locked up with. Let me tell you these were and are some of the toughest prisons and men in the country. When he was telling me about it, he was being flamboyant, had a sly look in his eyes and a big grin on his face. He then hit me with the punch line 'you wouldn't believe whose cocks I've sucked'. I pissed myself laughing at this and he laughed with me. He was trying to shock me and see if what he'd said had turned me on, but it hadn't. He soon learnt that I am not gay in anyway, but I did find him fucking funny.

One day I was walking down the landing towards my cell and I passed Sasha's door. He came out on to the landing behind me and shouted my name a couple of times in his camp way. I was about 25 feet away from him, I turned round and he was standing there in a bathrobe. He then opened up the bathrobe and well fuck me, he was wearing a black with red trim bra and knickers set, plus suspender belt and stockings! He then started walking towards me giving it his best supermodel walk and saying 'you know you want me, take me I'm yours'. I literally fucking cried with laughter, then told him to fuck off and walked away.

I was standing on the landing one day and a new bloke arrived and took the cell next to Sasha. Over time they became close and then lovers. This bloke was the complete opposite of Sasha, he was very quiet and didn't really speak to anyone. I was on a visit one day so was he and as we walked into the visiting hall two young kids ran up to him calling 'daddy, daddy'. He picked them up and they shared a loving cuddle. He then walked to a table, put them down and kissed a woman like he was madly in love with her. I was looking on in complete shock. This woman turned out to be his wife.

After visiting time, I made sure I walked back to the wing alongside him. I couldn't help myself and said to him 'mate don't take this the wrong way but what are you doing, you have a lovely family and you looked so much in love with your wife'. He then asked me to go for a smoke with him, so we had more privacy. He went on to explain to me that because it costs a lot of money to stay in prison, he didn't want to add pressure on to his wife because she had enough to deal with and he didn't want her to worry about him and what he needed. I understood what he was getting at and started to feel sorry for him. He also told me that if he was with Sasha while in prison he would get him everything he needed. That way his wife wouldn't have to worry about providing tobacco, phone cards, toiletries, trainers etc. for him and it was less stress for her. I understood it that it was just his way of serving his time. He had his way and I had mine. I didn't agree with his way because in my book it was wrong what he was doing but from the look in his eyes and his body language, it was his way of getting through it. There is also no doubt in my mind that this bloke was bisexual and I very much doubt his wife knew.

As I said earlier, there were a few oddballs and one of them who didn't come any stranger was a bloke called John Martin Scripps, known as Johnny. I'd seen him walking about and you couldn't miss him because he had a funny gait. He took big strides as he walked and was always in a hurry like he had to be somewhere. He sort of bounced on his toes and at the same time his head nodded and as a man being over six foot tall this looked even weirder.

Johnny kept himself to himself but did tell me he had been born in Wapping, but as a young kid had moved away from the East End. When speaking to him, he came across as slightly backward. I spoke to him a couple of times, but never asked him what he was in for. What I did know was that he wasn't a nonce but was a very dangerous madman who had a very deep dark side.

I was in his cell one day just having a chat making small talk because I wanted to know what he was about. In the corner, there was a pile of prison issue clothes, blankets, sheets and anything the prison issued, but it was all cut up, so I asked him what it was for. He then told me he would show me what he'd been working on and pulled out a bag from a cupboard and out of the bag he got a blanket and all sorts that he'd been stitching together. I was looking and showing interest but at the same time was thinking he isn't well! He was so excited when he was telling me and told me that by doing the stitching it kept him calm. I honestly did believe it did keep him calm in his mind and wondered what prison shrink had told him that stitching would work. It was obvious just by Johnny's walk that he was two units short of a phone card and would never fit into the real world.

Johnny was allowed home leave one weekend. Off he went, never to be seen back at The Mount again. He done a bunk to Singapore and some years later I read that he was on a murder charge. There were other murders in the Far East but they could not prove them all to be Johnny. He was dubbed by the British tabloids as "The tourist from hell" because after killing his victims, he stole their credit cards and cash and dismembered their bodies. He was eventually hanged in Singapore. These were the sort of madmen I was living with!

Kim had now thankfully been found and was back in the hospital, which I was so happy to hear. It was such a relief because I'd been worried sick. I was also told that I could have home leave in two weeks' time, so was really happy that I'd get to see Kim for myself in person. It had been far too long and all I wanted to do was hold and cuddle her. I knew I wouldn't have the time to talk to her in-depth about what had happened but at least I could see her. I was still speaking to her every day and sometimes two or three times, but it wasn't the same as being able to see her face and giving her a loving brotherly hug.

The week before my weekend home leave really dragged. I was allowed out for the whole weekend and had to be back at the prison by no later than 4:00 pm on the Sunday. I'd arranged for my brother Darren to pick me up so was all set.

That night I had a good night's sleep and was up bright and early the following morning because I couldn't wait to get out. I was taken to the reception area and given some of my own clothes to wear. There was a bloke from my wing also there for home leave. He was an older bloke who was coming to the end of a very, very long stretch.

I remember once I'd gone to use the phones and he had been sitting there waiting for someone to finish their call. I'd asked him if he'd been waiting long. When he looked at me, his eyes had looked dead and when he answered me he'd said in a tired voice '17 years, four months, two weeks and five days'. I'd only asked him how long he'd been waiting to use the phone! I didn't want to end up like him in that way. He was pushing 60 and was one of London's so called big time gangsters and was very high profile. When he'd said how long he'd been waiting, I wasn't sure if he was working his ticket or wasn't the full shilling. He was a nice older fella and very pleasant.

We were now ready to walk out of the gate and were standing side by side as the big gate was about to be opened. He turned to me and was white as a sheet and said he wasn't sure if he remembered how to drive. I laughed and said he must have someone picking him up to drive him home. He then laughed and said he had. As the gate slowly opened and a little sun shone through, I looked at his face and he was grinning from ear to ear and as the gate opened further the sun lit his whole face up with that big smile. I knew it was a big moment in that man's life, so I put my arm around his shoulder and as we walked, I told him I wished him a good weekend and he turned to me and said 'you too son'.

CHAPTER 31

Home Leave Turned Crazy Leave

Darren was waiting for me on the other side of the gate and I was so pleased to see him. As we made our way back to London, I tried not to ask Darren too much about home because he would suspect something was wrong. Darren wasn't at the hospital with the rest of us so didn't have a clue what Bin had told us on that shocking day. Until I knew the full facts, I wasn't going to throw his world upside down. I now had 48 hours of home leave to find out as much as I could. I had no plan in how I was going to do this and I had no idea if Kim was in any fit state to even tell me.

Darren drove me to North London where I was staying for the weekend so I could get cleaned up and change. I'd washed that morning, but I needed to wash prison off of me so I felt clean. I phoned Mark and he told me that he was taking me out that night and that I should be ready by 7:00 pm; our usual Friday night meeting time. I had a bit of running about to do but told Mark I would be ready on time. Darren waited for me while I changed and off we went.

The person I was staying within North London played a part in my life and to write about that would be a whole new book in itself. To write about that would be wrong so let me just say I made a very, very bad judgement at that time in who I chose to have around me. The reason I mention this now is because it is a part of this story within my book.

Darren drove me to Bin's house and I was looking forward to seeing my family and the one person I wanted to see most of all was Kim. I had it in my head that I needed to speak to Kim and if she told me the full truth about what had been happening, Bin was going to get it. Darren had warned me that she was not herself but slowly she was getting better. She was out of hospital and only had to return to hospital once a week so her progress could be monitored.

I walked into the house and only Jackie was there and I was so pleased to see her because Tracey and Jackie had been so good to me while I was in prison. They'd written to me all the time and if I asked them to do something they did it without question. I asked Jackie where Kim was and she said that Rodney had taken her to stay with him for a couple of days and also told me that Bin was down the pub. She said that everyone would be there the following day for a little party for my birthday. Now I may have been feeling paranoid but in my mind keeping Kim away from me had been planned. I hadn't seen either Bin or Rodney since that day in the hospital and Bin had admitted what a true vile low life beast he was. Since that day, the words 'I only touched her tits', had swam around in my head day and fucking night and I'd come to the conclusion that he wasn't telling the whole truth. The look of fear on his face that day, and for him to think I was going to kill him, told me that he wasn't telling the whole truth and was only partly admitting and playing down what he'd really done. I had a cuppa with Jackie, we chatted small talk and it felt good because it was another world from prison.

I didn't stay at the house long because there was a couple of things I had to do and sorting out some prison currency was one of those things. I wanted to be fully stocked up when I got back to prison. I'd arranged to meet various people all throughout the night in different pubs all over the East End and was going to have one or two drinks in each pub with the people I'd arranged to meet. I met with Mark and we had a few drinks on our own to start with and then our night began. I wasn't sure how long I'd last because I hadn't had a good drink for quite a while, but I was going to give it a good go.

I'd arranged to meet my cousin Johnny at 9:00 pm so we went to some pubs before meeting him. The drinks were flowing and we were having a good laugh. We then went on to meet Johnny and the pub he was in was full of blokes who I had grown up with on Chicksand and some I hadn't seen for years. They were on a stag do and we had such a laugh. I couldn't buy a drink for love nor money. My cousin had slipped a long'un in my pocket and wished me a good night and still wouldn't let me buy a drink. As we were having such a good laugh in the pub we were in, me and Mark decided we were going to stay there. I told the person I was staying within North London to meet me there and when they arrived I said that's where we were staying. They didn't like this and said they wanted to go to the Joiners on Hackney Road. The Joiners is a pub that I used all the time, but this particular night I didn't want to go there because I was having a good time where I was. After they kept on at me to leave for the Joiners, I explained to Mark the earache I was getting so we left.

We walked into the Joiners and as I looked around what I saw was strange. We got a drink and I stood with my back against the wall and soaked in the shocking truth of what I was looking at. It was clear why the person who I was staying within North London didn't want to stay in the previous pub, they'd set me up to be in the Joiners that evening. I had met a bloke in prison who I didn't think was right because he constantly asked me about people I knew so distanced myself from him. Well, every single person he had asked me about in prison was standing in that pub and some didn't look happy. I walked over to one bloke who was standing with his sister-in-law who I knew and bought them a drink, but as I took the money out of my pocket, she piped up and said 'I bet there is plenty where that came from'. I just dismissed this and laughed it off and went and stood back where I was. People were just looking at me, not saying anything and I could tell they weren't happy. They had worked out that I'd clocked on that the person I was staying with had set me up, so I told that person not to leave my fucking side.

I had completely forgotten that I'd met the bloke in prison in the Joiners some years before meeting him in prison. I'd met him after my mate's mum's funeral and he'd popped in the Joiners and taken the person home that I was now living with. It was only then, standing there in the pub that this had come back to me. I didn't realise until that point that they knew each other.

It was now getting late, or at least late for me because my body clock was in lights out mode. I thought if anyone was going to do anything they would have done it by then but no-one stepped up so I got on with having a good night. What I didn't know at that time was that when the bloke in prison was asking me if I knew certain people and I had said yes, he had gone back to that person and told them that I'd slagged them off, which I can say hand on heart I never did. Over the years, I've spoken to people in that pub and that's what they've told me and I've put them straight.

The bird I bought a drink for who'd said "I bet there is plenty where that came from' I have seen many times over the years and she has never said a word to me and finds it hard to look at me because of what she did that night. She bought me and Mark a drink that night but as she walked towards us she was being a bit strange and taking too much care not to spill a drop. At that point anyway I'd had enough and told Mark I was going to get a cab and I'd call him in the morning. I got a cab home, went straight to bed and woke up fresh as a daisy the next morning with no sign of a hangover.

I phoned Mark and he told me that he had been up all night tripping out of his nut and was seeing shit that had shocked the life out of him. As I was talking to him, the person I was living with piped up and said 'you were tripping as well Gal'; I wasn't tripping. I didn't tell Mark until some years later, but I knew that trip wasn't meant for him and he must have drunk the drink that was meant for me.

It was my birthday and I was off to see my family and the one person I was desperate to see was Kim. I arrived at the house and my whole family was there and I was so pleased to see everyone. Kim was in no fit state to talk to me because she was drugged up to the eyeballs on what the hospital were prescribing her. She could just about make small talk. This was killing me as I wanted to know from Kim the truth of what had been going on. I thought if I could get through to her, I could help her, but the state she was in from the drugs and with everyone around made it impossible. Bin was there and couldn't even look at me. I didn't talk to him or go near him because I was on the edge and ready to flip out. Everything was playing around in my head especially that day in the hospital including the brother bollocks hand pact of never mentioning what Bin had said again. They were true to their word, they were carrying on like nothing had fucking happened or been said. It did my nut in and I was a ticking time bomb ready to explode.

I knew I couldn't stay in the house for much longer and had to leave. My head was so far up my arse I needed a plumber to remove it. As I was looking at my big sister and searching her eyes for some life, they were looking at me dead and lifeless, which broke my heart. This was not the girl I knew full of fight for life,

life and soul of everywhere she went. This person was broken and a shell of the girl I knew and loved. I missed her smile. She felt so far away, I wanted to pick her up and run with her and get her away from all the madness, sadness and sickness that had made her this way and put her where she was in her mind. It literally was madness what was around me. Everyone was talking and laughing like everything was normal. Fucking normal, after what that monster had said in that hospital room and my sister was sitting there like a zombie. I couldn't handle it and got the fuck out of there, it was too much.

I kept myself to myself for the rest of the weekend and didn't tell anyone what was going on in my head, which felt like it was about to explode. I couldn't function properly going on like that. My weekend was then over and I was on my way back to prison. The whole weekend had been a head fuck and I now just wanted to get my sentence over and done with. I arrived back at prison on time, was booked back in, searched, given the all clear and sent back to my wing.

As I walked back on the wing the first person I saw was the bloke who had previously been asking me about people on the outside and such people had been in the Joiners when I'd walked in there two night previous. He had a big smile on his face he said 'oi Gal did you have a good TRIP'. What a fucking sad bloke. I know he thought I'd tripped out, but I hadn't. In my book if you dislike someone you stay away from them, or if the dislike is so bad, you straighten whatever it is out with them and be done with it.

That Sunday night, in my cell, I was up all night thinking of Kim especially her lost eyes. My head was fucked and for the following week my mind was running away with itself. I walked into the S.O.'s office and asked to be moved back to London as I was nearing the end of my sentence. The real reason I wanted to move back to London was because I felt like I was about to go fucking crazy and I wanted to be near my family. I needed them to visit me every day so they could tell me what the fuck was going on. Within two days, I was on my way back to Pentonville.

CHAPTER 32

Brain Train

I arrived back at Pentonville and was pleased to be back in London and nearer to my family. If I wanted someone to come and see me, it was only an hour out of their time rather than a day trip. I settled into my cell and there were a couple of faces that I knew but after a couple of days something wasn't right, people were looking at me strangely. I didn't take any notice at first. Days and nights passed and they were rolling in to one because I wasn't sleeping very well. In Pentonville you're banged up for longer than in any other prison I've been locked up in. This gives you so much time to think and it was all I did. I'd lay on my bed and go over things in my mind again and again and this was going on for 23 hours a day. The only time I left my cell was to get food because I didn't want to be around anyone.

The nights were bad because in the dead of the night, I would sit on my bed with the light off and my head felt like a speed train racing through a dark tunnel. I was in a bad way and could not stop this train inside my head. I was no longer the driver in charge of my thoughts and they were spiralling out of control. One scene that would not leave the tunnel was that day in the hospital and Bin's voice was all I could hear echoing around my head. I was seeing things that had happened in my life but at the time they had happened I hadn't taken much notice. One memory was of Bin holding something in his hand while he lay in the hospital bed, and in my cell I could see what it was clear as day. In his right hand, he was holding a small picture of my mum which I hadn't seen before. Following that memory I kept having visual flashes of my mum and to me, at the time, felt it was my mum's way of telling me that she was with me and by

233

my side. I felt it more than I ever had before then, and it felt so real. Kim was also etched all over the tunnel walls.

I felt that way while I was banged up for such long periods and needed to do something to keep my mind occupied to distract me from thoughts of my mum and sister. I decided to clean my cell so got some bleach, cloths, a mop and bucket and cleaned my cell over and over again until my hands were sore. I also started to work out to try and knock myself out of a night. I got two big empty bleach containers and filled them with water, got a broom handle and fixed it to the containers so I had weights to work with. I was working out like crazy, but it didn't slow my brain down and I couldn't get properly focussed. The brain train was still on high speed chugging through my thoughts and the fuel for the brain train was chain-smoking roll ups and drinking tea. Working out was not releasing the steam, the pressure was building and I could not change gears as much as I tried.

I left my cell one morning to use the phone and saw a bloke I knew, Bedford Ben. He was a bloke I knew living in the East End but was originally from Bedford, hence the name. He was a nice fella or so I thought and as I walked towards him he avoided me and walked back into his cell. As I passed his cell, I noticed a couple of other blokes in there but didn't take any notice and carried on towards the phones. The person I tried to call didn't answer, so I made my way back to my cell and as I passed Bedford's cell I heard COD mentioned and the surname of the bloke who had asked me if I'd had a nice TRIP and they were spreading the word around the prison that I was a grass. I didn't know what the fuck was going on.

That night I was out on the landing and everyone else was out of their cells. It felt like all eyes were on me and from hearing what I'd heard earlier I had taken out some insurance and had a tool down the back of my trousers. Bedford was walking towards me and I looked at him and told him I wanted a word. He could see I wasn't happy. As he got to me, I put my arm on his shoulder and told him to come into my cell. I shut the door so it locked so it was just me and him locked in and there was no way out.

I said to him that I was no fucking grass and that no cunt in the prison had better be thinking that they were going to do something to me. I told him if something did happen to me that when I got out of Pentonville, and when he was released, I would hurt him so bad that he would not be doing much walking or talking for the rest of his days and I meant every fucking word. He then shocked me and said OK, he then said he was the only one on the wing with a knife and he would get it back from the blokes who were planning to do me with it. When he said that, it done me and I was on one. I told him I didn't think he understood me and said that if something did happen to me inside, whoever done it had better make sure that they done a good job and I was dead because they wouldn't last five minutes when they got out of prison. He told me I had his word and that nothing would happen. I still see this man a lot and we shake hands and greet each other with respect. What he doesn't know that I do, is that he told one of my very best friends that I was slagging him off in Pentonville, which is a fucking lie. It seemed like people wanted to blacken my name, but the truth always comes out in the end and it all did.

There was another truth that I was set on finding out and it would not leave my thoughts. I couldn't stop climbing aboard the brain train because I knew there was so much more that Bin hadn't said and his eyes that day were telling me there was more. This became an obsession for me and was all I cared about. I didn't give a shit about anything else and in some sort of way I liked all the thinking I was doing, but sometimes it became too much.

At night I would be laying on my bed, fully dressed, deeply submerged in thought and I'd get a flash before my eyes of something that had happened, which made me bolt up and run to turn the light on because I couldn't handle what I'd seen. The sweat would be dripping off of me, my heart pounding and my lungs felt they were going to burst out of my chest where I couldn't catch my breath. Turning the light on helped the feeling stop.

I needed to know what had gone on in the home that I'd been brought up in and I was going over my life by each day trying to see something. Some awful memories were playing out in my mind like the beatings from Bin, having no food, being dirty and unwashed. I was on this train going through a tunnel and on the walls were pictures of my life. I wanted the train to slow down so I could study the pictures, but there were no brakes and no control.

I was asking myself why my brothers and sisters were the way they were and wanted to know what had happened to them. My brother Paul was and still is so unwell with a mental illness. I truly believe that something happened to him. For him to be so unwell, I think something happened and his brain shut down and drove him insane.

Once when I was a boy of 13 or 14 years of age and was at home, I came down the stairs and my brother who I will call X was in the kitchen talking to Bin. X looked at me and said 'I've told him'. This confused me so I asked what he was talking about. X said he had told Bin that my brother who I'll call Z had done things to him and when I asked what X said 'you know, sex things'. He then went on to say that Z had done things to me also. I looked at both Bin and X and they were looking at me wanting me to agree. I told them I had no fucking clue what they were talking about and said 'he might have done things to you, but he has done fuck all to me'. Bin then piped up and said 'I'm kicking that poof out of this house' and that's exactly what he did. My brother ended up living on the street and was homeless. The next time I saw him I cried, I could not believe my eyes. He was so dirty, the clothes he was wearing were falling off of him and he was talking to himself. I still have no idea to this day why X and Bin did this to him and it was now playing out on the brain train in my cell.

I didn't feel mad. It felt like it was a process in which I had to think that way so I could understand what had gone on in my life and playing it out in my head was my chosen process. For the first time in my life, I knew that my upbringing was wrong and nothing about it had been right. I came to the understanding that my mum's passing was the biggest factor for my path in life. I knew that if my mum had lived I wouldn't have gone down the path of crime. Without her love and nurturing that I needed as a young child I'd had no chance with Bin in charge. My life could have been so different.

The path I had been given and had no choice in I compare to as follows. If I'm your dad and I take you as a young seven year old kid, you trust me, I'm all you know and you believe in me. If I take you to the side of the road and tell you, I'm going to teach you an important life lesson and how to cross that road. We're standing at the side of the road and I take your small hand in mine so tight that you feel safe. The road is clear both ways, but I wait for a lorry to come along and drag you in front of the lorry to get to the other side and we make it without being run over. You would go through life thinking that's how you cross the road. You would take that lesson and master it. I realised that's what I'd done, I'd taken the bad lesson that I'd been taught and turned it into a way of life. The brain train was showing me that the lessons I'd been taught were fucked up and given by a vile man who had brainwashed his own children for his own gain.

A few weeks went by and nothing had changed, I was still having sleepless nights and over-thinking. I couldn't stop the thinking and focussing on the pictures on the brain train. I wasn't eating too well and the fuel for the brain train was chain-smoking. Another flashback that I had was being an 11 year old boy and knocking on the door to my home. There was no answer so I'd put my hand through the letterbox and let myself in. I was bursting to use the toilet, so ran upstairs towards the bathroom. Before going in, I noticed that Kim's bedroom door was shut which normally meant she was home. I put my hand on the doorknob, but it was locked. I did hear something on the other side of the door but didn't take no notice at the time and went to the toilet. On the brain train all these years later, sitting in my cell, I knew what I'd heard which was 'ssshhhh he will go away'. It was Bin's voice. I'd nearly caught the bastard. My subconscious mind had kept this from me but had now revealed to me what I'd heard all those years ago. I don't know what I would have done as a young child if I had caught what the vile creature was doing.

I started to re-read the letters from my sisters that I'd received over the time I'd been inside. I looked for clues for what had been happening and became obsessive and read them again and again. I was doing this every night but didn't find anything. Sometimes I thought I had found something but it was just me being desperate. One night when I was doing this and again found nothing, I started to rip and tear the letters and was screaming at the top of my voice over and over again 'you fucking slag I'm going to kill you'. My mind had now gone and rage had taken over.

I picked up the table in my cell, lifted it above my head and smashed it against the wall. I ripped off the table legs and smashed up everything in my cell. I picked up my metal framed bed and threw it, then jumped on it and started to kick it to break it up. I took the metal parts of the bed and bent them up. All the time I was doing this I was screaming 'I will kill you, you slag'. I was foaming at the mouth and desperately wanted to hurt someone. Anyone would have done, I had to pass on the pain that I was feeling and needed to offload it. Ideally, I wanted to offload on Bin's head.

I heard someone shouting outside of my cell 'Hutton stop now and there will be no nicking'. I ran towards the cell door with part of the metal bed in one hand and a table leg in the other and was screaming 'you cunt get in here and I'll give you something to nick me for'. The alarm then started to sound, I was going crazy and was ready to hurt whoever stepped through the door. I'd lost it completely and was smashing anything up that I could and was running and jumping around the cell. I could hear the sound of quickly marching feet and I knew anything from eight to ten screws were coming for me. It was getting closer and sounded like the rumbling of thunder and then it stopped.

I could hear my name being called, but I was in the zone and the madness going on in my mind. I returned to the door and told them to come in, I wanted them to come in, I needed them to come in. I was screaming at the top of my voice and carried on smashing up the cell. I was fit in body, game for them entering my cell and had told myself that I wasn't going anywhere. I could hear the screws questioning whether to enter and heard one of them say that I'd burn myself out shortly. I then went into mad overdrive and was screaming 'is that right you cunts'. Within a minute I was fucked, my arms dropped and were heavy, the power in my legs had gone and my brain started to slow down. Everything became slow motion.

The door opened and they ran at me wearing helmets and holding shields that are used in riots. I tried to lash out, but they ran at me with such force it felt like a wave had hit me and lifted me off of my feet. I was in the corner of my cell with a shield in my face and was being folded up. They were grabbing all parts of my body and it felt like I was folded up into a nice little parcel and was then lifted and ran off the block. I was taken to the deepest part of the prison and when we got there, I felt the fight coming back and I wanted to have a go. By now I was crying in frustration and screaming because I was being held down and could not move. The screws were all over me and told me to stop struggling as it was in my best interests. I told them that when I got up one of them was going to get done. I then spotted out of the corner of my eye a screw walking towards us and he was holding a little see-through plastic medication cup with black stuff in it. I was forced to swallow the contents and they let me go. I tried to get up, but I couldn't, my feet and legs had stopped working and I could feel a warmness rising up my body. I couldn't lift my arms and the warmness reached my chest. As I laid there, I thought they've killed me. I tried to talk, but my jaw wouldn't work. My eyes closed and I thought death had caught up with me.

I woke up and had no idea how long I'd been asleep for. For all I knew it could have been days. I tried to move my arms but couldn't. I was laying on my back but wasn't on a bed and tried to sit up, but couldn't. I looked around and noticed I was on the floor in a cell, but it wasn't a normal cell. The walls and floor were padded and when I looked down at where my hands should have been, they weren't there. Everything was hazy and weird and nothing was making sense in my mind. I looked down again and realised I was wearing a straightjacket and a pair of thick heavy shorts like boxers wear. I shuffled over onto my bum towards the wall and sat up against it. I thought I was in a fucked up dream.

The cell door opened and in walked a very tall screw. He bent down and looked me straight in the eyes and at the top of his voice asked me if I was OK. It was all surreal and I thought he was taking the piss because he was talking to me like I was foreign or had learning difficulties. He really over-emphasised his words. I nodded that I was OK and again he spoke loudly and very clearly and said 'OK Hutton I'm going to take the jacket off and you're going to get up and follow me'. I couldn't help but think why is he talking to me like I'm a cunt? He undone the leather straps on the jacket and my arms fell to my side because they'd been wrapped around my body in a cuddle for God knows how long. He told me to get up and I tried but my legs were wobbly. I looked like a horse that had just been born and was trying to find their feet, but kept falling. I just couldn't function and everything was so cloudy. After a few tries, I managed to get up and walk out of the cell which was only five yards but it took me a long time.

When I finally got outside the screw was sitting at a table and told me to sit down and again was shouting but slowly. I had no idea what was wrong with me, why I couldn't function properly and why this screw was talking and acting the way he was to emphasise his orders. I sat down and he told me that day was a new start in my life and it was my choice to take the fresh start. He told me I had two choices, one was to carry on the way I had been and they'd keep me in the state I was in for as long as I had left in prison, or two I could change my ways, get out of prison

241

and never go back. I was looking at him and just nodded because it was all I was capable of doing.

He told me he was going to get me a towel, some shampoo and some soap and that I was going to have a shower. When he returned, he handed me a cup of water and the other items. I wasn't sure whether to drink the water and checked the cup to make sure there wasn't anything else in it. My mouth was so dry I drank it. The screw then told me it was time to shower. The showers were right at the other end of the block and it took me forever to get there. I couldn't walk so was shuffling to move forward. When I got into the shower, I could see water coming out of the shower head but couldn't feel it on my skin. The screw told me he'd put some fresh prison clothes on the side for when I got out. He'd also given me my trainers but without the laces.

I left the showers and still everything wasn't right. I asked the screw what cell I was going to and as I did I started to dribble. I was now shuffling and dribbling and thinking I can't be like this, I don't want to be like this. I was taken back to the padded cell and he said he'd get me some food and if I was OK after that he would take me back to my old cell. I was sitting in the padded cell and was brought some food but before I started eating I did something I'd never done before in my life. I spoke to God but not in prayer. I looked up and said 'God look at me. I don't want to live my life like this, I'm worth more than this and if you get me out of here with a sane mind I don't care if I haven't got a pound in my pocket, I will change my life and will never take part in any crime that involves me trying to gain. I've become addicted to money and that has been part of what has led me to prison. If you get me out of here Lord with a sane mind, I will do nothing but good with my life as from today.'

As the days went by I could walk and talk better and the shuffle slowly went and I started to feel myself again. Within a week, I was hell-bent on getting out of prison. I put in for home leave with my chosen date and it was granted. They asked me if I wanted to see a nut doctor and I thought bollocks to that. What was I going to say? 'Oh doctor not so long ago I found out my sister has been abused by her dad. He tried to top himself and after being unsuccessful told me and my brothers what he'd done. Oh yeah and while I was on my last home leave my brothers acted like nothing had happened. Also, while my sister has been in the hospital Bin has been looking after her every day and she's now a zombie drugged up to the eyeballs sharing her life with Bin like the rest of my family'. If I had said any of that and they had questioned my family, they would have said they didn't know what I was talking about and I would have been locked up in some nuthouse and I'd also be a drugged up zombie, probably for life. Getting home leave and getting the fuck out of there was the better option for me. My home leave finally came and I'd decided I wasn't going back until I was better so once again I was on the run.

CHAPTER 33

Free in Body but not in Mind

I found myself on the run once again, but this time I'd decided I was staying out. I'd made my mind up that I wasn't going back until I was well enough. I found myself thinking 'when was all this going to stop, I just wanted to get off of the ride'. My head was all over the place, I wasn't myself and I wasn't feeling or looking myself. I went on to live on the run for 18 months which is a very long time for someone who doesn't leave the country. I wasn't running from the old bill or prison, I was trying to find the new me and to make myself better. I wanted to change my life and the way I lived in every way I could and it wasn't going to be easy.

I started to look at myself and what had just happened to me. How the hell had I ended up in a padded cell? I had spoken to God which I'd never done before and I had meant every single word. Don't get me wrong I'm no Jesus loves you born again type of bloke, but one thing I did know, I had asked and he had delivered, I was out of prison! I still wasn't sure about my mind being sane yet but being out of prison was a good start.

All my life up until that point I had spent getting money in any which way I could. It was all my life was about. I would eat, sleep and drink money and I was addicted to it. I now had to part from my lifelong money affair. All the money I'd obtained had taken me to a place I didn't want to be in life. I wasn't taught this when I was growing up. No-one had told me as a young kid that going out shoplifting, being able to do what I liked as long as I brought my gains home so my brothers and sisters could eat, would lead to me ending up drugged up to the eyeballs, wearing a straightjacket in a padded cell. No-one fucking told me that I'd end up shuffling instead of being able to walk because I was so spaced out I couldn't lift my feet up and certainly no-one told me I'd end up a drugged up dribbling wreck. If I'd been told this as an eight year old boy, I would have said 'fuck you, you do it because I'm going to school to better myself and my chances in life'. If I had of been given options as a kid would I have really have had a choice?

Now I had a choice. I moved houses but still within the East End and I stayed indoors for really long periods of time. I suppose you could have called me a bit of a recluse. For weeks at a time, I would lock myself away and not see or talk to anyone. I did so much thinking in that time and it was a calm and slow type of thinking which was just what I needed. I was suffering with depression in a big way, but I couldn't go to the doctors. Being by myself did help me. I started to get my mind back on track and eventually decided to find out in a calm way exactly what had been going on and get to the bottom of what had been going on within my family and to do it in the right way.

Kim had been taken on holiday because Rodney had moved abroad. He had moved to a few different countries over time; South Africa, Denmark and Cyprus and would take Kim on holiday for two weeks at a time or longer if she wanted to. I didn't see Kim or any of my family for the first few months I was out against her majesty's pleasure. I felt what I was doing was not about them it was about me first and foremost. I needed to sort myself out first and then work on them.

After a few months of locking myself away, I went for a drink with one of my older brothers. I really wanted to see him because I hadn't seen him since that day in the hospital when Bin had tried to top himself. We met and had a good laugh together reminiscing about old times and growing up. We both love football but tend to clash as he is sadly a Gooner (Arsenal fan) and I'm West Ham, but we have good banter and it's all good fun. The drinks were flowing and we started to get a little tipsy so I suggested we walk to another pub and the fresh air would do us good. As we were walking I asked him to stop and if I could ask him something. He said yes and asked what it was. I looked him straight in the eyes and said 'remember that day in the hospital when we and Bin were in the room and he told us what he had done to Kim about only touching her tits?' He looked back at me with total confusion on his face and without the slightest hesitation said 'Gal I have no idea what you're talking about. I wasn't there and you don't know what you're talking about. I heard you haven't been well but come on let's just go to the next pub'. He then walked off. We went to the next pub and I never asked him anything more that day. We carried on for a few more hours and both went home our separate ways, drunk.

I woke up the next morning and all hell broke loose in my head. What my brother had said to me when we were out was screaming out at me. I started to beat myself up thinking what a horrible bastard I was and how I'd made everything up. I thought I had lost my mind to make up something so wrong about the man who had brought us all up. I also thought I must have been some sort of evil sicko. I also questioned why my mind had done this to me and thought I needed help because I was a madman. I thought I was having some sort of mental breakdown. I questioned my sanity for thinking such terrible things about the one man in my life that I had placed high up on a pedestal and was a good man like everybody said. I also thought my brother wouldn't lie to me, he had no reason to. I was his little brother and he'd always looked out for me my whole life and I trusted him.

My mind was gone, lost, there are no other words to describe it. I was back on the brain train questioning my whole life. I was beating myself up thinking I was an evil bastard. I couldn't figure out at what point I had lost my mind and I'd started to make everything up. I had no fucking clue what was true and what my sick mind had created. I wondered when my mental illness had come into effect and why no-one had detected it before. I had now become my own doctor and diagnosed I was mental with help from my brother.

I hate to admit this, but suicide became an option in my mind. If you put yourself in my shoes for a moment, the person in my life who I trusted, loved unconditionally, worshipped and wanted to please the most had become a monster in my head. I had thought that he was the devil and had done the most awful things and then had found out from my brother that I had imagined it all. That must have been why all my brothers were acting like nothing had happened at the party they threw for me on my birthday when I was on home leave because nothing had happened. I really didn't want to live, I hated myself.

Instead of taking my own life, I started to drink. This blocked out my thoughts. Every bottle I touched I would finish. I started going to the pub at 1:00 pm in the afternoon and I'd stay until closing and some pubs stayed open well past legal closing hours. I was half sensible when I was drunk, I never fell about and made an arse of myself. I can't really call myself an ex-drunk because I didn't need to drink to stop withdrawal and the shakes. I had wanted to drink and there is a difference. I wanted to drink to block out the thoughts of what I thought my mind had invented. Drink wasn't ruining my life, my life was already ruined and drink was helping me forget that. A few years later I did get a wake-up call after a liver biopsy. Following a blood test my doctor detected an irregularity with my liver; I had smashed it up and beat the shit out of it.

One night I was out with my brother Darren and we ended up in a club which Darren's mate owned. I had been drinking all day and met up with him at this particular club. We were standing next to three young blokes and as I was talking to Darren one of them kept nudging me in my side with his elbow. This young fella didn't turn round once and say sorry and it felt like the force of the nudge was getting stronger. I asked Darren to do me a favour and have a word with his mate who owned the club to ask him to have a word with the young bloke because I was getting a bit irate and wanted to hurt the fella. As Darren went to find his mate, I was hit with another dig in the ribs. I turned and faced the young bloke and said 'steady on mate' but he didn't acknowledge me and carried on talking. Darren then came back and said his pal had said to move away from the young fella and his mates. This made me angrier so I asked Darren if he had explained I wasn't happy with the young fella and the situation he was pushing me into and Darren said he had. Looking back I now know I wasn't well and wanted to hurt anyone to release some of the madness going on in my head. Unfortunately, the pinnacle of that release was about to unfold in that club, it was just what I was looking for. I was in too much mental pain to be physically hurt.

The young bloke then dug me again and it was too much for me to take. I tapped him on the back and he turned round and asked me what the fuck I wanted. Because he reacted that way and spoke to me in that manner, I asked him if we knew each other. With an angry fucker look on his face, he said he didn't know me. I put my arm around his shoulder and in a very calm comforting voice I told him I wanted to have a chat with him. As I said this, I walked him off to a table full of empty glasses. As we arrived at the table, I pushed his head down with one hand and with my spare hand picked up a bottle and done him with it. I didn't stop, I was picking up every glass and bottle and smashing them over his head.

What I didn't know as I'd escorted him to the table was that he had a lot of mates in the club and the whole club turned on me and I was being hit bottle after bottle. I would not let go of the young bloke and was holding on to him biting him like a crazed dog. As I was doing this, I was being glassed, punched and kicked but I couldn't feel a thing. I was going nowhere and fought and fought and I knew if I went down I was a dead man, but I didn't give a shit. What can you do to a man that wants to die anyway, fuck all apart from give him what he wants.

I eventually let go of the young bloke and was fighting with another. I was being hit over the head with bottles and there was claret everywhere, but at the time I didn't know who was bleeding because everyone seemed to be covered. I was then grabbed from behind with an arm around my neck and as I tried to turn to see who had hold of me, the bloke glassed me with his free hand. He had glassed me in the eye and as he did, he let me go and ran out of the club door. Now I wanted this bloke but was still being hit with bottles from all directions. I could see Darren was toe to toe with anyone who got near him and I shouted to him let's get the fuck out of there. No-one could have stopped what was going on, the bouncers were also fighting and it was a free for all. All I wanted and was now fixated on was the bloke who'd glassed me in the eye from behind.

Me and Darren got outside of the club and the bloke who'd glassed me was standing on the corner of the street so I ran at him. I beat him with a car until he was unconscious. The car had no windows left and the bodywork was fucked. I had hold of his hair and was bouncing his head off of the car and I wasn't stopping until I heard someone shout 'oi you cunt stop, you're killing him'. As I turned around to look at who was shouting at me, I saw a bloke running at me with a baseball bat and just as I'd turned he had swung it. Bang, it hit me square in the mouth, but I didn't go down. I grabbed the bat and got it off of him and then put my hand to my mouth and was spitting out teeth. I walked towards this bloke with the bat and told him I was going to kill him. As I walked, he was walking backwards looking at me like I was crazy. He ran back in the club and shut the doors. I was gone, I was trying to kick the doors in, all the while the bloke was shouting sorry and that he'd called the old bill.

Darren was also now going mad and then the bloke shouted at him he was sorry he didn't know I was his brother. Darren told the cunt he was now in trouble. I then heard the sirens and told Darren we needed to leave sharpish. As we walked off, two old bill came running at me and asked if I was alright and asked what had happened. I said I thought I was OK, I'd been attacked by four blokes as I'd left the club and that they'd ran off and I was on my way to London Hospital to get sorted out. I was covered head to toe in blood, my teeth were hanging out and I wasn't a pretty picture. The copper asked for my name as he would be coming to the hospital, so I gave him the name I was using at the time and flagged a cab down.

There was no way I was going to the hospital because I would have been sent straight back to prison and I wasn't ready to go back yet. I went home and stitched myself up with a needle and cotton. I had head wounds, deep cuts all over my body and gashes around my eyes. I could stitch myself up, but I'm no dentist and needed one badly, as one of my front teeth was hanging out and I needed a shitload of other work done as well. As I was stitching myself up I made a phone call to the club.

Within two hours I walked back into the club and there were six blokes standing there waiting. As me and Darren walked in, the doors were locked behind us. There was one light on so it was dark, but I could see there was glass, tables and chairs everywhere. The owner of the club had told me on the phone that if I returned he would have a few of his mates with him and reeled off a few known names. I'd told him I didn't give a shit who he had waiting. We were now in this room and there was no way out for me and Darren, or them. I asked the owner if he wanted to phone anyone else. I knew they were tooled up with bats and hammers and such like, but he could see that me and Darren were not bothered by that and he knew Darren well enough to know he could look after himself.

I could tell by his demeanour that he didn't fancy it and then he said we could sort it out and he hadn't realised I was Darren's brother. He had just seen a bloke on the floor outside of his club being beaten to death and he'd just wanted it to stop. One of his henchmen who was standing there knew all of my older brothers so I asked him if the situation was anything to do with him. He was trying to be pally and said we should sort it out and stop the madness, so I asked him again if the situation had anything to do with him. He said no, walked away and sat in the corner of the club. Now they were a man down and looking worried, so I fronted it and asked if anyone else wanted to walk away. They were looking at me like I was a fucking nutter and to be fair they would have been correct in that assumption especially with my homemade stitched up face. I wasn't well, I was well past caring and at that point it was in for a penny in for a pound.

The bloke who owned the club then started to talk again, his speech had gone up a gear and he was talking quickly, which told me that he knew he was in trouble. He turned to Darren and asked if we could please sort this out and said he was sorry.

Then one of the other blokes said something similar so I told him to shut the fuck up. The owner had now turned into a little kid and it was quite embarrassing to see him pleading with Darren to stop the state of affairs we were in. I started to feel sorry for him and then Darren turned to me and said 'let's get out of here Gal, look he's lost his bottle and he's sorry'. I'm not proud of it because I was a horrible bastard, but I said if he told me he was sorry and I felt he meant it then I would walk out. The owner then looked at me and said he was truly sorry and asked if we could just forget the whole incident and apologised because he didn't know I was Darren's brother. I felt sorry for the bloke and said OK let's forget about it and we shook hands. We walked out of there and no-one was hurt. I just wanted to neck some pain-killers, get some kip and get my arse to the dentist in the morning.

The reason I have shared this story is because I want to share the way I was feeling at that particular time of my life. I hated the thoughts that were going through my mind 24/7, so I didn't mind getting bashed because I would have preferred physical pain to the mental torture that was embroiling my mind. I didn't have the bottle to top myself and really didn't give a shit if someone else done the job for me.

CHAPTER 34

New Set of Railings and Returned to an Old Pair

After a few days sleep my wounds started to close up and heal, so it was time to visit a dentist. I knew one that I could go to where no questions would be asked, but it would cost me a few quid, so I visited this dentist on Whitechapel Road a few days after the club incident and asked the receptionist if I could have a chat with the on duty dentist. She couldn't help but notice my front tooth was hanging out of my mouth so off she went to get the dentist. The dentist, who we'll call Rose, came back looked at my mouth and told me to follow her. When we were alone I told her I was on the run from prison, I would pay anything she asked but I could not put my name down on paper. Good old Rose told me not to worry, she would sort it and I wouldn't have to pay a bean! I knew she was a good girl and could be trusted and I always recommended her to people. Over the years she had many clients go her way, so was happy.

Rose had to pull the tooth out that was hanging down because it had been away from the gum and root for too long. She pulled out that tooth and took a mould of my mouth and that day I walked out of her surgery with a temporary front tooth. She told me to go back in a couple of days and she would have a plate made for me with a tooth attached that I could wear. Longer term I would need a bridge, but she told me that this would take months.

I'd now been on the run for over a year and had seen Kim a few times and she was doing well. She had now moved out of Bin's house and had her own flat on Commercial Street near Spital-fields Market. She was decorating her new place and I'd offered to give her a hand and do some painting. I was now getting back to my old self and pushed the crazy thoughts out of my head, so I didn't ask Kim anything. I had now accepted that I must have had some sort of breakdown and had made up the crazy thoughts that had swam around in my head. I spent more time with my brothers and sisters, got on with things and my crazy thoughts were never mentioned and family life was back to normal. I just thought Kim had also had a breakdown and left it at that. I was still drinking but had cut down a lot and was feeling good.

Months went by and I still had to be careful as I still wasn't ready to go back inside. The treatment on my teeth was going well, Rose was happy and after a while she fitted the bridge and gave me a new smile I was happy with. After fitting the bridge that day Rose gave me an appointment to return in one month and gave me an appointment card so I didn't forget. I left Rose's surgery that day, walked along Whitechapel Road, turned into Valence Road and heard a car tooting me up. As I turned, I saw it was someone that I really didn't want to see or talk to. I ignored them and carried on walking as they were shouting that they wanted to talk to me. The car then pulled over in front of me and this person asked me to get in the car, so I told them I was late and had to be somewhere. They said it wouldn't take long so I got in the car and told them not to drive off and to pull over onto the side of the road.

I was sitting in the car not really taking any notice of what was being said, but if what they were saying was true then I was thinking oh fuck. As they were talking, I was fiddling with the appointment card because they were winding me up. I then said I'd talk to them in a couple of weeks because I just wanted to get out of the car. I really didn't need it, they were giving me the hump so without thinking I chucked the appointment card on the dashboard, got out of the car and walked off.

I didn't think much of what had been said at the time, but it played on my mind and within a week I was back on the brain train because if what this person had said was true then everything I'd been through was also true. I was now doubting what my brother had said to me and questioned whether he had fucking lied to me that Bin was a nonce. I started to wonder whether I hadn't lost my mind beforehand. I started to drink heavily again, I began chain-smoking and again couldn't sleep. I felt like I was in a cell again.

I didn't know what to do to get to the bottom of everything, which is all I wanted to do. What I really wanted to do was walk up to Bin's door, boot it off and beat the living daylights out of him. I kept thinking of the pact that my brothers had made that day in the hospital and they were taking it to their graves, ready to protect Bin until the end. I wasn't unwell, it was my brothers who were sick. They were keeping their sick pact no matter what happened to their other siblings who were losing their minds in the process. They really quite obviously didn't give a fuck. I ended up locking myself away with my thoughts in my bedroom for a few weeks. This done me no favours as I was sinking into a deeper depressed state.

After those weeks locked away I then had the dentist appointment to see how I was getting on with the bridge and the teeth I'd had fitted. I managed to get off my arse and get washed and dressed for the first time in weeks and got myself to the dentist. I was not ready for what happened next. I walked along Whitechapel Road and through the market just as I'd done so many times when I was younger going shopping with my mum and as a street urchin on the prowl for unchained down goods for the take. I arrived at Rose's surgery and as I walked through the door two blokes were walking down the stairs and as I made eye contact with them I heard people shouting and then running from the street into the surgery behind me. I hadn't quite shut the door behind me and my hand was still on the handle. I then noticed that one of the blokes walking down the stairs put his hand in the inside of his jacket and knew they were old bill, so turned and walked out the door I'd just walked in. Within a split second, I was on the street thinking I needed to get on my toes and have it away. I know Whitechapel like the back of my hand and just as I put my left foot out to take off it was game up. I heard and saw further plain-clothed old bill coming towards me, they were on me within a second and I was manhandled and pushed up against the wall with five of them holding and surrounding me. All of the shouting then stopped and one asked me if I was Gary Hutton and said he didn't want any trouble from me. The other coppers were searching through my pockets, found nothing and said I was clean. They then put the bracelets on me and I didn't say a word. To be honest I was in shock and my mind was shot anyway. I was then asked again if I was Gary Hutton and had a photo shoved in my face. I looked at the photo and knew there was no way I was walking away from this one, but thought I'd give it a go anyway. I told them that the person in the photo wasn't me and they had the wrong person. I said I was a Hutton but wasn't the one they thought I was and that my name was Rodney my nearest brother in age! They then started to search my body for tattoos and scars that were on record and the game was up because they found what they were looking for on my arms. I was then told I was under arrest for being at large and on the run from Her Majesty's Pleasure.

I questioned in my mind why hadn't I seen the old bill on the street and the side street I had walked down. The side street had been blocked off for me and I also hadn't clocked the cars. I knew why I hadn't seen any of this it was because I was unwell and not paying attention to what was going on around me. This was strange for me because I'd always been so overly cautious with my surroundings – I hadn't been called a paranoid cunt for nothing! I'd walked straight into the old bill's trap that was set out for me. I was put in a police van that had been called and taken to Leman Street Police Station.

I was booked in, asked nothing and I said nothing. Is all I knew was that I was going back to Pentonville. I was put in a cell, given a cup of tea and I nutted out for a couple of hours. The next thing that happened was so strange and still to this day I have no idea what it was about. I was woken up by the cell door being opened and in walked a tall fella with brown slicked back hair, white shirt, red braces, a pin-striped suit and a polished pair of brogues. This bloke looked so smart and had a copy of the F.T. under his arm. He looked like a banker or broker, he looked that sort. I couldn't help but think 'who the fuck are you'? There was no need for anyone to talk to me because I was a straight forward transfer back to prison.

As he walked in the cell, he said 'Hello Gary, how are you?' I looked at him and had no clue who he was. My expression must have said this because he said 'you don't remember me do you Gary'? He was winding me up by calling me by my name because I would have put money on it I'd never met the fella in my life. I said 'no' and left it at that so he tried to tell me I should remember him because he remembered me when he was on the beat on Chicksand and who I used to knock about with. The person he said I used to knock about with I knew, but I told him he'd got me mixed up with someone else. He said he wasn't mixed up and that me and so and so would always be around Chicksand together. The bloke he was referring to likes to take rides in helicopters! I had no idea what this copper was after or

257

what he thought he was going to gain by talking to me. I told the copper I had no idea who he was talking about and asked him to leave so I could sleep. He then said he thought he'd just pop in and say hello, so I told him to shut the door on his way out.

The bloke the copper was talking about got nicked a while after that meeting in the cell. He'd apparently been a part of a bit of work involving £100m in bonds and been under surveillance for months. I believe this copper thought he would try his luck on me, but hit a brick wall because I know no-one.

While I was awake in the cell I started to think yet again and I knew I'd been set up and I knew by who. Leaving an appointment card in someone's car was not a good idea. When I left that car that day, I did think to myself at the time that I could not go back to the dentist, so why did I?

I was returned to Pentonville and was ready for help and ready to help myself. I was booked in, given prison clothes and seen by a doctor. I was given the once over and I told him that I needed help. I told him I'd been on the run for 18 months and for most of that time I'd spent it in a room locked away with my thoughts. I told him that the last time I had been in prison I'd been put in a straightjacket in a padded cell and I'd not been the same since. The doctor told me he would put me on the hospital wing so I could be checked out and that's where I was given a cell.

I knew I wasn't well but wow there were some strange people on that wing. All types of people shuffling around and literally in worlds of their own. There was no point in me thinking that I wasn't unwell and didn't belong there on that wing because I may not have been as unwell as some of those in that hospital, but I was unwell and in my own thinking bubble so in my own world kind of. I really couldn't be around any of the other inmate patients to see how bad some of their conditions were so settled in my cell and didn't come out.

One woman screw noticed that I was washing head to toe in the sink in my cell and asked why I wouldn't use the showers. I told her I'd had enough of prison and the bollocks it came with and that whether I was in or out of my cell I was still in prison all the same. I told her that I could drink, wash and eat in my cell and if I wasn't brought food I wouldn't eat. They brought food to my cell for months and that's where I stayed.

They would give me tablets and I saw a doctor a few times who I told I was so depressed I just wanted to be on my own. There was no way I could tell him what was going on inside my head and what I thought was going on in my family. I still didn't have 100% proof of what I thought was going on and fighting against it was making me unwell. I didn't know what drugs I was being given, but I was sleeping so my head wasn't on the brain train at least.

Weeks went by and I got to see three shrinks, one of which told me I was having a breakdown and it appeared to have been going on for quite a while. This doctor, who was the first to examine me, told me that in time, with the right help at the right hospital I would recover. To be transferred to a hospital and out of Pentonville all three shrinks would have to agree that I was unwell which they eventually did. I was informed that as soon as a bed became available I'd be transferred to a proper hospital. Up until that point one screw nurse did not believe that I was unwell and was a pain in the arse. He'd come into my cell and say there was fuck all wrong with me and each time he did I told him to fuck right off because I couldn't be bothered with the prick. On the last day before I moved to St Clement's, where Kim had been, he would not give me my daily prescribed medication. He told me that I wasn't going to make a mug of him and walked off and as he did I told him he was a muppet and not a real doctor and he'd better get back to my cell and give me my meds. I never did see that prick again.

The following day I was told to get ready and pack my belongings because I was being transferred to St Clement's. Walking out of that cell after being cooped up for months was strange but I was pleased I was going somewhere that would be able to help me. I'd started to think straight again and in my mind I knew what I knew and I was going to deal with it in my own way and in my own time.

CHAPTER 35

Reflection, Progression and New Beginnings

After packing my belongings I was on the move again but this time to a hospital; St Clement's on Mile End Road in the East End. I was handcuffed and escorted by two screws one on each arm who drove me to the hospital which is just around the corner from the home I was in as a kid. As with all hospitals there are many wards and I was chaperoned on to the secure ward where the other psychologically unwell patients were.

Most people fear sufferers with mental health problems because they don't understand it. It's something we're unsure of and uncomfortable with so we tend to stay away from these people which when you think about it isolates someone who is isolated in their own mind anyway. We're all busy in our lives and don't take the time to understand this disability. If someone is admitted to such a hospital, they are coated with the stigma of disgrace and this is feared and dreaded amongst 'normal' people. Very rarely will you see 'get well' cards in a mental hospital. Well wishes from your nearest and dearest also rapidly disappear. People naturally think 'so and so has lost the plot, best keep away'.

If you see someone who has a problem with another part of their body and they have to stay in hospital you naturally feel sympathy towards them and step up your show of love for them. For example, if I break my leg and am put in hospital to be cared for, my leg is put in a cast, and I'm given some painkillers and given time to rest. This is because I've attended the correct hospital, seen doctors who know and clearly understand what is wrong with me and know how to put me right. It is no different with

261

the mind as you are taken to a hospital to find the right care. The problem with a mental disability and the reason we fear it is because we can't see it.

Believe me, I take the time and always talk to people who suffer with mental illnesses and there is always a reason for their breakdown in life. They may not be able to express themselves in a way we would like and may not be able to talk about it, but something in their past has damaged them psychologically which is why they end up the way they do. Most of the time, help can be found but, unfortunately, this is not always the case.

I was processed on the secure ward, my transfer papers were signed and I was handed into the care of the hospital. I was no longer a prisoner as such but still had to serve out the remainder of my sentence at the hospital plus beyond my sentence if it was felt necessary. I arrived at St Clement's not having really told anyone exactly what was going on inside my head. I was being treated for my behaviour in Pentonville because I'd locked myself away plus locking myself away when on the run. They couldn't understand why I'd chosen to confine myself in my cell for months and why I'd chosen not to have contact with hardly anyone. In my mind at that time, it was the only way I could keep myself calm.

While I was in Pentonville, there was a bloke in there who I had known when growing up, Georgie. He used to take the time to come into my cell and talk to me over a cuppa. The nurse screw who looked after my tablets would question him because she thought I was pulling a fast one. Me and Georgie would talk and he never asked me anything too deep and I never told him what was going on inside my head. He was just an old pal there for me if I wanted to see to anyone. I have so much respect for that man and have a lot of time for him.

After I'd been processed at St Clement's, I was shown to a room where I'd be sleeping and I was also shown around the ward. I was taken outside and shown the garden which had a 30 foot wall surrounding it. I remember thinking to myself 'how the fuck did Kim escape over that wall?' I had no desire to do the same as I wanted to leave that hospital understanding my mind and moving forward with a way to get on with my life.

I was introduced to the other people on the ward. There were only four of us, two other men and a woman. Every day was pretty much the same, we were given our meds in the morning, had breakfast, watched telly, had lunch, watched more telly, given more meds and then it was time to sleep. The two other blokes on the ward were OK one was a younger fella and the other older.

The young woman on the ward was a funny girl and would talk to me all the time. She had lovely long blonde hair that she would wash three or four times a day. She was very unwell but did not have one bad bone in her body, she was so kind. She told me that she had had a very high powered job in the City and a great lifestyle but had lost it all when she became unwell. She would come and sit next to me when I watched telly and I was aware that she had taken a shine to me so I kept her at arm's length but still spoke to her. One day she lapsed and cut all of her hair off. I asked her why and she said it was too much to look after and it got on her nerves. Her hair was in a style of its own, there was long bits, short bits and bald bits. She looked like she'd had a row with a lawn mower and lost.

St Clement's was close to where my whole family lived, so they'd bring me food daily. I would phone and ask for pie 'n' mash, beigels and my favourite curries. One day two of my older brothers came to see me and both had confused looks on their faces. As they sat down they asked me what was wrong and why I'd been sent to St Clement's. I looked at both of them and told them they knew why. I told them that I could not get that day in the hospital out of my head when Bin had told us, his sons, what he had done to his own daughter. They had the gall to insult me further and look at each other and then say they didn't know what I was talking about. One of them went so far as to say that they had no clue what I was talking about and wasn't there. They then left the hospital and said they'd visit me another time. I didn't see them again while I was in hospital and I didn't want to.

In my mind I processed my situation as you can't break something that was already broken which was me, I was broken. They were not willing to help or going to help fix me so I didn't need them. I knew the truth and they were a barrier protecting a paedophile and I'd have to go about getting the truth without them on my side. I believe they knew what had been happening at home long before that day in Bin's hospital room. I questioned why one of them left our family home at the first opportunity he got. He must have seen something or come across something like I did that day when I was playing football and let myself in to go to the toilet and Kim's bedroom door was locked. I was too young to understand, but my brother was older than me so had he seen something and understood and knew it was wrong and that's why he chose to get out of our family home? Also, why that day in the hospital was it only me who reacted with hatred and why had Bin singled me out as the only one who would want to kill him? Why hadn't any of them reacted in the same way? They already knew before that day and nothing will change my mind on that.

What saddens me is the good old saying 'there is no love like a brother's love'. You can keep that saying because the four brothers there that day are animals. At one point in my life, I wanted to change my name because I may look like my brothers but our insides are made differently. I have courage, integrity, loyalty and soul and those four couldn't muster up one of those attributes between them. They are their father's children and I am my mother's son.

The time had come for me to be discharged from hospital. Before I was let go, I was called to a meeting with the doctors and nurses who advised me I would be free to go home in a couple of days. They asked me how that made me feel so I told them I had been on some train ride during the last few years of my life and I wanted to disembark. I wanted to go for a walk and find myself and see what life had in store for me and I was looking forward to it. I told them I was done with crime as nothing good comes of it because you find yourself spending long periods alone in a cell and it's a waste of life and I had a lot to offer the world.

They appeared to like my speech and bought it. For the first time in my life I wasn't selling anything, I was speaking from the heart and was completely sincere in what I had said. At one point in my life you could have dropped me off in the desert and I would have been selling the best sand anyone has ever sold and I could have sold a ton of it to an Arab. I was done with the fucked up life I'd been living and had really reflected on where it had got me.

It was now 1999 and I was a free man. I didn't have to look over my shoulder anymore and could now walk freely and I loved it. I was given an appointment to return to see a shrink after one month to see how I was getting on which was normal procedure. As a free man I got myself fit and began running. I knew a bloke who had two places for the London Marathon in 2000 and me and Mark took those places. I returned to the shrink for the last time, just before the marathon, and he asked me if there was anything in particular I was looking forward to. I answered that yes there was, I was looking forward to running the London marathon and he laughed at me. At the time, I thought the shrink must have thought I was having a delusional dream. After running and finishing the marathon I think I know why he laughed at me, the human body is not meant to run 26.2 miles and that's all I'll say on that matter. It was a new beginning and a new start in my life.

I got on with my new existence, bought a car and started mini cabbing. I was happy to be a 'normal' person and live as regular people do and I liked cabbing because I was talking to people and it kept me busy.

Kim had now moved to a newly built flat in Stepney Green which was very nice, but she had started to drink heavily and I really felt for her. One day she had got so drunk she went to Bin's house and started to kick off. I was told that it wasn't the first time she had done this but usually she turned up during the night and not during the day. I was told she did this most nights when drunk and she'd be shouting things like 'you nonce'. During the evening, it would only be Bin and one of my sisters in the house and they would take no notice of her. I couldn't understand how my sister could hear Kim and not do or say anything, but I believe the same may have happened to her. The neighbours told me they could clearly hear and understand what Kim was shouting. One of my older brothers lived literally around the corner from Bin's house and could hear Kim also, but he did absolutely nothing.

This one particular day my younger sister phoned me and asked me to go to the house as soon as possible because she was about to fight with Kim. I knew Kim would kill her and I managed to get to the house before that happened. Kim was going nuts and wasn't listening to reason so all I could was put her in my car and get her away from those she wanted to hurt and before she got herself in trouble. She was in the back of my car sobbing and not making much sense. I was driving and not taking much notice to be honest as I just wanted to get her home and talk to her.

We arrived at her flat, I turned the engine off, faced Kim and asked her to tell me what was wrong as I wanted to help her, and I was desperate to help her. She looked up, wiped the tears from her eyes, looked at me and then up to the heavens and said 'my mum knows I'm telling the truth, it first happened on her bed when I was eight years of age'. Kim wasn't talking to me, she was talking to our mum and asking for help. I told Kim that she needed to go and tell someone and needed to get help.

All the time that poor girl was in St Clement's that fucking bastard did not leave her side. He did that so she didn't get the opportunity to speak to someone about what was happening in her life and what was going on in her head. He made sure he was there when she woke up and stayed until she was given her medication and went back to sleep. I was in prison at the time and my brothers were free to help her but chose not to. They kept up their pact in protecting their evil twisted dad no matter what the cost even the sanity of their own sister. I'm not sitting here saying I done everything I possibly could, but I was unwell myself and was being told by the same cretins that it was all in my imagination and I'm twisted for thinking such a thing. I was now hearing directly from Kim for the first time what I knew to be the truth and that I hadn't been insane myself with my own sick mind.

I took Kim into her flat, made her a drink and told her that I would do everything in my power to help her and get her the help she needed. We talked for a bit and I told her I would be back in the morning to start the ball rolling in moving her life forward. When I left Kim, she was calm and seemed happy with what we had discussed in getting help and moving forward. I wasn't thinking about going to the old bill, I was initially thinking about getting her help to get off of the drink. She needed to speak to a doctor for help before thinking about talking to the old bill.

The following day I arrived at Kim's flat and she was as drunk as a skunk and could barely talk. I couldn't make sense of what she was saying, but she clearly didn't want me in her flat. I pleaded with her to let me help her and told her I couldn't do it without her. She would not let me in so I left and went about my day and she carried on with her routine of getting drunk and going to Bin's house and kicking off which she did most nights.

I saw Kim out one day and she was walking along arm in arm with a bloke who she introduced to me as her new boyfriend. Following that encounter, on 25 January 2001, I found myself standing in the labour ward of the London Hospital looking at a beautiful baby girl and Kim being this baby girl's proud mother. I thought to myself that hopefully Kim would now sort her life out and this was now a reason for her to turn her life around. I was more than willing to do everything I could to help her. While she was in the hospital me and my brothers clubbed together and decorated Kim's flat to make it nice for her to bring the baby home to and got her everything she needed. At this time, I knew what my brothers were and still couldn't trust them as far as I could throw them but if it helped Kim for us to be getting on at that time, I was happy to do that so she was settled.

I went to see Kim frequently at her flat the first few weeks she was at home with her new baby girl. I would pop in as I was passing to see if there was anything she needed. She seemed to be doing really well, baby was doing well and Kim was coping. At the time I had no idea that that beautiful baby girl would become such a big part of my life.

Three months had now passed since Kim had left the hospital with her daughter and I was told that she was drinking again and had been seen out late at night with the baby in her pram. This was not good and trouble beyond belief was about to ensue.

CHAPTER 36

Betrayal

Early one morning I received a phone call from one of my older brothers, he asked me to meet him in Stepney Green. It sounded important so I went to him and when I got there, he was sitting in his work van. I jumped in the passenger seat and asked him what was going on and why did he want to meet me. He told me to look down the street which I did and I noticed a police car and asked him what I was supposed to be looking for. I also said to him that Kim lived in the block of flats opposite the police car. He told me to keep watching which I did. I saw two policemen get out of their car, walk to another plain car and speak to the people inside. There were three people in the plain car who got out and walked into Kim's block with the police behind them.

Now I was confused and asked my brother what the fuck was going on. As I asked him, he pointed and said to look back in the direction of Kim's block. As I turned, I could see a woman running across the road with a baby in her arms with the police and other two people close behind. They all got into their cars and drove off with the baby. I asked my brother what the fuck had he done and why had he brought me there to watch. I knew it was Kim's baby that that woman had been carrying. I knew if I went to Kim she would have been going crazy and it would have been dangerous. He told me that it wasn't him but our other brother and his wife, plus his own wife who had made the phone to social services. I couldn't believe what I'd just witnessed and what my own brother had allowed to happen and asked him how he could do such a thing to his own sister, his own blood.

I was in total shock, absolutely heartbroken, numb and just slumped in the seat. To this day that scene still plays over in my head and I could cry every time. How sick is that to take your younger brother to watch as social services take your niece off of your own younger sister. What he said next, sitting there in his van, was the icing on the cake of our brotherly love. He sat there in the driver's seat of his work van and said he wanted to tell me something. He knew what I'd just witnessed had fucked me in a big way and then went on to ask me if I remembered that day we were in the hospital when Bin had tried to top himself and we were in Bin's room and he'd told us what he'd done to Kim. What a fucking question. Like I had forgotten that. I looked at him and didn't say a word and then he told me that it was all true and I hadn't imagined it. He also told me that when he had left the hospital that day he had gone home and told his wife straight away what had happened. I asked him, for my own confirmation, that I hadn't made that day up in my own mind and he confirmed that I was not mad and it had happened. That was all I needed to hear and I got out of his van. That just shows the make of the bloke, his father's son.

In one way I was happy to find out I wasn't fucking insane, but on the flipside there was Kim and what she'd been through and was now going through as a result. I needed to help Kim and her baby. After my brother told me that, it occurred to me that my brothers with children had not only put their own kids in danger but everyone else's kids. They had let a paedophile be around children. They had let the children of our family and our family friends to be around Bin. This is something they have to live with and I hope it eats away at them because that makes them as bad as him. These people, my family, have no moral conscience whatsoever.

I contacted social services after Kim's baby was taken and put myself forward to care for her. I was made to jump through hoops, but she was totally worth it. At first they had no idea who I was and told me that they had to be in contact with the informants who were family members and to see if they wanted to take and care for the baby. It turns out 'the family' had declined and some of the family had gone so far as to tell social services to never contact them again. One of the family members, who portrays herself as a saint, told social services it was not possible for her and her husband to take the baby because their jobs wouldn't allow them the time to care for the baby. This is a fair enough reason, but when I asked the saint's husband why he didn't put himself forward, he told me that the real reason was because their own kids were so young and it wouldn't be fair on them. He also told me that he didn't know what his wife had said to social services until I had told him. When we had that conversation, he came across to me as gutted and shocked. I can sort of see the saint's reason that her kids were young, but was it really fair to put that three month old baby girl into care, not to be with her family, was that fair? My brother had appeared gutted and shocked because I believe he knew he had been hoodwinked.

By this time, one of my sisters had married and moved out of the family house but still spent all day at Bin's house while her old man was at work. I confronted her one day about social services phoning Bin's house as they said they had spoken to a woman and she would have been the only woman in the house as my other sister would have been at work. She, of course, denied that she had spoken to social services. The young social worker, a nice young girl who had phoned the house, told me that she was told to never phone the house again and that the family wanted nothing to do with the baby, shortly before having the phone slammed down on her. If it wasn't her who was it?

The whole family would come up with such bullshit to make themselves look good and make themselves feel better, but the bottom line was they wanted nothing to do with their own flesh and blood. One excuse they would love to tell anyone who would listen was that Kim would make their lives hell. Kim didn't make their lives hell and she certainly hadn't made my life hell, they had made her what she'd become which was unwell and in desperate need of help.

I put myself forward for caring for Kim's baby girl because my sister needed my help and I would have done anything for her. I also didn't want, years down the line, an 18 year old girl walking up to me and saying 'hello are you my uncle Gary?' I played this scene over and over in my head and could picture an 18 year old girl, a stranger, telling me how she had been in and out of care homes and foster care and how she'd become a smack or crack addict and ended up on the game. I could never have lived with myself knowing my own flesh and blood could be out there somewhere going through such trauma.

I proved to social services that I was the right person to have the baby in my care. In the initial stages, I had to sit in a room with Kim for eight hours to make her see that it was a good idea for the baby to be in my care. This wasn't a permanent arrangement it was just until Kim sorted her life out and got herself better. I was hoping and praying Kim would sort herself out. In the meantime, it was parks, ducks and squirrels every day for me and the baby and we got to know all the animals by first name.

This went on for a few years and it was tough. In a selfish way, which I didn't think of at the time, but in retrospect it helped me as a person because it made me the person I wanted to be and gave me the life I longed for. The baby became of age to start school which freed up a lot of my time so I started to speak to as many people as I could to find out information from people around my family and what they may have known.

When Kim had left school, she found her perfect job as a youth worker. With Kim's personality being a youth worker made her shine and was her calling in life. Kim could play pool, table tennis and snooker all to a very high level and it's what some people would call a misspent youth! The place she worked was five days a week and was a 9 to 5 job. It was a great place for kids. It was a place where they were safe if they were bunking off school.

I found out that one day while at work Kim had lost the plot and freaked out and had told one of her co-workers what had been going on in her life. At this point, she was 19 years old. I don't know what had brought her to that point to make her lose it that day but what I did know was that Bin would turn up at her place of work on a regular basis and demand money from her so he could go to the pub. The colleague Kim had confided in, who knew our family very well and over the years became a mentor to me, was very upset by what they'd heard and didn't know what to do and suggested she phone one of her brothers.

Kim chose one of my older brothers that day and he turned up to find Kim in a right old state crying her heart out. She told him exactly what she had told her workmate that she had been sexually abused all her life. Kim at the time was still living at home and I can't imagine what hell she was going through. Our brother told her co-worker that day that they must keep what Kim had confided to themselves and that he would do all he could to help her get over it – yes you read that correctly – get over it.

Kim's workmate was not happy with this at all and told them both so, but Kim pleaded with her co-worker that it was the best thing to do so they respected Kim's wishes. Her co-worker agreed but wasn't happy at all and over the years supported Kim as best they could. From that point, our brother went on to make things worse for not only Kim but himself. After I found this out it confirmed to me that when Bin had tried to kill himself and we were all in that hospital room that particular brother knew for a fact what that evil bastard had done to his sister and still, he had kept it to himself.

As I had more time when the baby girl started school, I went into the flower game and set up a few flower stalls which went really well. I started off with a barrow similar to that of when I was a kid that we'd used to move homes. Again, it had big wheels and was red and green in colour and was common in every London market. The one I bought I turned into the Rolls Royce of flower stalls and placed it in one of the out of town shopping centres right in the middle of the big named stores. I was selling flowers to people who when they'd left home that morning didn't have flowers on their shopping list. I brought the old style street market to the new shopping centres.

I was doing really well with my street patter and gift of the gab and soon turned it into a flower show. I progressed and bought one of those fancy garden houses and turned it into a shop. On Mother's Day and at Christmas I was selling more flowers than a high street flower shop. During Valentines week, I was selling flowers hand over fist. On Valentine's Day, I sold 3,000 roses not to mention all the other flowers, cuddly toys and anything else I had which was red or had a love heart on it. I built the business up and got another stall and again started with a barrow and soon after replaced the barrow with a lock up shop. The only downfall was the hours as I would have to get up at silly o'clock in the morning to buy fresh flowers and wouldn't get home until 9:00 pm, but the money was good. I wasn't doing it for the money though, I was doing something with my life which was my payday.

On one Valentine's Day, it was so busy there were six of us working and we were selling bouquets of roses faster than we could make them. I was taking the orders and the money and passing on the orders to be made. A bloke walked in and I thought 'I know him' and within a split second the penny dropped. I didn't say a word and let him order his bouquet of roses and made small chitchat about how expensive roses are this time of year. He gave me his order and I charged him £80 and he gave me the money without a thought even though I'd charged him £30 over the odds.

As he was waiting I said to him with a big smile on my face 'you don't remember me do you'? He looked at me confused and was studying my face but said 'no I don't sorry'. Still smiling I said 'oh you should, how can you forget me?' What I said next turned him into a mumbling wreck. I said 'do you remember the words We Smash £5m Fake Racket, does that ring any bells?' His face turned to one of pure fright, but still he said 'no sorry'. I told him 'yes, you're Roger the reporter who once worked for the News of the World'. He looked at me and the penny dropped for him but not all the way. He said to me that he knew me and that my mate wanted to kill him and had chased him a couple of times in his car. I looked at him and had now stopped smiling and said 'Roger I am my mate'. He basically shit himself. His flowers were now ready so I took the bouquet and whacked him straight round the face with them. The heads of the roses flew off and I handed the worm of a man what was left of his loved ones bunch of stems and told him to fuck right off. He was only too happy to oblige and ran. I could have beaten the shit out of him, but what for?

CHAPTER 37

Cloud of Devastation

After Kim was separated from her daughter and the baby was placed in my care, my whole thought process changed. This little girl who could not fend for herself was relying on me for stability and to be raised in the best way possible and this kept me extremely busy as any new guardian will know. Kim was still getting drunk and had fallen into the highest level of alcoholism which is such a dreadful illness and heart-breaking to witness. What with the abuse, pain and suffering she had endured causing her unbalanced mind, I believe she drank to try and alleviate or forget the hurt and anguish she'd had her whole life. I know my brother Darren would try and help Kim but she wouldn't accept it. My other brothers and their wives had added to her torment by calling in social services. I know now looking back that Kim couldn't cope with a new-born baby, but they could have helped her manage better, not put the nail in the coffin by doing what they did and adding to her pain.

Kim was still turning up at Bin's house on a regular basis and shouting at the top of her lungs. I received a phone call one evening telling me to go to the London Hospital as Kim had gone there of her own will complaining of a severe headache which didn't sound good. By the time I arrived she had been put in a sedated state as the doctors feared she had bleeding on the brain. I asked if she was talking when she had admitted herself and was told that she had walked into the hospital and not arrived in an ambulance. For some reason, this gave me some comfort knowing this because she was up and mobile when she'd arrived.

I remember being at the hospital and my brother who'd made me witness Kim's baby girl being taken from her and my cousin Johnny were there and we were told by the doctors that they were going to keep Kim sedated for the time being and transfer her to intensive care so further tests could be done to find out what was happening. We were also told that following the tests they would advise us of the way forward, but they also said they were not too hopeful of the outcome because the scans they had taken so far were showing a very bad bleed on her brain. This was devastating to hear.

We spoke amongst each other and thought it best to go home and return the following day when more information would be to hand. As the three of us were leaving the hospital my cousin, who knew nothing about anything, was asked by my brother to go to Bin's house and inform him what was happening to Kim. Unbeknown to me, since my brother had confirmed to me in his work van that what Bin had said that day in the hospital was true, he had stopped speaking to Bin. As my cousin Johnny walked off I turned to my brother and said he couldn't do that to Johnny and that Kim didn't need the cunt Bin and fuck him. He said to me that if Johnny wanted to go there then let him. I reminded him that he'd just asked Johnny to go there to tell Bin. At the time, I knew it was wrong but I just had to get home.

The following morning I was up bright and early and straight to the hospital. I sat by Kim's bedside until late that night and did so for the following two weeks. I would ask lots of questions of the doctors and nurses and one day for the first time in my life I heard the word aneurysm. I was informed that Kim had one on her brain and it had burst. I was told in simple terms it was like a blister and that you could happily live with one for your whole life and not know it was there but also that one day it could burst. In Kim's case, it had burst and taken half of her brain with it.

All the time I sat with Kim I would talk and talk to her and tell her everything that her baby girl had been up to and how she was growing and the funny little things she would do. One day I was sitting there talking and all of a sudden was filled with so much hope, Kim started to pull the tubes out of her mouth and her eyes were open looking at me, they were begging me to help her. She was heaving where she had pulled the tubes out. I jumped up and told her to stop pulling them out as they were there to help her and I told her that she was OK. I ran to get the nurse and told her what had happened and as we got back to Kim's bed, she was in a sleeping state again. The nurse told me this happened a lot with patients in a sedated state. My hopes vanished that Kim was pulling through.

Time went by and the doctors told me that they wanted to talk to the whole family as a decision on Kim's future had to be made. I wasn't talking to anyone so left that to my brother to sort out. He pulled together every member of my family and we were put into a room. The only person who wasn't there was my brother Paul. I went along with, or should I say I had to go along with, Bin being there. It was the closest I had been to this man in years and every bone in my body was screaming at me to kick the bastard's head in, but of course, I couldn't, my sister was dying in the next room.

We were told that the tests had been completed and that Kim's brain stem was dead and there was no chance of her ever recovering. They wanted us to decide when, not if, we wanted the life support machine turned off which was keeping her heart beating and oxygen circulating through her blood. Kim's brain had died.

I left the room we were in and there in the corridor of the hospital I dropped to my knees and started to punch the walls while screaming 'why?' over and over again. I couldn't believe the crushing news we'd just been delivered. This was the ultimate blow like none I'd taken before. I'm not ashamed to say I cried like a baby, it was all I could do as the pain was unbearable. My head could only focus on Kim's painful life and how she would never see her baby grow up to be a lovely looking girl with buckets of personality, an image of her mum. This still kills me to this day as she is a mini Kim.

The following day I found myself standing by Kim's bed in a cloud of devastation at what was about to happen. My immediate family were there apart from my brother Paul. My cousin was also there and the hospital priest. My brothers and sisters were huddled around Bin cuddling him which killed me. I knew I couldn't say or do anything, but it sickened me to see them do this.

The doctors had warned us that once they turned off the life support, Kim would just pass. As they turned off the machine, my big sister Kim peacefully slipped away. I cried a sea of tears and prayed with the priest. I had never known pain like it, it was so deep and no amount of tears would take it away. I couldn't deal with it, the grief pulled me in like the strongest of sea waves. I made my way home because I had to be on my own. I cried and cried and was hit with guilt and 'what ifs'.

After a while, I started to concentrate on remembering the good times we had shared as kids. I had to pull myself together for Kim's baby who needed me now more than ever. Me and Kim had shared so many fun times especially playing football. Kim would do some crazy things just to get a laugh out of people which made me smile through the tears. All through focussing on the good times we shared, I couldn't shake off the darker side of what she had been through at the hands of that lowlife scum, Bin.

A couple of days after Kim passed my older brother who had been at the hospital with my cousin contacted me regarding funeral arrangements. I told him that I would not be involved in the arrangements, but I would speak in the church about Kim's life and I would carry her to and from the church and I would also place Kim in her place of rest of which I wanted the deeds. I also told him that I would not be getting in any of the funeral cars with him or any of my other brothers and sisters and I would have nothing to do with them. I told him that the fucking nonce had better not come near me and that he should not even be there. I also said during that phone call that when I spoke in the church I would be telling everyone present what that vile bastard had done to Kim. In my mind, Bin killed my beautiful sister. If she hadn't been drinking, she may have gone to the doctors or hospital sooner. Drink stopped her from doing this and Kim's excessive drinking was 100% Bin's fault by him raping her mentally and physically for years.

My brother begged me not to say anything in the church as it wasn't the time or place so I asked him when the right time to speak out was. There was no point in us carrying on the conversation as I was feeling irate and had nothing more to say. The following day I'd had time to calm down and promised him I would not say anything in the church with regard to Bin's violation of our sister but told him that I would be talking and would be giving the farewell a brother should give.

Over the next few days, I struggled and really couldn't handle the thought of Bin being at Kim's funeral and I couldn't believe my brothers and sisters were happy about this. It played over and over in my mind and drove me mad that that pig would dare show his face at the destruction he'd caused and I had to do something about it, I just couldn't let it go.

One night I got in my car and drove to Bin's house with a lock knife in my pocket. No-one knew what I was doing, but I knew what I had to do. I pulled up at the paedophile's house knowing he would be sat in front of the telly, got out of my car and without breaking my step as I walked towards the house kicked the front door off its hinges. I was in the house walking towards the end of the hallway and one of my older brothers appeared with my younger brother Darren in tow. My older brother's face expressed fear and he knew exactly why I was there. I told him to get out of my way as I wasn't there for him and didn't want to hurt him and said the same to Darren. Before I go any further, Darren was not at the hospital the day Bin tried to top himself, so didn't know what his dad had done to his sister. They both asked me what was wrong so I told them to fuck off as I ran at them. They both grabbed me. I went mad and lost the plot. I was shouting for Bin calling him a nonce but, of course, the cunt didn't show his face.

My brothers both had hold of me tight and ran me out of the house. I asked my older brother how he could sit there with that fucking nonce and he told me he didn't know what I was talking about. Darren was confused and didn't have a clue what was going on, but said that if I wanted to fight someone he was game. This statement made me flip. By this time both of my sisters appeared outside the house and my younger asked our older brother who I was calling a nonce. He turned to her and said that I was calling him a nonce and that I'd lost the plot, he was still protecting Bin even though we were about to bury our sister. This sent me over the top and if Darren was game so was I but we were kept apart with our siblings pleading with me to get in my car and go. My older brother who lived around the corner then came running from around the corner with a baseball bat in his hand. He lived less than 50 yards away so could hear the shouting from his house.

When I think about this, it pisses me off because when Kim used to scream and shout outside Bin's house he never came running to help her, but as soon as he heard someone was threatening his dad, there he was. A couple of months after that incident when I went to Bin's house, the same older brother who chooses when to hear and when not to asked me something which completely sums him up. He said to me one day that he knew I was telling people about what Bin had done to Kim to which I replied yes I was because it explained her life and the hurt she was feeling by what that man had done. He turned to me and actually said I was right because it did explain her life but then asked me not to tell people that he knew what had gone on. I could do no more than just walk away from him.

In the week leading up to Kim's funeral, I saw one of my older brothers for the first time in a very long while. I told him that I knew he had known for many years what Bin had done to Kim and I knew about the day that Kim had lost the plot at work and he'd been called to help her. As I said this to him the blood drained from his face as he didn't know whether I was going to knock him out or not and to be honest I don't know how I didn't. I questioned him why he'd never done anything about it or told anyone and why he still treated Bin like a king by giving him money and buying him clothes and I told him that his sister was dead because of that animal. He couldn't answer me, so I told him he was a cunt and no better than Bin and I later found out that he was telling our brothers and sisters he'd spoken to me for the last time in his life.

I did speak to him again, twice. Once, to say sorry to him. The reason I said sorry was because I found out that he had also been a victim of Bin. Unbeknownst to me when I'd had a go at him before Kim's funeral he'd had a breakdown. He'd climbed up six flights of scaffolding and tried to commit suicide by jumping off. What he'd kept secret all those years was too much inside his mind. After jumping, he had to have metal plates inserted in his back and was in a bad way. He also spent time in the Priory as he is fortunate enough to go there.

What he told the doctors though shows he is not of sane mind. He told the doctors that he was a paedophile and every time he washes his nieces and nephews he touches them inappropriately. This is utter bullshit because I swear on my life that if he passed them in the street he wouldn't even know who they were and vice versa and he was never near them as babies and certainly never bathed them. My sister told me this as the doctors had contacted her and she told them the same thing. I believe one of two things. Firstly, he was abused by Bin also or secondly he couldn't live with what he knew about Kim and not getting Bin put away for it.

Why do I think Bin also abused my brother? I found out that Bin swings both ways or was gay trying to live a straight life. He had been caught a few times in the company of men which were words that had escaped my mum's mouth all those years previous. My mum had been in the garden hanging out washing one day and had been upset and ranting and our neighbour had called across and asked her if she was OK. My mum replied and said she was OK but had only caught that bastard with a man again.

This also made me question why Paul was so fucked up and forced to live on the street at such a young age. I found out that

Paul was living in a street off of Whitechapel Road so went to see him and tell him about Kim passing and give him the details of her funeral. I knocked on his door and he opened it but only enough to fit his head through. He looked at me like he didn't know who I was so I told him I was his brother Gary and he said hello and that was it. I told him about Kim and his response was 'OK thank you' and shut the door in my face. I think that Paul had been subject to Bin's disgusting ways also and this explains his mental problems.

CHAPTER 38

Hardest Day of my Life

A week before the funeral my brothers and sisters were busy preparing for the day. I had made it clear that I would not put a penny towards costs because not one of them had tried to help since I'd taken care of Kim' baby, so it was their turn. I didn't want or need money from them, but the offer would have been nice and if the boot had been on the other foot, I would have made sure I'd done my bit to help them out but they're a different breed of people.

One memory that still haunts me on how sick they can be was when I was walking along one day taking Kim's daughter to an inner-city farm and bumped into one of my cousins. We stopped for a chat and I was gobsmacked at what came out of her mouth and what she had been told by one of my sister in laws.

My cousin said she thought it was a lovely thing that me, my brother and sister and law were doing by looking after Kim's daughter so I asked her what she meant. She had been told that I cared for the baby three times a week and my brother and sister-in-law had her for the other four days. I told her it wasn't true and asked who had told her that because she had been lied to. My cousin told me it was my sister-in-law who had told her and said to me that she believed my sister-in-law because why would she lie. I informed her that my sister-in-law is a liar, who like the rest of them have a lot of guilt and that they'd never cared for or helped with the baby.

My cousin was looking at me like I was nuts and feeding her bullshit. I could see from the confusion on her face that she'd been lied to and there standing before her she thought I was the liar because my sister-in-law is church going. She likes to give the impression that she's a saint when in fact she's a hypocritical, slippery, evil woman so much so that a few years later when Kim's daughter started school at St Anne's I had to take her out and change her schools. My sister-in-law worked at St Anne's and started to tell Kim's daughter things about Kim. Why she felt the need to tell a five year old child that her real mum was a drunk is beyond me and beggars belief.

The day of Kim's funeral arrived. I knew it was going to hit me hard and I was worried about holding it together for when it was my turn to speak about Kim's life in the church. I made my way to St Anne's by driving myself in my car. This church holds so many memories for me all throughout my life. It was also the school we went to as kids and where me and Kim found our love of football and honed our skills with the ball in the play-ground. I arrived at the church early and it was a lovely sunny day so I waited outside. People started to arrive and one person came over to me and told me they had been to the family home and everyone was there. I held my tongue.

Hundreds of people attended to pay their respects and not only was the church packed but also the street outside. I stood by my-self outside the church doors and greeted and said hello to peo-ple I knew and hadn't seen in a long time. I was smoking fags and eating mints like no-ones business. The emotion running through me was a rollercoaster of up and down. I wasn't sure in my own mind whether or not when it came to my turn to give my eulogy that I wasn't going to say anything about what Bin was because I was desperate to tell the world. I kept telling my-self that I'd given my word that I wouldn't. I was truly torn be-cause in my world I believe in life you can have it all money, houses, cars, love and friendship but without your word you have nothing. Your word can get you all you need in life and I will never break mine once it's made.

My mum's sister, aunt Nora, walked towards the church with her family and I could see that my uncle Michael was very upset because Kim was his favourite. We greeted each other and as me and my aunt hugged each other I could feel her fighting to hold on to herself. As we were about to part from our hug, I looked up and could see the funeral procession arriving led by the hearse carrying my big sister.

They came to a stop outside the church and the car doors were opened and my family got out. One of my sisters was in the first car and helped Bin out which made me feel sick. She held Bin's arm as they walked into the church and he tried to look sad. I just kept thinking to myself that I couldn't do it, I couldn't watch my brothers and sisters comfort this man, but was also telling myself that I was doing it for Kim and I must let it go for today and give her the best send-off possible.

As everyone entered the church me and my brothers were told to hang back, were paired up and asked to stand in two lines behind the hearse. We lifted our sister's coffin on to our shoulders and slowly walked into the church as Kim's favourite song played; Greatest Love of All. The lyrics of the whole song are special, but the words 'I believe the children are our future, teach them well and let them lead the way' are so special and so apt for Kim.

Fighting back the tears we reached the altar and placed our sister down where a very large beautiful photo of Kim was standing so she could be seen throughout the service. I left my brothers' sides and sat on the opposite side of the church, separate from all of my family and my older brother, Michael, did the same and sat next to me.

The priest began the service and I struggled to focus on what he was saying because I was fighting back the tears and shaking. I felt like I was in a dream state where I could hear and see everything that was going on around me, but it was all unreal. I then heard the priest call my name to the altar and inform everyone that I was going to say a few words. As I approached the altar, my brain was screaming at me not to look at anyone especially my family and Bin. All throughout the service so far I'd heard them crying and I knew if I looked at them I would say something.

I had written down what I'd wanted to say and I opened up the piece of paper and read the first line, but I couldn't read the rest of what I'd written and just talked off the cuff. I told stories of Kim when we were kids and the fun we would have and the things we had got up to. As I spoke I focussed on and talked to the faces at the back of the church and could see them nodding, smiling and laughing at the things I was saying. One thing I did say and everybody nodded and agreed with was that Kim could play football and it was the first time I openly admitted that my sister was better than me at the game to which everybody laughed and agreed with. Kim was so talented and gifted at a young age at football and better than anyone in St Anne's that day and they all agreed.

Closing what I had to say I asked and told everyone to keep and hold good memories of Kim and to remember she was a youth worker and gave a lot of her time helping people. I said that Kim had gone through some bad times in her life like we all do, and asked her friends to remember her as the life and soul of their nights out as she loved to sing and dance and made sure everyone around her had a good time in her company. Kim was loved because she was a lovely girl and that was proven that day by so many people turning up to pay their respects.

Since the day Kim passed, I had been looking for a song that could be played once I'd finished my eulogy. The song I wanted played was sung by someone I knew. Johnny K's little brother by that time had become a pop star and was at Kim's funeral that day and I'd chosen his song. I introduced the song and told everyone it was for my sister from me and her daughter. The song I chose has a line in it 'I'll be loving you forever deep inside my heart you'll leave me never'. I know this to be the case for Kim's daughter and in my case Kim will never leave my heart. As I left the altar, I fought back the tears, kissed Kim's coffin and returned to my seat where Michael grabbed my hand and told me 'well done'. The song played and I could hear tears all around me. I was numb and sat slumped staring at the floor, what I'd just done had completely taken everything out of me.

It was now time to take Kim to her resting place so we carried her out of the church. It was so hard with everyone so upset, seeing Kim's friends, girls that she had grown up with tears streaking their faces. I went back to my car, drove to the cemetery and walked behind the hearse focussing all the way on the photo of Kim. Everyone else were sat in cars and driven to Kim's place of rest.

At the time, I didn't think about what people thought about me having nothing to do with my family on the day of my sister's funeral. I wasn't near my family, grieving with them or getting in the cars with them, I didn't think about what people thought and even if I had of done, I wouldn't have cared. There was no way on this earth I was going to go along with that circus of a family comforting and cuddling a nonce, an animal, a subhuman who should have been put down at birth. All of them upset, playing victims – pure guilty tears from all of them.

As Kim was lowered to rest I walked away, I couldn't watch these vile bastards allow this man stand over my sister's grave. They should be ashamed of themselves.

The week leading up to Kim's funeral I had disagreements with my family and one particular disagreement was the plot in which Kim would be laid to rest. I wanted the deeds to the plot because I found out that the plot my siblings had acquired held two people. In my mind I knew why this had been done, I honestly believed they wanted to put their dad in the same grave as Kim. This was never going to happen in my lifetime and would have had to be done over my dead body. At the time, I told my brothers and sisters my thoughts in ways that was probably wrong, but I would have rather spent the rest of my life in prison than let that animal not let my sister rest in peace. What made it worse at the time was that one of my older brothers stole the deeds and as far as I know still has them to this day.

Following Kim's funeral some of my brothers and sisters started to question what they had done. One of my sisters questioned my brother who had stopped talking to Bin why he no longer wanted anything to do with him. This brother was now ready to tell the truth and told my sister what had happened in the hospital when Bin had said what he'd done to Kim.

My sister then knew some of what had happened over the years and made calls to the rest of our siblings apart from me and another older brother who she didn't contact at first. When she called my older brother who had been called to Kim's youth club and who later ended up in the Priory, she informed him she was going to confront Bin that day when she returned from work. He did no more and called Bin and told him what was going to happen, to get out of the house and go to the pub and he would pick him up later. My sister was none the wiser at the time of this and didn't know what a lowlife our brother was.

I have no idea for a fact what my sister knew apart from what our brother had told her, but to this day she knows what she knows and is willing to live with whatever that may be. Some things are best left unsaid and I will leave certain things that way.

When she arrived home, of course, Bin was nowhere to be seen and had scarpered like the weasel he is, so she was unable to confront him. She made some phone calls and in the end found out that Bin had moved in with our lowlife brother who had warned Bin. No surprise there.

After a couple of days, I went to this brother's house and knocked at the door. He took a while to answer and through the window I could see Bin running and looking for somewhere to hide. I knocked a few times and eventually the door opened just enough for my brother to poke his head through. When he did answer his face was pale, worried and he was shaking and stuttering. I told him I had come to his house for one reason only and that was to tell him to get that evil bastard out of his house. My brother's reply was that he'd called the police and that they were on their way. I told him I wasn't there to hurt anyone and that I thought he'd been through enough and it was time to tell the truth. I could hear police sirens drawing nearer so walked back to my car and left. I couldn't believe that he knew what Bin had done to Kim and still he'd taken him in and was protecting him. This told me a lot about him and apart from he is not well in the mind, he must be holding some very big secrets.

Since my sister had taken her stand, nobody could get hold of one of our older brothers to tell him what had happened. My other sister phoned me horrified that our other brother's wife, who had been previously involved in calling social services, had taken it upon herself that she should be the person to inform our brother's children about their granddad. Her reasoning for doing so was pure evil and the only person who should have been speaking to his kids was him.

Neither me nor my sister could get hold of him which we needed to do before our evil sister-in-law did, so we drove to our brother's ex-wife, who lived in Essex as we wanted to tell her to not let her kids take a call from evil sister-in-law because she was set on hurting our brother in any way she could. The short story is that evil sister-in-law was engaged to one brother, it fell through and she married another brother. She has a lot of hate in her.

When me and my sister found our ex-sister-in-law she was at work and we told her we needed to speak to our brother. She could see something wasn't right because my sister was very upset so we told her about evil sister-in-law's plan. She asked us why everyone had turned on Bin, so I told her about the day me and my brothers were at the hospital and Bin's curbed confession. She said that what I'd told her made a lot of sense as to why her marriage had broken down because my brother was always drunk. She said that she would make sure that her children did not answer the phone and she would speak to our brother. We were happy with this because it was right that they heard from their dad, not some twisted woman point scoring.

After a little time passing my sister who had taken the stand called us all, apart from our brother housing Bin, together at Bin's house. I turned up, walked into the front room and found

Darren crying so I walked over to him and put my arms around him. Darren told me he was sorry and that he thought I was mad because he had no idea what Bin had done. I told my little brother it didn't matter because now the truth was out and we now all had to deal with it but had each other. I let Darren go and as I turned round, I saw one of my older brother's sobbing. I couldn't help myself and shouted at him 'what the fuck are you crying for you cunt, you told me it never happened and that I was mad'. The sobbing prick looked at me and disgracefully said the words 'can't we just make out it never happened and let daddy live here'.

During that visit to the house, one of my sisters also asked me about my beating of nonces in Bullingdon and asked whether I knew about Bin at that time when I'd visited her. She pointed out that Bin had acted peculiar and looked scared that particular day when I was talking to her in the kitchen. I told her that I didn't know at that time and just thought he had the hump because I was puffing. Looking back, me talking about beating nonces that day had probably shit the life out of him and was why he'd pointed me out in the hospital and said I was going to killing him when he admitted part of what he'd done to Kim.

During that gathering, I took one of my sisters outside because I wanted a quiet word with her. When we were outside, out of earshot, I told her I wanted to be honest with her and that I thought she needed to go and see someone because if at any time she had been abused she would need help. She looked at me like I was a nutter and would have none of what I'd said. I know deep within me that this didn't just happen to Kim but that day she was adamant so I said what I had to say in way of support and left her alone.

Not long after our talk she was married. She had never had a boyfriend in her life. She sold the house for a lot of money of which some was Kim's money as Kim had bought into that house also. The house sold for £350k, but not a penny was given to Kim's daughter.

I could go on forever about my family and the things that have gone on, but I'll stop there apart from to say I do not speak to anyone in my family and as far as I know Bin still lives with my older brother who had warned Bin he was going to be evicted. One thing I am grateful for is that brother does not have the deeds to Kim's grave.

CHAPTER 39

Giving Back and the Key to Life

In chapter one, I said I'd let you be the judge of whether I'm a product of a postcode and I'm sure now you'll appreciate why some names have been changed or not mentioned. It was never my intention when starting this book to name and shame but was to speak of the truth. I'll now turn to how my life is today and explain my giving back.

The answer to the question 'am I a product of a postcode?' is yes, but the tail end of that answer is we are all products of our postcode. Wherever we are in the world, we all try and want to better ourselves in whatever way we know how. We are taught by our parents, peers and mentors growing up and these people are our strongest influences. These people set out a path in our young minds because that is what we are taught, so in my case, or part of my path, I was taught to steal and went on to further that path – it was all I knew and I wanted to better myself in that field.

While reading this book you may have thought that there would have been a different future if my mum hadn't passed away when I was so young. I have asked myself that question many times but that wouldn't have changed Bin and the way he behaved, things may have been slightly different in some aspects. At the end of the day my mum sadly did pass away when I was a small boy so I can't and shouldn't live with 'what ifs' because 'what ifs' never helped anyone. Me, my brothers and sisters didn't stand a chance and still live with the pain that Bin caused to this day. Some of my brother's drink daily and one of my sisters chooses to forget her past, but trying to forget and drinking to block things out is unhealthy because memories always return.

Eventually, I washed my mind of everything that Bin taught me because anything he did was for his own gain and protection from the evil things he had done. I took a long hard look at myself and questioned what does a person do who has come from a similar background? Many go through life moving from crime to crime and prison to prison and it becomes their way of life. Sadly, most of the time (not all), their children follow the same path. In my eyes, it's all about breaking chains from natural progression. The key to building futures is through education. Education leads to a better path in life and not just for the learning experience which is key but also for self-motivation, confidence in our own abilities and self-worth. I'm not rose tinting it, we're not all clever enough to become doctors and lawyers, but each have something we should channel our energies into in a positive way. My own personal path is teaching and educating people where I went wrong, so hopefully they will listen and don't follow in my footsteps.

My way of life has completely changed. I've turned it around and crime is a thing of the past and giving back is the way forward for me. The way I look at it is, if I do nothing to help youngsters out there growing up the same as I did, then I didn't learn anything from the way I'd lived my life. In my mind, it makes no sense to do nothing because I have the knowledge to benefit those who are heading towards the mistakes I made. Me and my sister, Kim, were similar in that respect but at different stages in our lives. Kim was hell-bent on giving her time which is why she decided to become a full-time youth worker. Even with all the shit she had had to deal with she still wanted to help kids have a better life than the shit one she had been dealt early on in her life.

Trust me, there are many young Gary's and Kim's all over the country, in every postcode, who are lost in life with no real role models or mentors to guide them into building a better life. That was something I'd lacked as a youngster and my poor sister Kim had faced the ultimate betrayal. Not once in my earlier years did someone sit me down and tell me the key to life or about the right path and how to go about it. I decided I wanted to find a way to help young people and knew I'd found my path, a path I chose for me.

I have a very good friend, Abddie, who I grew up with who works for a local council in South London. He has a past like me but turned his life around and now works for the council's Youth Offending Team. He works with young people who have come to the attention of the police and courts and have been given community service or similar as punishment for the crimes they have committed. I wanted to get into the same line of work as Abddie so started attending an evening college class to study counselling. I was looking to understand and learn how young people tick because I wanted to give something back long term. I hoped for an insight into how to deal with young kids, who were a younger form of me.

The first class I ever attended, I was sat in a group of people and we each had to say something about ourselves and why we were attending the course. I had never done anything like that before in my life and was sitting there shitting myself, having no idea what I'd say when it got to my turn. Those who spoke before me were all doing as asked and talked about themselves. There was no set time, some went on longer than others and I found it all very interesting what they were saying. It came to my turn and I was nervous. I stood up and started by saying I was there to understand young kids as I wanted to work with them. I told the group I knew I had something to give as I had been one of those kids and no-one knows street life better than a street urchin which is what I am. I carried on talking and could see the room were listening to every word I was saying so I knew I had them hooked. Time flew and before I knew it class was over but everyone then started asking me questions.

After class, the tutor told me that because of my background and upbringing I would make a perfect counsellor. She had thought my introduction had been great. I didn't have a clue, I'd just stood up and told those people parts of my life and the journey I'd been on which had felt great and given me further confidence in knowing that I had something to give. I attended the classes for a while but soon found out that counselling is all about working on yourself and that bored me because by that point in my life I had done so much work on myself I couldn't do anymore. The tutor was a lovely woman and when I told her I couldn't attend her classes any longer as I needed to find a different way to help young people, she told me that she thought there was something out there waiting for me and she was sure I would be helping a lot of young people in the future. I was more than keen to find out what that something was.

Abddie told me that his job ran a mentoring programme and they trained people to become mentors to troubled youngsters. While you're trained you work with young people who have been given community service orders by the courts. This was right up my street because you're meeting the youngsters while you're training and not just being trained in a classroom. I started on the mentoring programme and to start with it was great. We'd sit around and be asked all sorts of questions about the law, drugs, street life, gangs, crime and all manners of things and I found it interesting and found myself settling down. The people in the group were new to such way of life and I sometimes couldn't get my head around what some of them were coming out with. They came from all walks of life, but not one of them had lived an inch of what I had. They were there to be given an insight into the way of life that these troubled kids lived but I had lived it, it was my every day and had been my way of life.

I did the mentoring programme for a year and a half, but it wasn't for me. It was a great start into what I was looking for, but it wasn't what I was looking for. I got to meet many young people who had found themselves on the wrong side of the law and had been given court orders. Sometimes their court orders were to paint a wall in their local area, or do some gardening and I'd be right there painting or pulling weeds with them. Whatever they'd been told to do, I'd be there with them talking to them and initially they thought I'd been given a court order also and that I was one of them. I'd talk to them and be real. I'd tell them where their life was going and because I'm on their level they got it. I knew I could change lives which is all I wanted to do but didn't know how to make it happen.

When I was younger I had a very good friend I grew up with who had lived next door to me and who went on to run a very successful sports company providing PE teachers in schools. One day he asked me to give a talk in a school and that was my opening. My mission turned to going into schools and talking to the whole school. I started to go into schools and talk to the kids and they'd never heard anyone like me talk. I developed a way of talking about my life into a way of teaching that the kids could learn from, and it was and still is a powerful tool. Teachers would sit in my talks open mouthed as I talked to the kids in a real way so they respected me and what I was talking about. After a while, the teachers started to bring the so-called 'naughty' kids in their classes to have a chat with me and we'd have a one to one. The kid got what I was talking about and went about changing their ways. I'm not someone who walks away so I'd give the kids my phone number and stay in touch with them and if they came across a pitfall they'd give me a call and I'd help them deal with it.

In my talks I don't paint a rosy picture of the so called gangster bollocks bullshit that some kids seem to aspire to and believe in. I don't talk about the crime I got away with and boast that my mate is Al Capone, I tell them about the downside and the real truth about crime being a waste of life. I tell them about the time spent behind bars when you're sitting on your bed and cry like a baby because you miss the people you love most in the world and those people are the people you're really hurting and I tell them the truth in how I've seen some real tough men cry. I'm genuine and factual when I talk to the young men and women and that earns their respect.

After getting into schools, I then started going into youth clubs and on to housing estates and talking to the teenagers who were not going to school and I'm proud to say I've helped some kids out there turn their lives around. I would give a talk about a life without education and how education is the key to life. As I've said, we can't all be bankers and lawyers but we all have a passion for something. The significant point is to work with that passion, develop it and turn it into a path that leads to a better way of life. In many cases it is music, dance and art but it can all be built upon and these kids need to learn not to let opportunities pass them by.

When I talk to youngsters, I have a link into their lives because I've lived it and I turn that link into a tool which engages them. As mentioned earlier in the book, I was nicked quite publically and slapped on the front of the News of the World. I have a copy of that paper and got it laminated which I take into my talks. The kids are hooked by this and I use that hook, because it grabs their attention, and then get to the reason I'm giving the talk. They know I'm one of them, not against them and they can tell I'm from the same streets as them. I don't stand there in a suit and tie and preach about a way of life I know nothing about, but I talk about what's real and they relate to me. I talk about a life without education and the pitfalls and also talk about the benefits of a life with education. It has become a powerful tool and has changed lives including mine. The next chapter you will read a few words from some people I have met, talked to and guided. I'm not blowing my own trumpet by doing that but as I'm talking about guiding and helping people, I thought you should hear from some of them as evidence, seeing as I've asked you to judge me.

Apart from going into schools and youth clubs, I also went on to work with a number of London football clubs and got involved in their projects with communities and charities. I've just finished working on a government project called Youth Contract working with Not in Education, Employment or Training (NEET), working with 16 to 24 years olds all across London. Along with my lifelong friend and another pal, we used my talk to engage kids. We helped change lives by helping so many young people move into something positive whether education, employment or training, all part of the key to life.

CHAPTER 40
Wisdom and Hindsight

Emily

I was working at a place where kids go for help when they're in trouble and Emily walked in. I was there working on a project called Headstart with young people and using some office space. I was sitting at the back of the room, minding my own business and looking through some paperwork waiting for some young people to turn up that I had appointments with. Emily sat down and started talking to someone at the main desk and I started listening in, as you do. She was talking about what she had been nicked for and low and behold she'd been nicked for trying to spend moody money in an expensive shop in the West End. The seven or eight people in the room all turned round and looked at me and told Emily she needed to speak to me. I knew I had to help her because in a way I felt responsible for her crime even though I'd had nothing to do with the crime for years, it felt like my life had come full circle. Not long after I started this book I did work with Emily and hope in some way changed her life's path for the better. Emily's foster mum, Jenny, recently wrote to me as follows:-

"I first heard of Gary when my foster daughter went to Baseline in Lewisham, for help and support. Due to the nature of her being there, Gary decided he would like to help her. The sort of help he was offering was both practical and emotional support. Gary telephoned me almost immediately after meeting with Emily, to introduce himself to me and offer his support regarding finding appropriate courses and also being available to attend court. He came across as a very caring person. He made it very clear from the start that he would make himself available any time and place, if he possibly could. I found this to be very unusual, in a world where most people are only out for themselves that Gary, who had only met Emily once was prepared to go out on a limb for her.

Emily went to see him over a number of weeks, in which time he encouraged and guided her, through his own life experiences. He also attended court with her as further support.

I can only thank Gary for being there for both Emily and myself, at a time when we both needed it. His support and advice have been invaluable."

Emily also wrote a note:

"I had been arrested for using fake twenty pound notes when I first met Gary. I walked into Baseline (youth services) to tell my key worker what happened and as soon as I mentioned I was getting done for fraud all the people in the office sent me over to Gary assuring me he is the one to talk to. I told Gary everything that happened and about things I'd been through in the past as well. He said he wanted to help me get back into college and discuss different pathways for me to go down in my life. Gary helped me to get interviews and supported me in filling out forms and was always there for me to talk to no matter what the problem was.

My court date for the fake notes was approaching and Gary helped me prepare for court. He came to my trial as I pleaded 'not guilty' and he stayed there with me, my foster mum and my social worker. We were there all day. I got found guilty and a few weeks later I got sentenced to six month's youth rehabilitation order, two months on tag and a four hundred and ten pound fine.

Gary carried on to support me and is always there if I need any help or advice. When I first met Gary, I was a typical teenager with a not caring attitude, but he didn't give up on me, he still believed in me and my potential even when I didn't believe in myself. Thanks to Gary's help I am now in college studying to be a Personal Trainer aspiring to one day open my own gym and I hope to do mentoring for young people in the future."

Randy Osei-Owusu

I met Randy as a young boy and he was a keen footballer. I took him and some other young boys under my wing and got them to play for an under 16s semi-pro team. I could see Randy was a mini-me and one day I sat him in my car and mapped out his life for him with the way he was going and told him he was going to spend long periods of his life behind bars. His response to this was 'nah not me'. He was a nice young kid, but I could see where he was heading as it was written all over him.

"Gary Hutton is someone who've I've known for over 6 years. I first got to know Gary through football.

I've played with his oldest son in the same team and Gary also introduced me to semi-pro football which I found a very good experience in which I learnt so much. I see Gary as a lifelong friend and since I've known him, he's always been a role model and someone I've looked up to and respect so much.

He's always been there for me whenever I've needed him whether that's been for football or my personal life.

During my whole life I have had so many up and downs and I've made mistakes which have leaded to me serving long prison term.

I remember sitting in a car with Gary and him telling me to reevaluate my life, but I never listened cause when you're young you always think you know best.

I was hanging around with the wrong crowd and to be frank I thought and acted way beyond my years. To the average eye I was a respectable, well-spoken young man but it was almost as if I was living a double life involving gang violence and crime. In 2008 I was part of a group of people who went to rob a store which involved someone dying. I saw that as a big eye opener in my life as you would never in your wildest dreams believe you would be involved in such a thing.

A year later I was arrested and charged with murder and conspiracy to robbery which absolutely changed my life.

Gary was so supportive during this period even when most friends had turned against me.

He regularly visited me, and made me realise that mistakes should be learnt from.

Gary has become family to me and I have nothing but praise to speak of whenever he's name is mentioned.

He too knows how it feels to be young and almost feel as if the worlds against you in which you to become a rebel.

He relates to me even when my own family struggled to relate to me, he knew how I felt and always tried to help me better myself.

Having served almost 5 years in jail I've learnt so much and bettered myself physically and mentally and now see a brighter future for myself. And part of this was due to Gary Hutton's non-stop believing in me. When you're doing time in prison all you can do is sit and reminisce o past times of your life, it either breaks you or makes you. At times you feel as if the walls are squeezing in and you become restless.

It is very easy to be misled or influenced into more crime. Earlier on in my sentence I use to let temptation get the better of me.

Now I find it easier to say no. I've realised that the word friend can sometimes be overrated. As a young man who's coming to the end of my sentence, I'm filled with positivity and high hopes and believe this has been contributed by the love of my family and the strength and wisdom of Gary Hutton.

My advice to anyone reading this book is value life and respect and listen to those positive influences in your life. And if you have someone like Gary preaching to you make sure you listen 101.

I would like to end here with saying thank you Gary for not only being a friend but being someone who believed in me when I didn't believe in myself.

Gary Hutton and Zoe O'Leary

To the legend Gazza lol"

Amanda Smith, Senior Youth Worker, Hounslow Early Intervention Service

I was working on a government project called the Youth Contract to help 16 to 17 year olds. It was a project working with young people that are not in any form of education, employment or training (NEET). My role was to make contact with youth clubs across London and Mandy was the youth worker in Hounslow. She had lots of young people who needed help and not all were in the age group that were entitled to help from the project I was working on. Mandy was so helpful and really understood the young people she was working with and their needs, so I never turned anyone away and went out of my way to help. Mandy has the drive and passion that many youth workers lack and she is an all-round nice person who really cares so working with her was a pleasure. I started off giving my talk to 30 to 40 young people and then would go back each week as part of the project and would work one to one with people who needed help and I'd guide them on to the right path in life. I would at any time and at the drop of a hat help Mandy or any of her flock. She has an absolute heart of gold. Here is a note from Mandy:

"My name is Mandy, I am a Senior Youth Worker, working for Hounslow Early Intervention Service. I manage a Youth Centre in Hounslow – on a disadvantaged estate, with the majority of residents receiving some form of Welfare Benefit.

I met Gary through a Government run scheme – the project was to reduce the number of NEET's. We had good numbers of young people, helped greatly by Gary. He engaged easily with the young people as he had the ability to relate to them.

He made conversations interesting, young people wanted to listen to what he had to say. The sessions were good fun and informative, he was able to relate to their issues and help them find solutions to their problems. He always did what he said he was going to do and was always reliable – showed up when he said he would.

His life experiences made him fascinating to listen to – young people would sit and talk for ages. It also made young people realise that anything is possible if you put your mind to it and work hard. He made them understand that life needn't be boring, you can still have fun, go out and have a good time, but it is important to find employment/education and better yourself."

Zoe O'Leary

"I met Gary in August 2013 and I'll be honest sometimes I wish I hadn't, ha! I've worked in the City for 20 years and have always worked hard and played hard. When I met Gary, I was playing hard, drinking too much and had party after party to go to and he sort of mentioned this to me, but didn't say too much he just dropped in conversation here and there. I didn't think much of it but did think to myself 'who the fuck does he think he is nagging me'. As weird as it sounds Gary saw in me that I wasn't right and wasn't on a good path with my drinking ways. Friends and family had seen this but God help them if they tried to tell me, I wouldn't listen and would be defensive, but all of a sudden I listened to a stranger.

He said something to me one day when I was pissed and it hit a nerve with me, but it didn't hit me straight away. The following day I woke up, I didn't have a hangover but I was tired. I was tired of parts of my life which was all based around alcohol. Alcohol led me to doing things I wouldn't dream of doing sober. For me, alcohol put an unhealthy bubble around me which was destructive and made me feel like I didn't care. I didn't care about myself. That day I woke up tired, I said I was going to have a month's detox and at the time I didn't believe myself because my birthday was in three weeks' time and who doesn't drink on their birthday? Fucking hell I'd drink to celebrate it being a Wednesday, it didn't matter what it was. Gary took the time to talk to me and listen to me and still does to this day. He didn't do it in an overbearing way because he's savvy enough to learn about people and know how they tick so he knew by being in my face I would have ran a mile and would have told him where to go.

The day I woke up and said I would detox was the first time I'd ever used the word in that way. My mates after a big night out would say 'I'm never drinking again' and I'd say bollocks. I never said it because I knew I'd be lying and wanted to drink again no matter how bad I felt. The last day I drank was Sunday 11 August 2013 (my sister's 30th birthday party with her friends). I like to say the last day I drank instead of the first day I didn't because I like to be different and awkward! I can honestly say with my hand on my heart that I've never ever felt so good and I'm doing so much more with my life. I wanted to do some volunteer work but had never really applied myself and Gary suggested I help the homeless who I've always had a soft spot for and told me about Whitechapel Mission and I've been volunteering there ever since, the place has my heart. I've also worked together with Gary on writing his book and now we're looking to get Product of a Postcode, the charity, off the ground. It's all hard work, but I love it and feel like I'm doing something positive

Before Christmas Gary invited me to observe one of his talks in a school and I jumped at the chance to watch him in action and see how he engages with the kids. We met on 3 February 2014 at Island Gardens station to visit George Green's School, Isle of Dogs.

I'm not sure what I expected to be honest. I expected probably half of the teenagers attending to be interested in what Gary was saying and the other half to be rolling their eyes, disinterested and just there because they'd been told to be. I've known Gary for months now and know he's an interesting character, but was amazed at how quick he had the whole room watching him and listening. He doesn't use gimmicks, notes, PowerPoint presentations and has no idea what is going to come out of his mouth, but it works. Gary calls his talk 'A Life without Education' and talks about his life. He speaks to the kids like they're people and in real terms and it's blatantly obvious they respect that. He doesn't flower around anything and tells them straight up the realness of what's out there in the world.

With the group he gave an introduction to Brick Lane, his family upbringing and being an eight year old thief to feed his family and moving on to being 14 years of age and into major crime. Gary's hook was the News of the World clipping and the students were engaged, and then he would speak of the awful shit that came with his way of life when he was younger. He jumped from the path of crime to the path of education and how important it is.

He told those in the room that they wouldn't know they had an addictive personality until they try whatever it is they tried i.e. puffing. He explained in an animated way the process of skinning up a joint to the injection of heroin. Gary informed the room that he could tell in the room by their body language who

311

had tried what. He actually went so far as to point out two boys in the room but he didn't pick on them and moved on swiftly. Gary told the group how there were young kids out there hanging around in gangs in the local area on estates and how they walk about thinking they're big time gangsters, but really they are prison fodder and told the group of their path in life if they lived that sort of life. One of the boys he did point out, I kept my eye on, and this boy would not look at Gary, was chewing his lip and kept his head down, looking at his hands on the desk.

Gary then moved on to talk about his own addiction which was money and his addiction to spending it. He said he had no problem going out and getting £10k, the problem was him keeping hold of it. One of the best analogies he came out with, which was the first time I'd heard him use it, was how easy money doesn't mean anything. He asked the room if he gave them £100k or they went out and nicked it, what they would spend it on. They all said they'd give some to their families and probably squander the rest. Gary then said that if they'd worked 60 hours per week for a long period of time to earn that £100k, they probably wouldn't give it to their family and certainly wouldn't squander it because it would mean something and they'd worked hard to earn it.

The kids and the teacher who was present were absolutely gripped by his realness, openness and frank way he spoke and to be honest so was I even though we had written most of the book by then. We had written the book by emails, I hadn't heard Gary in front of an audience and this will make his head swell, he was great.

He moved on to doing an impression of a so called gangster sitting back driving his car so he's in the boot of the car and then doing an impression of a bad boy with his trousers round his arse which cracked the kids up. This was Gary giving the group messages and planting seeds as he does. He told them that the wideboys might have the cars, watches and clothes, but they wouldn't have them once they're nicked and banged up and to keep it all you have to work for it. He was then telling them about being in a straightjacket in a padded cell drugged up to the eyeballs. It was impressions and laughter followed by this is what it leads to so was a massive eye opener for these kids and they understood what he was saying.

Gary explained the prison system and gradings of prisons and levels of criminals in each prison. He went on to tell them his mission of not wanting to be around paedophiles and rapists. What amazed me was he didn't hold back and told the kids what was what. All the while explaining things that had happened in his past he kept bringing it back to the path of education and doing the right thing. It was done so cleverly. I honestly sat there and thought to myself you've either got it or you haven't because personally I would have shit myself standing in front of those kids and they would have ate me alive.

The kids lapped up the helicopter story especially how it was used like a cab. He went from making them crack up to then telling them how he was shitting himself at the time and how being incarcerated really messes with your head and how he had been groomed as a kid into that way of life and didn't know any other way. He explained it with another analogy of being taught to cross the road which is mentioned earlier in the book. Gary certainly uses his life as a tool for teaching the kids and that's all he wants to do is help young people be the best they can be in the right way.

Gary asked the kids in the room if they'd want his way of life for their kids and when they said no, he asked them why they'd

313

want it for themselves. He drummed it into them that they needed education to get what they wanted out of life. Gary's ultimate message was education is the key to a better life and the path they must be on and he wasn't there to enlighten them about the ways of crime, but he used crime as the hook for their attention. He asked the students what they wanted to be in their future lives and what subjects they had to take to lead to their goals and showed real interest.

After the hour was up lots of kids gave me their email addresses as they wanted to know more about Gary and were interested in his story. What happened next really touched me and actually showed me the realness of what is happening to kids out there. While I was taking email addresses one of the boys who Gary had picked out earlier who had been chewing his lip made a beeline straight for Gary. I could see the boy hug Gary and then they were talking between themselves. Gary told me afterwards that the boy had said to him that he couldn't believe he had picked him out of the group and the boy had said Gary had him spot on as he was one of the boys sitting around on the estates. He went on to tell Gary that on 28 February he was being sentenced for affray. Gary told the boy to come and see him after his talk to the next group and Gary did hang around waiting for the boy. Mr Anderson then appeared and said the boy had left the school after Gary's talk. The boy had walked into Gary's talk a bad boy but Gary's talk had shown him the reality of what he faced and he walked out a lost boy. I'm gutted that boy didn't hang about because Gary would have helped him anyway he could especially with support. I hope he tries to get in touch."

Mazharul Islam

Mazharul was one of the students who was at my talk at George Green's School and following my talk I asked those who attended a few questions.

When you walked out of the room what did you think, either about one of my experiences, my upbringing or the way I deliver my talk?

"I think you have been through a lot of things and you learnt from all your mistakes. Also, I think you had the hardest time ever when you were young as you experienced everything. I liked your talk a lot as most of the things you said were funny and made me laugh. Not only that but the things you said made me think that you're so sick and you got a lot of guts and like no one would do that but you. Also, you going to schools and talking about your lifetime and what happened is great as it makes people realise what life is about. After everything you've been through, you have made something of your life which impresses me as it made me realise what we could make of our life and what we can do with our lives. Also, your talk has made me think about the steps I need to take to get to where I want to be in the future to ensure I have a good life."

What did you expect from my talk and did I meet your expectation, or was I nothing like you expected?

"At first, I expected you to talk about your life and the things you did in your life. I also wanted to hear why you went to prison. You did meet my expectations as you talked about your life and why you went prison. The talk impressed me a lot actually as you also explained to all of us about what life's about and how we can do what we want to do."

Did I hit a nerve i.e. did something I say remind you of something you have done, or have thought about? If it was something you have thought about or have done, would you now think twice?

> "When you said something about walking down the road acting like a gangster reminded me of something I done in the past as I used to be part of a gang which made me mess up my life and my education. However, I got out of the gang and started sorting my life out. Your talk made me realise that me getting out of the gang was the best thing i have ever done. Also, when you said you never got no education. It made me realise how lucky I am and how I have got the chance to be something and hopefully I will change attitude towards education."

What did you think the talk was going to be about?

> "I did not really know what to think the talk was going to be about but all my friends told me it's a person coming into school saying why he went prison and what he did in his life."

Do you understand why I give these talks and do you think they're a good idea?

> "I understand why you give these talks. I think it is a fantastic idea as it made me realise what life is about. Your talks will help young people understand what life is and how they can improve their life. It will make people think that no matter what they've done, they can still be something."

Can you see the importance of such talks maybe being rolled out into schools all over the country? If you think yes, why do you think that?

"Yes I can see the importance of these talks because telling people about what you went through will make them think about the mistakes they did. If their strong enough, they will take the talk on board and will try to change and hopefully will make something of their life."

David Anderson, Deputy Head of Sixth Form and Geraldine Naughten, former Sixth Form Head, George Green's Secondary School

"Gary Hutton's presentation about his life and experiences in the criminal justice system has frequently had a profound influence on some of our 'at risk' young students. The glamour of making 'big' money through criminal activity promptly fades as Gary graphically describes the fear, indignity and risks to personal safety associated with imprisonment. Most of our students, having been raised in the East End of London, are very streetwise but even they quickly realise they could not cope with these consequences. Gary, having grown up in the area, can engage with the young people because he can identify with them and is familiar with the challenges they face, be it from peers or from the all-pervading influence of the media. His authentic approach, wisdom and above all Gary's firm grip on reality often has a profound effect on many students at risk of being led off the "straight and narrow". For these reasons, we have Gary as permanent guest speaker, and every year word quickly gets around that his Social Education session is the one not to miss!"

EPILOGUE

I've spoken in schools, youth clubs, helped with mentoring schemes and government projects and now want to do something different and get even more involved. I have co-founded a charity called Product of a Postcode (POAPC) which is just starting out. This charity has been set up in memory of my sister Kim.

POAPC has been set up to help children achieve their dreams through education. Our aims and goals are to work with underprivileged children through schools, sports clubs, youth clubs and community centres. We will help underprivileged talented young people fulfil their ambitions and go-get their dreams. As an example, not all parents can afford for their kids to travel to a sport they love or pay for kits and equipment, pay for gym fees, acting school, music classes etc. so that's what POAPC is about, helping families and dreams. Kids become focussed on what they're passionate about and don't fall wayward and hang around on the local estates wasting opportunities. We want to teach young people that they have self-worth and boost what they're aspiring to be so they can better their life. Not everyone is academically clever but has a passion for other things like sport, music and art. We want to channel all that passion so they live a productive life away from crime, prison, drugs and all the other pitfalls.

Not all kids have a stable home life and don't have real mentors so need guidance. Our main aim ambition at POAPC is talking to kids about a life without education and the pitfalls that go with it. Speakers will be going into schools in London and talking about their life experiences without education and where the wrong path can lead. As you have read, I found myself in a padded cell, drugged up to the eyeballs, wearing a straightjacket – that's the reality and that's what we're about, real life stories and turning what was a negative into a positive. We will work closely with young offenders while they are in prison and support them on release. We will train them to become mentors and speakers so they too can give back and change lives and it works.

We are passionate and care wholeheartedly on the development of young people into a better life than that of gangs, drugs and crime.

Please look us up on Facebook (Product of a Postcode) and Twitter (@ProductPostcode) and follow our development and success stories and, of course, please feel free to donate. Please do let us have your comments on the book and look out for when our website becomes available.

Sales from the book also goes towards helping POAPC, so tell your friends!

Lastly, I'd like to say we are all a product of a postcode whether good or bad.

Take care,

Gary

Printed in Great Britain
by Amazon

87622322R00181